Dear Steph,

Wishing you the best of health and happiness.

– Glen xx

Sept. '23

BEFRIEND GRAVITY

The Commonsense Approach to Rebuild Your Happy Spine

Glenn Duffy, D.C.

BEFRIEND GRAVITY

This book may be purchased for business or promotional use, or for special sales. For information, please use the contact form at www.glennduffy.com

Published by Healthy Choice Publishing Ltd,
3 Wood Row, Throop Road, Bournemouth BH8 0DN, United Kingdom

www.glennduffy.com

First Press Edition, 2022

Disclaimer
The information presented is the author's opinion and does not constitute any health or medical advice. The content of this book is for informational purposes only and is not intended to diagnose, treat, cure, or prevent any condition or disease.

Please seek advice from your healthcare provider for your personal health concerns prior to taking healthcare advice from this book.

Although the author has made efforts to ensure that the information is correct at the time of writing, we do not assume and hereby disclaim any liability caused by errors or omissions, whether such error or omission result from negligence, accident or any other cause. No warranty is made that any of the information is accurate or up-to-date. All warranties are disclaimed, express or implied.

Any examples or cases used in this book are based on real life challenges and situations, but not on any individual client. Names, characters, business, events and incidents are the products of the author's imagination. Any resemblance to actual persons, living or dead, or actual events is purely coincidental.

Cover & Copy Design: **Alan Cooper Design**
Diagrams & Illustrations: **Jose Lebron**
Author Photograph: **Prisca Laguna**

Hardback ISBN: 978-1-915741-00-4
Paperback ISBN: 978-1-915741-01-1

About the Author

Dr Glenn has spent two decades working to change lives by rebuilding happy spines, for life.

Glenn realised that the care patients were receiving was not the same as what family and staff were getting. Healthcare was run by budgets or expectations of "quick fixes". Meanwhile, the families of Chiropractors were getting the best care and enjoying a higher state of health and wellbeing.

He opened a group of clinics near London, growing a team of Chiropractors, Physiotherapists, Nutritionists and Coaches. His waiting-list practice helped recreational and olympic athletes alike. His research in biomechanics had him invited to lecture at postgraduate level, and he later taught with the Royal College of Chiropractors in the UK. He has since pioneered accelerated spinal care protocols, producing long-lasting results for his clients.

A sought-after speaker on spinal health and personal transformation, Glenn is cofounder of the not-for-profit ChiroWild, a nature-based transformational experience which grows health professionals to better serve their profession and patients.

A "retired" competitive sportsman, he is always seeking nature. Be it on the water, or in the mountains, you will find him there with his dogs, family and friends.

Glenn lives in Marbella, Spain, with his wife and two kids. He runs a thriving private practice, attracting clients from around the world.

You can learn more about Glenn at www.glennduffy.com

To my family;

Noor and Ayan, my angelic children, and truly my greatest teachers. Farah, my wife and soul-mate. Our waggy-tailed Mexx, and our family's recently departed member, Tokaji… our beloved Hungarian Viszlas. You inspire me to be the best possible version of myself, and you give me real reason to leave a legacy of a better world for future generations. Love does not describe what I feel for you; you are my world.

Contents

Preface

I got my first "health" job, as a part-time gym instructor, at the age of 16. I was paid lower than minimum wage, in cash, and not officially on the books. I was excited to share my knowledge (or lack thereof) to the unsuspecting public. While I undoubtedly have learnt a lot over the past 27 years of non-stop work and study in health, there is one thing that I hope will never change: my passion for empowering you to better understand and seize control of your health and happiness.

In my professional career, I have spent countless hours explaining a different understanding of health and wellness. A model which is as alien to our medicalised world, as it is basic common sense. Every time I explained it, I could see lightbulbs switching on in my clients' self-awareness. But it is hard to make a big difference in a person's understanding of health and wellness one conversation at a time. It is hard to undo decades of medicalised thinking and conditioning in one conversation. Moreover, I have always struggled to find a concise way of explaining decades of learning and insights in…just one conversation.

In order to get my message to more people, I moved into public speaking, explaining some or even many concepts in each session. I even developed a series of basic and advanced workshops. After each workshop, I would receive the same feedback. Someone new to the concepts would ask where to find out more. My only answer was a *reading list* of multiple books. Not exactly very accessible. The other feedback would come from someone who had already attended the same talk in the past. They would always comment that I covered more of one topic, or less of another, and could I please explain that topic in more depth next time.

I am surely not alone in this challenge: the challenge of travelling the long road of conscious discovery, "evolution," and hard learnings. Learnings that culminate in a very different, critical view of the illness care system. Many of us travel a journey which births an enlightened, optimistic view on how healthcare can be, but leaves a gaping chasm between our vision and our ability to explain it in a single conversation.

People suggested that I record videos of these concepts, challenging people's current beliefs and explaining the logical, proactive model of health which I wish not only for you but also for your friends and family. I quickly learnt that the world of Youtube requires a level of skill and time-commitment which was beyond me. Despite this, our videos have been a success. All of our new clients and practice members watch videos which explain their condition and the process of recovery. But this is still only a part of the picture. A very small part of a very big picture.

So this book is an attempt to highlight the flaws of our current "health" assumptions, both in global "philosophical" terms, but also relating to individual choices. Addressing topics such as "why did I get carpal tunnel syndrome?" or "should I go for surgery?" The next step is to construct an understanding of the undoctored life, where you know the ingredients for your body to function at 100%, in health *and* happiness. The secret is recognising that a healthy nervous system and spine are the core to all health. And understanding how to build health and resilience from the inside out is crucial.

I had intended to write this book from the perspective of an "objective bystander," but it proved impossible. Although I have a strategic, objective overview on these topics, in my everyday life I am a practising Doctor of Chiropractic, and I would never have it any other way. When you dedicate your life to such work, you get to meet good people who have been sold short with bad health recommendations and are now paying the price. A lot of this bad advice comes from laziness, by just doing what we always did, even though it has never worked very well. Some of these bad recommendations are driven by profit margins, which does not sit well, when your health is at stake.

So I resolved to write the truth. My truth, of course, but to say it as it is. If this book serves the wider public, then that is fantastic, but my first and foremost goal is to fairly serve my clients: the thousands of people who have trusted my judgement and advice with only brief explanation. Herein you will find a lot more context and explanation, so that you can come to the same logical decisions about your own health. Or you can pass this book on to a friend or family member, so that they may do the same.

Either way, I hope to give you concrete, inspiring insights and knowledge, freeing you to make enlightened health decisions.

Introduction

I hope that you can open any chapter of this book and quickly learn how your spine loses health and how you can restore it. Yet, you will most benefit if you understand the underpinning arguments set out earlier in the book. Want to know about scoliosis? Just open up that chapter and enjoy. Want to understand how to rebuild a healthy spine, despite having scoliosis? I recommend you head back to the start and read the whole lot. It is designed for you to cut in and out as you wish, hopefully returning to certain sections should you forget, for example, the keys to spinal health. You will probably find yourself trying to explain a particular condition or concept to a friend or family member, so at the back you will find an index to help you to quickly find any given topic.

The book is divided into four parts.

In Part I, we look at how to seize control of your health, your destiny. We first review the current assumptions in what we call the "healthcare system," which is really an illness care system. We learn of our subconscious biases, of how we are conditioned to react as the media, our families, and this illness system has taught us. Armed with this understanding, we can head off these biases before they make bad health decisions on our behalf. Then we visit real health philosophy.

My belief in *your* ability to heal changes how I would approach you as a client, and it should also change the level of trust you can have in your own body. After reading this section, you will see your friends' and family's health decisions through a different lens. You will have a more strategic perspective on what seem to be minor decisions. Consider it as explaining the *"Why?"* of our illness beliefs and health decisions. I choose to use the word "client" instead of "patient". This is not a mistake. Instead of discussing how to remove illness from you—as a patient, we will discuss how to restore health in you—as a client.

Part II deals with the *"How?"* of a healthy nervous system and spine. We go into a lot of detail about how your spine is designed for perfection, learning there are four key bones which need to "sit right" to keep your system in balance. We also explain how losing this alignment can cause a multitude of direct and indirect injuries, from herniated discs to indigestion. After a quick overview of scoliosis, we explain how your spinal condition may have defined your personality. And how rebuilding your spine may liberate a new, more genuinely happy, version of you.

Part III addresses and guides you through the process of healing. This is the *"What?"* of your health decisions. Consider it a field guide to rebuilding your spine. We go over the effects of adjusting your spine, what you can expect, and when you need trust and/or patience. We also talk about some "easy strategies" for exercise, sleep, and sitting, to instantly change your spinal stress and help the healing process. We close by deconstructing some of the myths surrounding when drugs or surgery are a good idea.

Part IV is about making the best decisions for your own health. Once you put this book down, you may need to get support in order to achieve your health goals. We discuss what to look for in your doctor or therapist. If this person is going to guide you from recovery and into lifelong health, this is worth some thought. We often take this "action" with little consideration, going to see the closest Doctor, or the one who is suggested by our health insurer. When we make this step a more conscious decision, then all else follows. When we align our "What, How, and Why," we can enjoy lasting, abundant health.

We close with a vision of what role you, the health-enlightened enthusiast, can play not only in your own health journey, but by supporting those around you.

This book will not go over every nutritional supplement you can take or exercise you can do to support your spine. It does not go over every spinal misalignment or technique, but it gives you the basic scientific understanding, from which everything becomes common sense. There are big, conscious omissions of important health themes, which I write about elsewhere. There are also liberal oversimplifications of complex matters. It is not a treatment or a diagnosis for you or anyone else. You should still seek professional advice to guide your decisions.

The content that you will read here is backed by science, clinical experience, or both. I have included some references to guide you to further reading and resources, but this is not intended to be a chiropractic textbook. In fact, some sections are backed wholly by this rare thing called common sense. And you may notice that all of it is garnished with a dash of satire.

In this book, you will read and feel my passion for certain topics. Yes, the current healthcare landscape outrages me, and you may feel my emotions as you read on. If you were to take some sections out of context, you may feel I lack appreciation for my medical colleagues or even physiotherapists, osteopaths, or other chiropractors. This could not be further from the truth, as each profession has a valuable role to play. I will liberally criticise how *all* health professions, including many chiropractors, are failing their clients. The health of you and your family is too important for me to "pull punches," and I hope to serve you by being transparently honest about how short-sighted most "treatment" approaches are. This book will arm you with the discernment to choose a brighter vision for your long-term health.

This book puts you back in the driver's seat so that you are conscious of your health decisions and the motivations behind the recommendations that you may receive, for better or worse. It arms you with a comprehensive, accessible understanding of the core elements of your spinal health, and how to rebuild these as a priority in your health journey. I may never have met you, yet I have total confidence that you have a magnificent ability to self-heal, and that somewhere in this book lies insight or information which will allow you to do this with greater ease and happiness.

If your Chiropractor has asked you to read this book, that is a good sign. They obviously care about your long term plan. They want to empower you with an understanding of your health, so you can take back control. It looks like you are in good hands.

PART I

Seize Control of Your Health Destiny

"Where we put our awareness, and for how long, maps our destiny."

— Joe Dispenza

Chapter 1

The Cycle of Death

"What we call the secret of happiness is no more a secret than our willingness to choose life."

— Leo Buscaglia

Waiting to Die

As he sat in the corridor, waiting to be wheeled back into his room, John wondered how he had gotten here. It felt like a matter of days since he last played with his grandchildren. In fact, it felt like only a few days since he was dropping his own kids off at school. But they had all grown up. Hopefully, they were coming to visit soon. It had been far too long.

In contrast, it felt like a different lifetime in which he was a dynamic young man, known for his sharp wit and sprightly laugh which could light up any party. He was once told he was "quite a catch!" But now, at 84 years old, the world felt so small. It felt like the whole world consisted of himself, his wheelchair, the corridor, and the closed door to his room at the end of the corridor. It felt like an eternity of boring loneliness. How long would the nurse take to come back from that phone call? Perhaps she had stopped for a cup of tea en route...or gone to tend to Mary in room 5. "She is so bloody selfish; she always keeps the nurses an age," he thought to himself. The drab corridor seemed to darken further.

Realising that the nurse had probably forgotten him, he instantly felt a desperate need to wee. These past eight years had been the most boring of his life. Waiting for the weekly, sometimes fortnightly visits from his brother's daughter, Jackie, seemed almost more painful than hoping for no visits at all. If anything, it just reminded him of how much better his brother's life was. If his brother needed to pee, he only needed to find a nearby tree on the golf course.

If he had kept up sports when he could have, if he had sought a different treatment for his chronic headaches, perhaps life would have been more fun today. Perhaps he would have enjoyed his kids more, rather than finding and treating them as a nuisance. Maybe they would have kept him more active and fit...? Either way he had spent over half his life sitting. What if that had been different? Maybe he would not have undergone that back surgery which left him bent over double and in even more back pain. Perhaps, if he were more fit, healthy, and in a better posture, he would not have had that fall which broke his hip. That hip fracture was to blame for everything. "Bloody hip," he mumbled to himself, then coughed a few times as he partly cleared his throat. The clearest thing he could remember is that after that surgery and anaesthetic was that everything became ... unclear. Memories disappeared as fast as they appeared. He could still remember his kids and family and things from a long time ago, but his family convinced him that it would be safer for him in a care home. Safer for whom?

Which one of those things could John have changed to still be walking, staying fit, perhaps playing the occasional round of golf, or at least socialising and seeing his family as normal? One of them? All of them? And when was Mary from room 5 going to let that bloody nurse go so that she could bring him to the toilet?

What was for sure is that his identical twin brother had made better choices. They had long since drifted apart, but the Christmas and birthday cards, Jackie's visits, plus the occasional phone call, told of a very different life. Perhaps it was all lies. Pat had been prone to lying since he was a kid. Halfway across the world, yes, but he was in John's mind every day. Pat had stayed fit and healthy, spending money on his health while John worked overtime. He still enjoyed golf and other sports, and was even still travelling on holidays regularly! John knew that Jackie had been to see Pat, as she talked lots about her father. "Lucky bugger," John thought to himself, "maybe one day he'll see fit to come visit his twin brother!" He was disgruntled, but he knew it was not luck. His brother had made better life decisions. Not only had his brother had more fun and fitness in his life, but now, he was living longer to rub it in.

At her last visit, Jackie had laughingly said, "Well uncle, we all know you have no regrets," but it was not true.

John knew he was dying, and he shared the same regrets with most other dying people.

He wished he had not worked so hard, especially in those magical moments while his wife was still alive, or while the kids were smaller. He wished he had expressed his feelings more, mostly to his wife, but also to his family. He wished he had stayed in touch with his friends, perhaps he would not feel so alone now.

He wished he had cared more for himself, both in health and happiness. After all was said and done, no-one gave a shit about how much money he had made or how many times he had stayed working late at night. It counted for nothing. Work and "business" just got in the way of those things that really mattered. In fact, thinking back on it, a lot of life was full of unimportant bullshit. He wished he had looked after himself more, lived a little more, loved a little more.

At once John was overwhelmed by it all. He had a good life. He got lots done. Had some good times on the way. But shit, it could have all been so different. He took a deep sigh of relief and felt his thighs getting warm. "That'll teach them to forget me here in the corridor."

Are We There Yet?

By the age of 17, I had already had been anaesthetised seven times, had six surgeries, and spent a week on an intubator in intensive care with pneumonia. I had clocked up more medical appointments for rugby injuries, eye problems, and asthma than some people would in a lifetime. Bless my parents for putting up with it all. I knew the medical system pretty well from a first-hand perspective. And from those experiences, I knew that I wanted to work in healthcare.

I cannot express how deeply grateful I am for the medical system. It has possibly saved my life in the past. Despite this, ever since childhood, I knew that the medical system we called the "health" system was broken. The saddest part is that its brokenness was too difficult for most people to see until it was too late.

To put it another way, I realised that most people were so trusting in the system that they were slowly committing suicide by lifestyle. Putting out the occasional fire in their health with drugs or surgery until the list of drugs got longer and longer. And eventually, that long list would become their very own death sentence.

John's story is the most common pathway to death in our western societies. In fact, at the jolly retirement age of 65, your life expectancy is a further 20 years, until age 85. Good news, no? But of that, about HALF is due to be in a state of chronic pain and/or disability. That means, be it at home or in a care facility, you will need assistance with your daily activities for the last 10 years of life. A *decade* of disability awaits the average person before death. This is a shocking statistic and explains why so many people are scared of ageing.

Having chronic spinal problems radically worsens that picture. For example, if you have chronic back pain at 55 years old, the disabled part of your life will be about 5 years longer. That's 15 years of disability. Depressing, right?

We have this huge issue with life expectancy, sometimes called our lifespan. In fact, we have become so obsessed with it that we have kind of forgotten what the point of life expectancy is. The word *life* would infer it should have something to do with living, but it does not really. Life expectancy is going up. Woohoo!!! In fact, over the past few decades, life expectancy in Europe has been rising by two years every decade.

But so does the disability expectancy... That means that we are living longer, but we are living more *sick* years than *healthy* years. So the real picture of "progress" is pretty bleak.

When I present to large audiences, I often ask, "If I were to pass you a sign-up sheet, and all you need to do is put your name down, and we will ensure you live to 100, how many of you would sign it?" Guess how many hands go up? Usually, no hands go up! Why would people not want to live to 100? Guaranteed longevity sounds great, does it not?

In reality, when you think of living to 100, most of us instantly picture our grandmother or grandfather or another older person. Our "John." Living in disability. Possibly living in solitude. Living in a way which we don't want to have to face. When you close your eyes and think of life at 100, how does that look?

What if we were to change that image? What if that image were an active, happy, smiling, socially engaged 100-year-old? Playing some light sport, doing fun things, traveling and seeing children, grand-children, and even great-grandchildren?

So I ask again, "Now, if I pass another sign-up sheet around, just put your name down, and we will ensure you live *healthily and happily* until 100, how many of you will sign it?" Now nearly all the hands go up.

It's time to forget about *life* expectancy and start to concentrate on *health* expectancy. Instead of talking about our lifespan, let us talk about our healthspan. That is, "How long can I live a happy and fulfilled life?" not just, "How long can I live?"

There is a huge difference. If you want to live a full and happy life for years to come, start focusing on your *healthspan*.

Let's say that you have now put up your hand. You are interested in living to 100 or more, *in good health and happiness.* The question is *what next?*

If you are looking for something that is going to instantly change your life, then please put this book down. Because if it instantly changes your life, it will almost certainly change back a few weeks later. If you are seeking quick-fixes, then a future similar to John's might be on the cards.

If you are looking for something that changes your direction for your *journey of health*, then read on. This book can orient you from where you are today and guide you on your journey.

Are we there yet?

I personally am not "there" now. I believe that none of us will ever be "there." In fact, there probably is no "there."

It is a journey through health, happiness, and time. And you, your knowledge, your health, and, indeed, your happiness will evolve on that journey. There will be uncertainty, mistakes, and failings. There will be a few tears and hopefully plenty of laughter, and you will come out the other side stronger, happier, and more resilient than before. And those around you will learn from your actions, attitude, and growth. And so will their friends. And so will their children. Your personal investment in your own health may be one of the most impactful things you will do while on this planet.

The Biggest Decision You Never Made

"Pain is inevitable, suffering is optional."- The Dalai Lama

2 Steps to a New Life
Step 1. Get injured
Step 2. Seek help. Choose to change direction

So, what next? As with any journey, the only way forward is to take the first step. May that step be in the right direction.

95% of what we all do every day is "automatic." It takes no consideration or reflection. This allows us to cruise through life, journeying through health and happiness and time, rarely conscious of the steps we are taking. In fact, taking most of them for granted. From waking in the morning to arriving at work, we have been mostly on auto-pilot.

How much conscious thought do you have to put into the process of getting showered, brushing your teeth, making breakfast, getting in the car, and driving to work? Very little. That is good news; it would be pretty tiresome if we had to think about every step every morning. Autopilot is brilliant. But not when we autopilot our relationship with our body and how we view our health.

The average kid sees a mind-boggling 40,000 TV and digital adverts a year.[1] Three-quarters of advertising spend is by pharmaceutical companies.[2] Are those messages teaching us that our bodies have an ability to self-heal, that you can become and stay healthy simply through clever lifestyle choices? Of course not. They teach us from a young age, and repeatedly, that signs like pain can be solved with pills, that we all need drugs to heal. Like it or not, protest or not, your and my subconscious have been bombarded with this, and it forms a part of our world-view, and therefore, our health decisions. It is only when we make a very conscious and committed effort to self-check that we really take control over our health philosophy. Despite this being my life's work, and even after years and years of being aware of health philosophy, I still battle to stay conscious to this conditioning. Most of us need a big motivation to stay conscious, and often, this comes from a moment of crisis.

Step 1. Get Injured

Every now and then, life throws us a warning call. Like a stubbed toe. Ouch.

The stubbed toe means you were walking the wrong way, so you need to change course, right? Obviously. So let's say your warning call is acute low back pain. Or debilitating headaches. Or general tiredness to the point of not being able to focus and study or work. Or lack of flexibility to put your socks on in the morning, meaning you cannot play a round of golf. In other words, *something inconvenient enough to catch your attention.*

Your friends and colleagues share their condolences. "Bad luck," they say...

"Lucky you," I say. You have just been given an opportunity. Just about every huge life-changing decision has come on the back of some pain, loss, or crisis.

So pain and injuries are lucky? Yes. Just like the stubbed toe told you not to walk into the furniture, your pain or problem is giving you a choice. Most of us assume pain is, well, painful. But pain does not have to cause suffering when you make a conscious choice.

As the above quote says, *"Pain is inevitable, suffering is optional."*

For most people, the problem with pain is not just the feeling, but how *inconvenient* it is. It stops us from carrying on as we were. Our lives are busy enough, packed enough, without having acute back pain or headaches to deal with at the same time. A paracetamol is easier and faster than extra hours in bed, a visit to the chiropractor, or exercise.

And it is very clear that in the western world, we live a life of *ultimate convenience.* The toilet is indoors. The carrier pigeons are well behaved and live inside your telephone. You don't have to kill and fillet a chicken to get your evening meal. You have a refrigerator which means you can just go to the shops once a week and that the beer is always just the right temperature.

But when something becomes painful enough, inconvenient enough, we are eventually provoked to act. To make a choice.

Step 2.Seek Help — Make your Choice

There are three choices you can make at this stage.

Choice 1) Self Medicate
Choice 2) "Treat" the pain with natural therapies
Choice 3) Change direction: look to the cause and restore true health

1. What do most people choose? What have our parents, friends, and those thousands of subliminal advertisements told us to do? Self-medicate.

Yes, most people will *first* reach for a drug. Like ibuprofen or similar.

About 80% of people with back pain will reach for this type of drug. 1 in 4 people pop these pills for more than 6 months a year! It is almost certain that you have one or many close friends who take anti-inflammatory painkillers year-round. They don't even count them as medications when they fill in their health history when they go to the doctor's office.

They may get some relief. Close call. For a moment, that pain was going to force them to change their lifestyle habits. It might have caused them to get off their chair and move more. Or to seek professional help aimed at correcting the cause of their problems. Now, they can get back to doing exactly what got them injured or ill in the first place.

In chapter 12 we look at the *factual evidence* about painkillers, but for now, let me highlight three simple facts:

Taking these drugs, even short-term, can be dangerous and damaging to your health.

Many painkillers are no different, or barely more effective, than placebo.

Masking the problem today fixes nothing, but means that tomorrow you will have more suffering and illness.

These are facts which are brushed under the carpet, in the name of convenience for the user and profit for the manufacturers. People may continue in and out of this cycle for their whole life.

2. Others will choose an alternative "treatment" option. That is, to use a natural therapy. Drugs and surgery are the tools of medicine. Diet, supplements, exercise, and manual therapies are the tools of the natural therapies.

Although the media hype around isolated stories might lead you to believe otherwise, I know of *no* natural therapy which can compete with the risk levels of drugs and surgery. Medicine and medical error continues to be one of the leading causes of deaths worldwide, in comparison to which, natural therapies are extremely safe. Natural therapies are a safer, more body-respectful way to respond to the inconvenience of injuries, pain, illness, or disability.

There is a huge problem with most natural therapies. They are *less convenient* than drugs. Because they are safer, more gentle, it is normal to take longer to feel better. This approach respects your body's need for time to heal. Rather than pop a few pills a day, you may be asked to change your water intake, your diet, your exercise pattern. And moreover, you may need to physically drive to a clinic for treatment, perhaps multiple times a week. In our convenience culture, this grates. Many people will quickly say, "This isn't working," and give up on the natural option. What they really mean is, "I don't have time to wait for this to work," or, as I would put it, "I don't value this enough to patiently invest in my health."

There are a few reasons for this. One is the obvious comparison of natural therapies to drugs. They are not comparable, and so expecting them to "work" on the same timescales is not reasonable. Another reason is that *most* natural therapists and/or natural therapies have fallen into the trap of "trying to play doctor." They take a set of symptoms and try to treat them just like a medical doctor, only using natural approaches. While this, in my opinion, is far less toxic than sticking drugs into your body, it succumbs to a pathetically poor vision of health for you, for our communities, and humanity as a whole. We can do better.

3. Choose to change direction. Look to the cause to restore true health.

How could so many yogis, gym instructors, gurus, and "health junkies" have missed this? Is there a flaw in their health model, or have they not fully interpreted their model? Or is all of that subconscious conditioning just too much? They have diligently invested in their health and done a pretty good job of it. When they come in as new clients, they feel that they "know their body," and in many ways they do. Yet, they will never find real health or happiness until they change direction. At least, they start from a great place compared to many others. All that lacks is a small change in direction.

Making this change depends on being ready and on having the right guidance.

Being ready might mean that you are "fed up" with "treatments that don't work." Or that the loss and inconvenience that your injury or lost health has caused is so shocking that you are ready for a big change. Maybe you have seen a photo of yourself and realised that unless something changes, you will age like your mother, father, or grandparent; hunched over and in pain. But in all cases, being ready involves humility. It requires being humble enough to listen constantly to your body and to

---

* *The choice of the word "client" instead of "patient" is explained on page 192*

listen to alternative views, even when they surprise or disappoint you. This humility is essential if you want to learn about a different level of health. The type of health which is defined by a dynamic learning relationship with your body; as a journey, rather than a destination.

The right guidance typically comes from a book or a health-enlightened doctor or therapist. I hope that this might be that book for you.

The fundamental difference in step three is the choice to *stop trying to treat the condition.*

Most illness, injury, pain, or disability is a symptom of a *loss of health* rather than a *gaining of illness*.

It may sound like semantics, but this is an *epic* leap into a different realm of health and happiness. Shifting this perspective can be inconvenient, because rebuilding health often means changing habits that have taken decades to develop. Let's say your gut has been unhealthy for decades. You finally get symptoms. Some drugs, supplements, or therapies may "treat" the problem, and you may feel better. But until you go through the process of "rebuilding" your gut, you will never experience full health, and this process will take months, maybe years. Or you have had a forward head posture since you were a teenager. Now you are 35, and you have headaches, or a herniated disc in your neck, with shoulder and arm pain. "Treatments" like drugs, surgery, or even chiropractic may relieve your pains. However to recover from the 20+ years of postural damage which caused the problem, it may take a year or more.

When we see illness as lost health and focus on gaining health rather than removing illness, our whole perspective on life shifts.

Unfortunately, even when this third step sounds logical, most of us are too busy or get distracted en route. I have seen many clients, already past their pain and well en route to true wellness, abandon their journey. Why? Because they lost focus, they got lazy, and most importantly, they lost their motivation. Because their motivation, in truth, was no more than getting rid of their pains and problems. As their pains had gone, so had their motivation. Choosing life-long wellness is a journey. Like eating healthily, it does not make you feel good every day, but it makes you feel good over years and decades. It makes you age differently. Just because eating one healthy meal does not make you feel good instantly, does not make healthy eating ineffective!

The foundational principals of chiropractic philosophy honour the innate instinct for every living thing to strive for perfection. And the job of a good chiropractor is to free up that ability in you and then keep it free for life. Chiropractic, though an "effective treatment option," is at its most powerful when you make it a lifestyle choice.

How will you look a decade from now? Some people argue that you age according to your genes. And that is about a quarter true.[3] But the other three quarters really depends on your health philosophy: how much you are willing to invest your time, money, and effort into being a healthy and happy person. For life.

The great news is that any day, including today, you can take back control of those three quarters. It may seem daunting at first, but no endeavour can bring you greater rewards. Living through a journey of wellness is a richer experience of the world, not just in terms of bodily mobility, but in everything. Better sleep, better relaxation, better sex, better fun, better relationships. Better Life.

Health v Illness care

"Create health, or forever fight disease." — Unknown

It is important to note that, as long as there is no *real* money in wellness, there will be no government or corporate interest in wellness. The money made from setting up a chain of wellness centres pales into insignificance compared to drug and surgery profit levels. And yet, all the evidence clearly shows that a wellness lifestyle radically reduces sickness care costs.

Clients sometimes say that care is too expensive. This normally means that it is too expensive for their value system. When they really need it—for example a self-employed person can no longer work—they find a way to afford health care. But for many people, other things matter more than their health to them. Sadly, they will one day find out that sickness is far more expensive than health.

Crisis care is high-cost, high-impact, and short-term. Bills are huge, the stakes are high and *urgent,* and the intervention generally lasts days or weeks. Wellness care is low-cost, high-impact, long-term. Bills are lower but more sustained, the stakes are even higher, but not as *urgent*, and the intervention lasts years and decades.

It is not that all of this crazy investment in illness care is not working. We *are* getting better at treating chronic illness. The problem is we are also getting better at *creating* chronic illness, even faster than we can "treat it." Who stands to gain from this? Your parents, you, your children? No. Only people who profit from sickness care profit from this model.

In 2005, I sat with a friend, a doctor in the UK's National Health Service. We were talking about the healthcare system, in particular, the culture of overworking. Despite the reorganisation and reclassification of shift lengths, emergency doctors were pulling shifts way beyond the clear, rational thinking capacity of any human being—up to 40 hours at a time. It had been all over the media. He explained that, although it seemed to have been "fixed," the only thing that had changed was when the doctors were signing off. They were signing off after 20 hours, but still working 40 hours. Only the appearance to the public had changed. We talked about how to fix this "illness juggernaut." His point shocked me. He said that the only way to fix it was to first break it entirely. As in, the system needed to totally collapse and be rebuilt from the ground up. Decades of habit die hard, and the habit of such a juggernaut cannot be turned around without a clean slate, a fresh start. I fear that our recent lessons prove this to be true. Despite pouring more and more money into emergency facilities to fight acute sickness, we still fail to stop smoking in the community, get people exercising, reduce obesity, and boost vitamin D levels. Some of these things are just so damn easy that it feels that some part of the illness care system is invested in stopping doctors from making their clients more healthy. The saying goes that "just an ounce of prevention is worth a pound of cure." But what profit is in an ounce of prevention, when compared to a pound of cure?!?! It is no wonder that the better you know and understand the system, the more cynically you tend to view it.

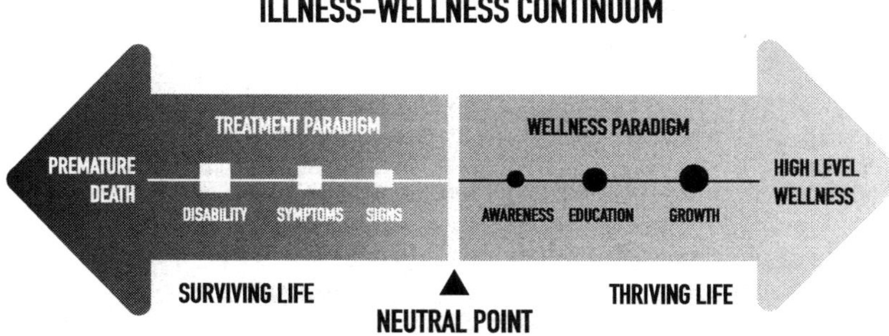

Figure 2. The Illness - Wellness Continuum

Where are you on this scale?

You, your family, your friends, everyone you know, and I sit somewhere on the "Wellness Spectrum" in *Figure 2*. In fact, when you understand how it works, you will start to "categorise" your friends and family on this scale, and it might irritate them!

Imagine a friend or family member who lives in the same place as most people, somewhere in the middle of the spectrum, in what we call "neutral point." Things are "normal." They can live their life without any real inconvenience. They can exercise, work, socialise, eat, and sleep without pains or limitations. They "feel fine."

But one day, they get symptoms—they cannot do something they love, or they are in pain when moving. So they make an appointment with a doctor, and they get a diagnosis, a label, an illness, and with it, a treatment. It does not matter if that treatment is drugs, chiropractic, or any other therapy, natural or otherwise. Their symptoms go away. They return to neutral point on the spectrum, and with it, they return to... exactly the same behaviour as before...

...until they get ill again, seek more treatment, and feel better again. And this cycle goes on with greater and greater severity, with more and more loss of ability, and less and less health, until one day they die.

Sound pretty dramatic? Well that is how our society currently works. That is what you and I are statistically most likely to do. That is what our friends are family are doing *right now.*

What do we currently name this process in our society? When someone gets ill, recovers with less vitality, then gets ill again, gets more treatment and recovers weaker still? And over the coming years or possibly decades, they get weaker and weaker, they hunch over, lose mobility, are in chronic pain, and ready to die? We call it ageing. Ageing. That is the accepted, normal way for people to age and die in our society. But there is another way.

Very few people actually invest in moving up the spectrum. To the wellness end where you are not just further away from illness, but also closer to happiness, flexibility, adaptability, and capacity to deal with good new things like happy moments, falling in love, and having fun, but also, resilience to deal with bad new things, like illness, tragedy, lost jobs, tax bills. Resilience allows you to survive injuries which cripple others. Resilience improves the changes of surviving viruses which kill others. We all have this choice, once we are aware.

Many people at some point in life get some form of health insurance. The theme, if not the price, is the same in all developed countries. Where we live in Spain, it is easy to get private "health" insurance for as little as €12 per month. Imagine you take out this €12 euro per month health insurance. You call them up and say, "Hi, I want to use my health insurance in order to be more healthy. What can you do for me?" What services are they going to offer to make you more healthy? None. Or imagine you visit your medical doctor. You walk in and he says, "What is wrong with you?" You say, "Nothing, but I wanted more health in my life. What should I do to be more healthy?" What would he say? He might well give you a referral to the psychologist!

What we currently call our "health" service or our "health" insurance deals with nothing other than *illness*. Sometimes, they can help with *illness prevention,* but it is still focused on what we don't want; that is, *illness*. I think it is wise to have some form of illness insurance, especially if you live somewhere that the state provision is lacking, but recognise that illness insurance cannot make you healthy.

If you do want to actually become more healthy, who is going to insure you? Who is responsible for getting you more health, resilience, adaptability, happiness? Only the person who is reading this paragraph can do this for you. Yes, you are the only person who can actually health-insure yourself.

It is a big responsibility. Most of us are unaware that we have this responsibility. We unconsciously choose a life of illness, waiting for the next symptom rather than becoming healthier. As you understand that there is another way, you can certainly help your family and friends and colleagues by awakening them to other choices.

Take the journey very seriously, as your life depends on it. But not too seriously, as your life depends on it. By that, I mean that the journey should be *fun*. You will never do a perfect job of this. Real health and wellness is a direction, a journey. And if it is a fun and pleasant journey, you are likely to travel much further.

If you ever visit my practice, you will notice that it is full of music, fun, life. Sure, most of our clients start in pain, but they soon learn to focus on restoring their real health. And that is because we choose life. Living a healthy, fulfilling life should be *fun*.

Choose or Suffer

Pathogenesis v. Salutogenesis

Medicine is the study of disease, what makes man ill, and how man dies. This study of the origins of illness is called pathogenesis.

Chiropractic is the study of health, what makes man happy, and life. The study of the cause of health is called salutogenesis—how to generate health.

The choice is really simple. What pathogens can you eliminate from your life? What salutogens can you add to your life?

As we discussed, many of these decisions are subconsciously programmed. The friends we keep, our families, and the TV we watch will all form our views. Be careful what company you keep!

I have a number of friends who are medical doctors. Most medical doctors cannot understand what wellness is. It is not that they are not intellectually capable, but when you learn the body and the world through the lens of pathogenesis, it is almost impossible to see salutogenesis.

Wellness is not a lack of illness. Salutogenesis is the only way to wellness, health, and happiness. It is up to you to build your own wellness team so that the only time you need medical care is to save you after a life-threatening accident.

In Chapter 11 we discuss how to make the most "salutogenic"—"health-generating"—life choices.

Imagine that you have seen better health. You know it. The idea of "recovering health" can feel like a big task, even overwhelming. As you progress through this book, you will start to realise how better health is more achievable than it appears. No matter how you have treated your body, it still wants to heal, cure, and grow. And you are not alone. Many others have walked this path with the right guidance. It may not all happen tomorrow, so be gentle and patient with yourself. It may not be an easy run, but it will be easier than letting your health gradually slip away. With patience and persistence, you can do it.

Chapter 1 Checklist

- Our over-medicalised culture has most of us doomed to a future of premature ageing, immobility, and dependence on drugs to keep us going.
- Our biggest health decision has been made for us already, programmed subconsciously. That decision removes our control of our health destiny.
- We can make a conscious choice to reverse that. Instead of avoiding illness, we can choose wellness. Instead of removing disease, we can add health.
- This conditioning runs deep, and we need to stay alert to "relapses" into the illness paradigm.

Action Points

- Take stock of your historic health decisions, from long ago to recently. Which of them were proactive? Which were reactive? Which of them just aimed to dull symptoms? Which aimed to improve your health?
- As you recognise your awareness and skills to build an abundance of freedom and wellness, you can cultivate better lifelong health. You can "water these seeds," to keep focusing back on your best decisions. Celebrate your best decisions, and resolve to continue to choose life, health, and happiness.
- The more you read around this topic, the more you surround yourself with happy, healthy, living people, the easier your journey becomes. Order another health book after this one and schedule a coffee with a like-minded friend to chat about your intentions.

If you are near Marbella, Spain, go to www.duffyquiropractica.com to find out how to work with Dr Duffy.

If elsewhere, go to www.chiroalliance.org or www.chiropractic.org to search for subluxation reducing chiropractors.

Chapter 2

The Flow of Life

"Nature needs no help, just no interference."

— B.J. Palmer

Respect Mother Nature

I have been in practice for over two decades. But just over a decade ago, I become sufficiently "qualified" to write this chapter. In around 2010, after studying health for about 15 years, having had multiple successful multidisciplinary practices, and having myself been a chiropractic client, I was still ill-qualified to write about a true health. Two things conspired to open my eyes to some very obvious facts. So obvious, and yet I was pretty unaware of them for most of my life.

Nearly ten years into my practice career, two key things happened, which changed my perspective on myself, my health, my family's health, your health, everything. A client called me out, and I took a leap of faith.

I Got Called Out

The client in question was only 35 years old and was in the "maintenance phase" of her care. She had a disc hernia ("slipped disc") at the base of her spine, which had worsened suddenly after having her first child. Her diet was not ideal and she was slightly overweight, plus she had a stressful job working from home and did not get enough exercise. I was seeing her once a month, adjusting her *to "treat" her symptoms,* and doing just enough to stop her back from getting worse. This is the "maintenance" model of care, but it was far from ideal. One day she came in, doubled over in pain. She was angry. She said, "If I had come in just a week ago, this would not have happened. Why do you keep recommending that I come in once a month, leaving me to struggle through the last two weeks of each month?" I tried to calm her and said of course, that she could come more often. Then she turned and asked, "How often do you get adjusted?" I proudly announced that ALL of the staff in our team got adjusted about once per week, and sometimes I got adjusted even more frequently. At the time, I had no symptoms of spinal problems, but I knew it kept me healthy year-round. I thought I had impressed her. She carried on. "And what about your family? How often do you recommend that they get adjusted"? Again, I proudly told her that I recommended that my family get adjusted about once per week, but to never leave it more than two weeks between care. And then she hit me with it. "And why don't you recommend the same for your clients. Do we not matter so much?"

Since that moment, I have always treated my clients as if they were a member of my family. I will always recommend to a client the same care that I would recommend to my wife, kids, siblings, or parents. Whether people value it, can afford it, or can find time for it is their own business. Who am I to offer a client less than the best of health and happiness?

A Leap of Faith

The second big shift was a leap of faith into totally changing the care goals I set for my clients. I attended a conference where one of the key speakers spoke of his practice. He spoke of setting goals, then adjusting his clients for many weeks before reviewing them again. It's not that he didn't care about how they felt in the meantime. It's that he cared *too much* about his clients' *long-term health and happiness* to be distracted by how someone might feel on a particular day. He spoke of setting goals which were *independent of how his clients felt.* He said that, when you focus all of your attention on reducing spinal misalignments, on freeing the nervous system, you would awaken to things in the client's body to which you are otherwise blind. Only then would miracles occur. And he told stories of remarkable healings in his own practice, things which sounded impossible to the medical mind.

I had studied chiropractic in a Medical Sciences school. I was outraged. I was still stuck in the model where I would ask the client at every visit how they felt. In fact, in medicine it is called "patient-centred care." I now know that it should be renamed "problem-centred care". Based on what they said, I would proceed to poke and "chase" their pains around their body. They would get relief, but their pains would come back. Or they would get injured elsewhere. Then we would go into further detail, give them long lists of exercises to do, and treat them more. And then they would have another problem. We would give supplements, orthotics, and everything else you could imagine. In fact, despite having a waiting-list practice and doing the best job I could, I could see our clients getting older, less mobile, and having more problems year on year. It was like a constant fight with gravity, age, and illness, and we were losing. This is the normal model of "treatment," not only in medicine, but also in the natural therapies. I was doing what the majority of therapists worldwide (and about half of the chiropractic profession) still do. I was trying to remove the problem rather than release the power of healing. Trying to contain illness, rather than release health. I would soon learn that I was not yet a real chiropractor, but only a "symptom-practor".

With full intent to prove myself right, I went to visit this doctor's practice. He was a loud, pretty in-your-face, slightly intimidating, Texan guy. Larger than life. At first glance, you could mistakenly think he did not care about the details, including the details of *how* his clients got so ill. My hackles were up, and I was ready to prove that what he was saying was impossible, unethical, or both.

He had an extremely busy practice. I observed him over two days. I had never seen so many happy clients. People who had been under care for years. They looked half the age that it said on their files. There was a feeling of love in the air. They looked flexible, at ease, in a state of effortless abundance in life. They looked connected to themselves, to their bodies, to their possibilities. I watched his new client exams. I watched the client reviews. I heard client after client celebrating their healings. Disc hernias? Of course, that was not new to me. But countless other "impossible" recoveries. From paralysis to autoimmune disorders, one after another client told of miraculous healings. His wife had even written a book with some of these stories.

Doctor Marc Hudson, in Mallorca, Spain, *did and does,* care about his clients. He cared too much to waste time on irrelevant details. He was too focused for small talk. He knew that chasing a pain from your left shoulder to your right ear was never going to change your life. But freeing the power of healing would rid you of pains *and* change your life. He had seen the power of healing in his clients. He knew how to free it, and he was on a mission to release the miracles in each person.

But I had one big problem. I was not sure if I could achieve the same results as Dr Marc. So I had to take a leap of faith. I had to do the same with my own clients. I explained this to some of my trusted clients, and they agreed to stop telling me what their symptoms were, and instead let me adjust what their body told me. They soon improved in ways which left them and me in amazement. The biggest challenge, in fact, was "forgetting" what pains the client had. When someone told me where it hurt, my instinctive nature to care meant that I again became blinded to the greater goal. And when clients did not tell me what hurt, not only did their pains get better, but a whole lot more. They started sleeping better, their chronic gastro-oesophageal reflux magically disappeared, along with a myriad of other seemingly unrelated "diseases", and most importantly, they became happier people. Perhaps I am a slow learner, but it took years of practising in the "standard" model to realise that the power of healing inside your body is capable of miracles. Yes, miracles. Sounds mystical, no? I even feel uncomfortable writing the word, but that is what they are.

Today, I base my recommendations and care on reconnecting your healing power, *not* on your pains or symptoms, and in so doing, we see miracles every week.

The rest of this book is the scientific explanation of how and why these miracles take place. But if you don't want to read all the science, you can put the book down after this next paragraph.

There is an innate intelligence in your body. It expresses itself as nerve impulses (electrical power) from your brain and through your nervous system. It organises and co-ordinates your growth from embryo to adult. It gives life to every single cell in your body. Little toe, heart, genitals. Every cell. And when it leaves your body, when that electrical impulse is extinguished, you are dead.

That life power travels through your spine. You were born free and full of life and love, with a supple spine. But your spine lives a tough life, with accidents, injuries, sitting too much, and bending over at computers. It becomes stiff and twisted, causing subluxation between your vertebrae. Subluxation interferes with the nerve impulses traveling to your body. Interfering with these impulses reduces your expression of life. In every cell in your body. This power that made your body heals your body.

Reducing subluxation frees the power to heal your body. It restores your very own life force.

Physics or Spirit, it Matters Not

Whether someone calls these principals Universal Intelligence, the laws of physics, God, Allah, Nirankar, Yahweh, or Mother Nature is not relevant to me. But recognising these principles is pivotal in how healthy you will be. Knowing there is an innate intelligence within you determines the medicines you will take, how you will treat your body, and how you will age.

Why? Because the medicalised society in which we live has taught us some pretty ridiculous things, things totally to the contrary of the above facts. We have been taught (and we continue to teach) that the cleverest thing is our own intellect. That through science, we can understand everything, then manipulate everything, and dominate everything. That the world is literally our domain to play with as we wish. This is the dogmatic paradigm of "science as God" which dominates our society. Farcically arrogant. And this has dire health consequences. Not only for planet earth, but for your health and mine.

Imagine two 30-year-old identical twins walking side by side through life. Twin A believes that science knows (or will soon know) everything, and humans are clever enough to safely manipulate nature, including the human body. Twin B believes that there is an innate healing power in her body, that science can help us to understand parts of it, but that we humans are light years away from understanding all of the details and nuances and that trying to manipulate nature is fundamentally dangerous.

Yesterday, they were sitting together at the traffic lights in their car when they were hit from behind. Today, they both have a headache. Twin A thinks, "Nuisance headache. Let me reach for a pill to silence it, so I can get on with my day." She just took a small step left on her health journey. Twin B thinks, "Mmm. I must be healing. Perhaps, I should drink more water and rest." Twin B drinks some water and heads to bed early, and so steps off to the right on her health journey. They are now headed in different directions.

The next morning, they both awaken with neck pain. Twin A thinks, "Damned neck pain. Lucky I have some more Ibuprofen from yesterday," and pops another few pills. Twin B thinks, "Wow, my body is expressing more symptoms. I must be healing. Let me drink more water and change my posture to care for my neck when I work today." Again they separate their paths a little more.

Jump forward two weeks. Twin A is frustrated with the recurring pain and headaches, plus she has started to get indigestion from all of the painkillers. She books an appointment with her medical doctor. Meanwhile, Twin B has increased her water intake, improved her working and sleeping posture, and books an appointment with her chiropractor. Twin A receives omeprazole to calm the acids in her stomach, as her medical doctor prescribes stronger painkillers. Twin B starts getting adjusted with her chiropractor to free the damage in her neck. Their health and happiness are now on two very different paths.

Jump forward twelve months. Twin A has been suffering shoulder and arm pain and has surgery booked for a herniated disc in her neck. She is taking multiple painkillers and even sleeping pills. She is chronically tired and irritated, and her relationships are suffering. She just missed out on a promotion at work and is feeling depressed. Her doctor has suggested she start on anti-depressants. Her general health has declined severely, mostly from the side-effects of the medications she is now taking. Things are not looking good. She assumes that the car accident is to blame for her bad health, and that otherwise, she is just unlucky.

Twin B now uses an orthopaedic pillow to sleep and has a great posture at work. She drinks plenty of water, and gets adjusted regularly. Her posture has improved under chiropractic care, and life feels full of opportunity. In fact she just left her boring job to set up her own business. Her relationships are flourishing, and she feels happier and more fulfilled than ever. Reflecting on it, she feels that a small car accident just a year ago gave her the chance of greater health and happiness, and she feels grateful for it. If only her sister could join her on the same journey...

I have seen a pair of identical twins with a very similar story to this. Our life beliefs shape our health philosophy. And our health philosophy determines our health and happiness.

Life is expressed in your body from Above Down, from Inside Out. It happens no other way. When we acknowledge and respect this healing intelligence in ourselves, when we respect that nature heals us, then we choose more life. At any point in time, we can change our health direction. We can choose more life. It just takes one choice.

Your Earth Suit

Lights On=Life, Lights Out=Dead

Figure 3. It is this simple. The better connected the electrical circuit from your brain to your body, the more life you have. 100% Connection = 100% Life. When there is no electricity flowing from your brain, you are declared dead.

You were once but a twinkle in your parents eyes. They got together and did some unimaginable things, and a single cell was born. You. Just one cell. Simpler than a bacteria cell. You started slowly. After three days, you were just 16 cells.[4] Things were not looking good, as at this rate, you were going to take 50 trillion years to become an adult. But then, as you started to bury yourself in your mother's womb lining, you started to gather speed.

Early on, your spinal cord and brain "outgrew" the rest of your body. Your brain started at the tip of a three millimeter tube of cells.[5] This tube formed as the centre of your brain and spine. As each body part opened out, migrating towards its final position, it tugged its own spinal nerve with it, trailing out from the centre. So your kidneys and your feet, pulled their cables from your spine as they grew. If this did not happen, your brain could not connect to your respective body parts, and they would all die. You then grew at a rate of 15 million cells per hour over nine months, into the 30 to 100 trillion cells that your mother thankfully brought into the world as YOU. But none of those cells were, or are, really YOU. How can we know that?

Most of the cells in your body are constantly dying and being replaced. In fact, when you do the maths, the *average age* of the cells in your body is no more than seven years old.[6] When you remove the longest lived cells, your body mostly replaces itself every three months or so!

Most of the things we identify as being "me" or "you" are constantly being replaced. While your outer skin sheds in days, your whole skin layer is new every month. Some blood cells only last days. Bone cells can last 25 to 50 years. Your eye lens cells should last one lifetime. So the "me" that you look at in the mirror in the morning will be thrown out in the coming months. Touch your hand right now. Seriously, take a moment to say hello to it. It looks familiar, right? It will be a new hand a few months from now. Admire your charming looks in the mirror in the morning, but say goodbye when you leave, as your face will soon be replaced! It is mind boggling, but it is true. The body you so identify with is not YOU!

There is ONE set of cells which are with you from start to finish, and they have a predicted lifespan of 200+ years. They are the strongest (by weight) and longest cells in your body.[7] Most of them have little or no ability to regenerate. Yet, they use disproportionately more energy than any other body cells, and they generate their own electricity. You got it, your central nervous system is the only thing which you will take from birth to death. The rest is all disposable.

This "disposable body" is made of up to 100 trillion cells, performing a potential 600 octillion tasks per second. Let me write that down…

600,000,000,000,000,000,000,000,000,000 possible functions. Hey, plus or minus a few octillion. But you get the point. That is a lot.

Imagine I gave you a big bag, full of 100 trillion live cells and asked you to look after them and their 600 octillion functions for me until tomorrow. Lung cells, kidney cells, foot cells, hand cells, blood cells, and of course, ear cells. A whole body's worth. What would you do? How would you keep them all alive? Put them out in the sun? Throw a bit of water in the bag? A burger and a few beers? Our conscious minds, even with the world's biggest instruction manual, would have no idea how to keep your body alive. So, the momentous, magical task of your 100 billion brain cells is to manage the 100 trillion body cells. In science, we call this your innate intelligence. Your innate intelligence manages your earth suit while you are alive.

So where is the real "you" in all of this? In your thumb? Kidney? Well, I am not going to pretend to answer that question properly, but I can say that the real "you" is expressed through this innate intelligence and your body. Everything you see, feel, do, experience is collected by sensors, passed through your nervous system and registered in your brain. The skills you have, your ability to read, do maths, walk, play tennis, remember history, feel empathy, feel anger, feel love, is all generated, managed, and expressed through your nervous system. By the electrical impulses coursing through it. This is neither hypothetical nor spiritual—this is scientific fact.

You learn to ride a bicycle at eight years old. 40 years later, you remount a bicycle, and a totally different body, a different set of cells, are instantly commanded to ride again, by the memory in your nervous system.

Your continued existence here on earth, in your "earthsuit" body is all dependent upon this central nervous system. And the life in this system is the electricity which flows in it. In fact, your brain produces some 20 watts of electricity. That lightbulb of electricity *is* the life in your body. When the electricity stops, your body loses life, and you leave your earth suit.

This book is about your spinal health, but in truth, it is about how to maximise the clarity and speed of signals between you (your nervous system and brain) and your earth suit, to maximise both the quality and the length of life you get out of your earth suit.

Your body is far more intelligent than all of the doctors and scientists in the world, and millions of times more powerful than any computer ever built. The greatest doctor is the one inside you.

Subluxation- What is it?

Vertebral Subluxation

Vertebral Subluxation is an abnormal alignment, posture, or movement of one or many vertebrae, putting abnormal stress on your nerves, and in so doing, interrupting the speed, clarity, and balance of the messages going to and from your brain. Interrupting the signals which control ALL of your health, ALL of your curing, ALL of your life. Vertebral Subluxation can be like chronically choking your very own doctor.

How often do you brush your teeth? At least a couple of times a day, I would hope. And how often do you do something to specifically care for your spine? I don't just mean exercise. Exercising your spine is like eating apples. Definitely good for your teeth, but not quite the same as brushing your teeth. Our teeth are replaceable. Our spines are not. And yet most people spend lots of time caring for their smile and virtually no time caring for the thing which protects the life inside them. What would have happened had our spines been as visible to the public as our teeth are? Would we look after them differently? For sure.

My job often involves looking at beautiful people with ugly spines. It's a funny thing to try to explain, how a person who appears in great shape might have a damaged and degenerated spine. No matter how beautiful your face, character, or soul may be, the state of your spine tells a lot about your health; past, present, *and* future.

So what does a Vertebral Subluxation look like? What really happens in the spine?

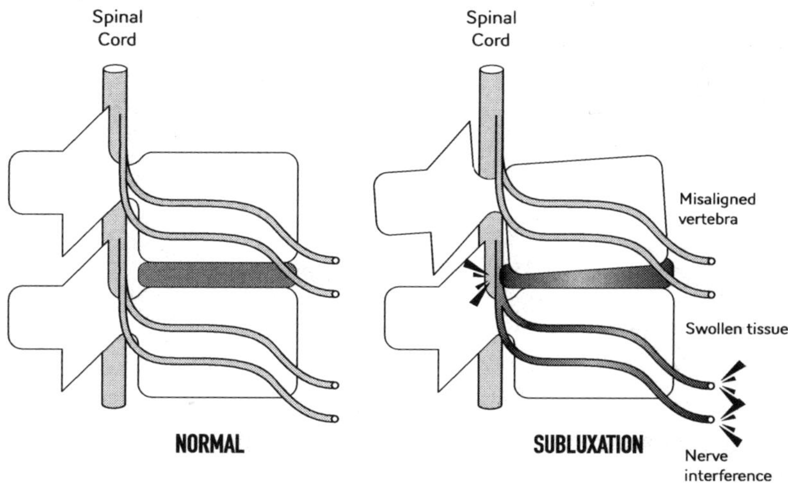

Figure 4. Normal vs subluxated spine, showing 1) Misalignment 2) Inflammation 3) Nerve interference.

Bone: The first element is the most obvious. A vertebra or a group of vertebrae is out of place or not moving normally. This might be detected on x-ray, by palpating (the doctor feeling your spine), or through a whole host of what we call "indicators." Indicators are like groups of changes in your body which, when put together, show where the subluxation or subluxations are. It takes years of training and skill to accurately detect vertebral subluxation.

Nerve: The abnormal position or movement changes the pressure on the nerve. This is how a "local" problem can affect every part of your health. Because the effects travel up the nerve to your brain and also down the nerve to the "end organ[8]" The end organ could be your foot, heart, genitals, wherever the nerve goes. Locally, this pressure triggers a cascade of further changes.

Brain: This is the most important part of a subluxation. Your brain now has to get used to a different set of feedback. In fact, subluxation causes "noise" in your brain, making everything a little more difficult.[9] Not impossible, but more difficult. When you are subluxated, you can do everything, but nothing at 100%. It is like the dimmer switch in your brain has turned the power down.

Muscle: Your muscle tension now changes. This can happen adjacent to the subluxation, or further down the nerve path. This is why people so often mistake subluxations for muscular problems. If you have a muscular problem, it should heal completely within days to a week. Why would a muscle injury persist or recur in a healthy person? If it persists or recurs, you have to look to the spine. A one-year muscle spasm does not exist. What controls your muscle tension? Your nerve signals. What controls your muscle healing? Your nerve signals! Nearly all chronic "muscle problems" are really "nerve problems."

Chemistry: This reason is far more subtle, and it is that the chemistry of the area changes. Rather than having a nice blood supply and drainage, your nerves now sit in a bath of inflammation. The cables to and from your brain sit in a bath of toxins, the effects of which are often silent.[10]

Ligaments and Joints: The sixth part is what we get to see on X-ray when people don't act soon enough—if you don't get adjusted regularly. Flexible spinal joints and tissues do not tend to scar and degenerate, but blocked, subluxated joints do. If the joints remain stuck, the ligaments and tissues scar, and eventually calcium deposits and grows "bony spurs" around the discs and joints. Sometimes, this is passed off as "normal wear and tear." If it really is "wear and tear," it should be *even* throughout your spine. All of your vertebrae are the same age, so wear and tear should be evenly distributed. If it is focused at one level or area, it is not normal, but subluxation-degeneration.

That is the medical explanation. Like most great things, science only starts to fully explain them decades or more after their discovery.[11] Some would say that subluxation blocks your Prana. Chi. Ki. Ruah. Or whatever else you want to call your life force. On the most obvious of levels, it disconnects you from your very own healing magic and from the fullest, best expression of yourself.

3 Ways to Get Subluxated

In this section, we are going to briefly explore what can cause subluxations in your spine. A good chiropractor can change your spine, reducing subluxations and allowing you to heal, but if you are doing things to re-injure it every day, then your progress may take longer than you hoped for.

These causes are independent of the symptoms you may be having. By that I mean, never mind if you have migraines, neck pain, asthma, a herniated disc, or hip arthritis—they can *all* be caused by a combination of the same things. This may sound bizarre at first, but when you get used to looking at your health (or any lost health) in this way, it empowers you to take control.

Taking control of these factors very literally will add years to your life and life to your years.

Three Ts

There are three causes of subluxation. In fact, ALL stresses in your life and your body can be grouped into these three categories. They are; Trauma (physical exercise and posture), Toxins (nutritional status and toxic exposures) and Thoughts (stored stress and current thoughts). I use these categories to plan the health and fitness of not only myself and my clients, but also my children and my family.

Trauma

The first is the most obvious. Trauma, or physical stress.

Car accidents, sports injuries, falls as a child, even the birth process, can cause damage in your spine, which causes movement habits and postures. As those habits and postures scar, they become a part of you, causing chronic subluxation. The longer ago they happened, the more *normal* this subluxated pattern has become and the more problematic they are. This means that a fall ten years ago may be affecting your health more today than a fall you had yesterday. Counterintuitive? The ten year old fall is now "a normal part" of you. The fall yesterday can still be dealt with so it leaves little or no long term scars, but the ten year old one is a far bigger deal for your health.

Then, let's say you have a bad posture at your computer, you fall asleep on the sofa, or spend too long gazing at your telephone. And you do that for hours, weeks, years, decades, and now your posture is *stuck* where it should not be. And that produces a lot of subluxation stress. Contrarily, if you don't have postural stress, and you move and exercise your body in a healthy way, then you reduce subluxation stress.

Toxins

There are two ways in which your nutritional status or toxic load can damage your spine.

The first concerns your general physical state, your general ability to heal. The benefit to improving your health through nutrition is obvious. If you drink too much alcohol, smoke, or eat junk food, the severity of your subluxations increases, and it is more difficult for the inflammation around the subluxations to settle.[12] If you don't drink enough water, recovering from subluxations takes longer and is more uncomfortable. If you have insufficient sunlight exposure and vitamin D, your whole nervous system is in a state of stress and defence.

The second concerns how toxic loads can irritate your nervous system. We live in a world which is loaded with toxic stress. Microplastics or mercury in our fish supplies, pesticides on our fruits, caffeine or alcohol, sugars, medications, chlorinated water, cosmetics, cleaning agents, air pollution—the list is endless. Your nervous system perceives these non-physical stressors to be threatening and directs your muscles to react, defend, and brace your body. This factor in subluxation is harder to recognise and often takes longer to improve.

The most common toxic stresses that I see "holding clients back" in practice are hormonal changes and medications. People who are undergoing hormonal changes or are on stronger medications may respond more slowly to care.

"If my body is so clever, why does it not adapt to all of these stresses?," you might ask. Your body *is so clever.* And it *does adapt* to all of these stresses. This is how our ancestors survived, and how you and I continue to survive. If you are only interested in *surviving*, there is no reason to deal with subluxation. But what if you want to *thrive?* The environment we live in has changed a lot faster that we have evolved. Which means that our bodies, designed to be cavemen and cavewomen, have to deal with caffeine, alcohol, grain and sugar intake, toxic pollution, media stress, computers and telephones, office jobs, sitting, and reduced activity levels, to name just a few. We *survive*. We store stress in our spines as subluxations. And we pay the price, sometimes with pain, often with ill health, but always with living a less fulfilled life than we might have. Choosing to *thrive*, choosing to reduce subluxation, is a choice to live closer to 100% life.

Thoughts

The third category is not so obvious, but is every bit as important. For some people, this is more important than physical stress. Thoughts or emotional stress show in your spine, through your nervous system. They change your posture, muscle tension, and cause subluxations.

You may have already felt this. Have you ever been concerned about something at work or in your studies? Or had an argument with your partner? Or worried about a financial problem? You sit reading a document or tapping on your phone or your computer into the night and suddenly realise that your neck or shoulders ache or that the front of your hips has gotten very tight or even that your back pain and sciatic nerve has gotten irritated, and your buttock is tight and sore?

Emotional stresses anchor to your spine in different patterns, depending on who you are and what the stress is. In Chapter 9, I explain this in more detail. Emotions are a great way of finding our "weak spots," and when emotional stress overlays physical problems in your spine, then things get complicated.

Among the three causes of subluxation, the easiest to assess is your Trauma/Physical status. In Chapter 14, we discuss how to choose a good doctor, but it's worth noting that if your chiropractor gets your care recommendation wrong, it is very likely because of one of these "hidden" stressors. When I "misread" a client, I have missed a hidden level of emotional, chemical, or hormonal stress, which means that your physical recovery may take longer than expected.

In Chapter 12 we look at some easy ways to reduce subluxation stress.

Chapter 2 Checklist

- Your body, wishing the best for you in every moment, is born to heal. Your brain is the most complex system known to science. The intelligence and scale of its task is very literally awe-some.
- Honouring the cleverness of your body produces radically different health results. Be it through scientific understanding or blind faith does not matter. Treating your "inner doctor" as the best doctor you will ever have means better health and longevity.
- Vertebral subluxation—stored stress within your spine—interferes with the intelligence which manages this wonderful healing power. It chokes the ability of your inner doctor to heal you.
- Vertebral subluxations can be caused, sustained, or worsened by three stress categories: postural and physical traumas, nutritional and environmental toxins, and emotions and thoughts. These stressors are simply a fact of modern life, meaning we all live with constant subluxation stress.

Action Points

- Scan this QR code with your phone. It takes you to a self-test for subluxation, which you can do at home in just 10 minutes. The results may surprise you! also at www.duffyquiropractica.com/am-i-subluxated/
- Consider one action which you could change from each of these categories… (Trauma/Physical, Thoughts/Emotions, Toxins/Nutrition).
- Put a note in your diary three months from now. Revisit the same self-test in three months.

Take a moment to write each of those titles (Trauma/Physical, Thoughts/Emotions, Toxins/Nutrition) at the top of a page. Write your name above them.

If 10 were perfect, and 0 were appalling, score your overall lifestyle "performance" in each category. Consider the last six months as a reference point.

Below each score, write down one to three things you could do to improve that score over the coming three months. The simpler, the more achievable, the better.

Put a note in your diary three months from now. Repeat this exercise in three months time.

Consider repeating this task every three to six months. It helps you to build an awareness of your health habits and growth over time.

If you are near Marbella, Spain, go to www.duffyquiropractica.com to find out how to work with Dr Duffy.

If elsewhere, go to www.chiroalliance.org or www.chiropractic.org to search for subluxation-reducing chiropractors.

PART II

Innate Design

"Design is intelligence made visible."

— Alina Wheeler

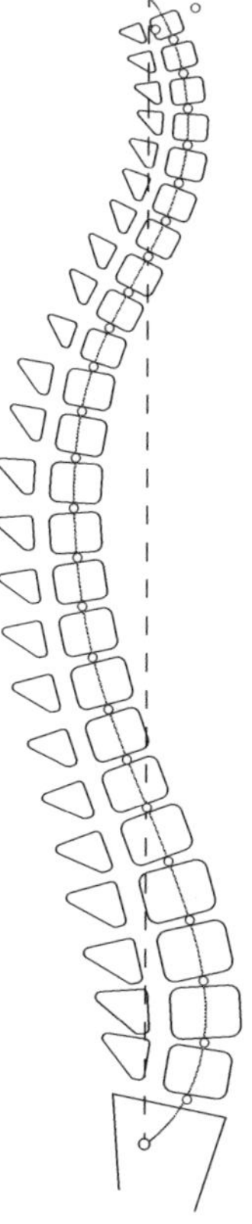

Chapter 3

Rebuild Your Spine

"It's only when gravity starts to take over you begin to think about your body."

— David Soul

Four Ingredients of Spinal Health

In Part I, we looked at our health motivation, the "*Why?*" of our health decisions. Now we are going to look at *How* we can rebuild our own health. This is the section where I might make myself a little unpopular.

We all know that good posture is key to good health. But what is the science behind this? Is the mantra "sit up straight" enough? Can we have too much of a good thing? Is posture just a cosmetic thing or does it really affect my health?

If I am young, I can choose to change my posture any time, right? If I am old, it is too late, and my posture won't change. I'm better off leaving well enough alone, correct?

Anyone of any age can move closer to a perfect posture. The younger you are, the greater the impact on your overall health and longevity. The older you are, the more it will affect your mobility and experience of the rest of your life.

Here are the four key ingredients of a healthy spine. You can add icing to this cake, or even add other flavours, but these are the KEY ingredients, without which you cannot have cake!

1. Connection. A clear brain-body connection makes finding a good posture easy. Your body wants to be healthy! This is the flour (or gluten-free equivalent) in your cake. Without it, you can bake something, but it will never pass as a cake.

2. Alignment. "Stacking" the four keystones of your spine one on top of the other turns good posture into a gentle balancing act, rather than a strength and endurance competition.

3. Movement. Movement is a team job. When you bend over, all of your vertebrae should play their role evenly. When they work as a team, you are strong and resilient. If a dozen of them are subluxated, they are not playing, and something is going to go wrong.

4. Load. The lighter the load, the healthier the spine. There is no getting away from gravity. The more you load your spine, the faster it ages.

This is a hierarchy. If I were to gift every back pain sufferer just one of these, it would be connection. Followed by alignment, etc.

One thing that separates us from our primate cousins is our bipedal stance. When we moved from four to two legs, we became more energy efficient and more mobile than any of our near evolutionary competitors. Volumes have been written about our upright stance, our balance, and movement efficiency. The idea behind these next chapters is not to give you a PhD in spinal mechanics and remodelling, but to explain the principles so you understand how to get healthier and stay young and well for life. If you go in for heart surgery, you want to understand the basics, but you don't need to go to medical school to study cardiology before the surgery, right?

The Balancing Act - Connection and Alignment

Be it the latest electric car, an eco-house, or the absolute marvel of your human body, energy efficiency always makes sense. Why would you spend more energy to stand upright than is necessary? So evolution designed your bones and ligaments to "balance" on top of each other with beautiful architecture. This is the *ideal* spinal model: a set of marvellously engineered curves which poise in elegant efficiency when you stand. That is the *passive* part of your spinal system—the support structure.

But if it were that easy, and only the structure mattered, we would all have one big, rigid tube for a spine, instead of individual bones. We could easily maintain perfect posture. So why does it all need to be so complicated? Alas, we also need to move, so this same structure also has the ability to bend forward and back, twist, and lean side to side. You have 33 spinal bones, of which five fuse at your pelvis and four are in your "tailbone," leaving 24 mobile vertebrae. And between each one, making up a quarter of the length of your spine, are cartilage discs. All of which means that your spine is far from "locked" in this perfect balance.

So what *should* keep it there?

Most people answer "muscles!" Yes. Those friends, muscles. And how much muscle do you need to keep your spine poised in an upright posture? A tiny, tiny, tiny amount!

Now I can hear some people shouting; *"WHAT? I was told that I needed to strengthen my spine because I have disc problems,"* or *"WHAT? I was given pilates and core exercises to strengthen my spine, and they worked."*

Let's repeat that. The strength needed to maintain your spine poised in that ideal posture is *minimal.* As in, your forearm muscles would easily be up to the task of holding your spine upright all day long. But this assumes that you have good spinal alignment. This assumes that gravity is your friend. In poor postures, your deep spinal muscles, designed to *balance and control,* now get charged with *holding up your weight!* It's no wonder that people have become obsessed with strengthening the spine. Don't get me wrong, I like icing on my cake, so it is nice to have a strong spine for lifting and sports, but it is even nicer not to *need a strong spine just to get through the day!* A healthy spine is designed to *balance* in a good posture and does not need strength to achieve this. So what does it need?

Earlier, we said muscles. But that is not really true. Because no amount of muscle can keep your spine upright if it does not receive fast and accurate instructions. In fact, you and I know many people who have a lot of muscle, but who have major postural and spinal problems. Is their problem a lack of muscle? Should they hit the gym? No.

A more honest answer is *nerves,* or more precisely, nerve feedback. We called this feedback *proprioception.* So muscles are only any good when they are *accurately connected and co-ordinated by nervous function.*

When you have clear communication between your brain and body, these sensors—your proprioceptors—tell your brain where each bone is in relation to the vertical axis. Your brain instantly co-ordinates the best response to pull that bone back into the best posture. This is a core element of your brain-body connection.

Without clear feedback from your nerves, the postural reflex in your brain has only a fuzzy idea of what your posture is. This is what happens when your spine is subluxated. That highly tuned part of your brain which magically balances your spine, coordinates your walking, and catches a ball has no idea what it is doing. Rather than befriend gravity, it picks a fight with gravity. It *tries* to respond correctly. But it now sends messages down your spine, telling muscles to contract where they do not need to. Other muscles relax when they need to protect you. Some go into spasm unnecessarily. It's all a bit of a mess, frankly. Do those muscles have a problem? Do they need massage or strengthening or core stability training? Those are nice ideas and will probably feel good, but without a clear connection between your brain and spine, no amount of massage or strengthening is really going to fix your problem. This is where chiropractic looks like it works miracles. It's not rocket science. Chiropractic adjustments clear this communication. They restore your proprioception. By reducing subluxations, and reconnecting the sensors in your spine, those muscles start getting used efficiently. Suddenly what seemed like a weak back is strong without any strength work. Chronic muscle spasms relax and soften without any massage.

Millions of people use Yoga and Pilates practice to improve their spinal health every year.[13] They are both very healthy practices, which can add a lot of strength to your spine. I recommend some form of regular practice for our wellness care clients, and personally practise both yoga and pilates. But you will also hear countless stories of people getting "injured by" yoga or pilates. In fact nearly 80% of yoga practitioners sustain an injury at some point.[14] 21% of pre-existing injuries are exacerbated, most of which are back problems,[15] and 1/3rd of yoga injuries last over 3 months.[16] Some of these are caused by a bad exercise, like a shoulder stand, which is an obviously bad idea and causes injury.[17] But most of these injuries are just highlighting an unhealthy, subluxated spine that cannot tolerate healthy exercises. This is most often the case of a problem being highlighted, rather than an injury being sustained. It is not the fault of the practice, but a symptom of an unhealthy spine. Most people with a healthy spine should be able to do such practice without ill effect, once their subluxations have been reduced.

Time to Move

Stretching is dumb. Does that sound offensive? No, I don't mean that people who stretch are dumb. Nor do I mean that it is a bad idea. But I mean that stretching is not specific. It takes one whole *area* of your body and moves it until the joints and muscles stretch. It's a pretty blunt instrument. But what if some of those joints were not moving in the first instance. What if some of those muscles were tight because of pressure on the nerve supplying them?

Stretching is dumb because the quality of the stretch depends on the quality of the movement, and the nervous control of the area. And these depend on the *history* of your spine. So a perfectly performed stretch in a spine with perfectly equal and healthy spinal movement, and normal nerve function, is a beautiful thing. Now show me a spine with perfectly equal and healthy movement. Show me a spine without any subluxations. My spine, for example, does not have such health, so I need to be careful with how I stretch.

Stretching cannot remove subluxations; it can only lessen the muscle tension and soreness caused by subluxation. If I could stretch my spine well, I would stretch all day long, but instead, I take three or four hours out of my life every other week to get my own spine adjusted. I also stretch every day, but that is because I like icing on my cake.

Load - there is no escaping gravity

You know how this works. Your spine bears the load of your weight for an average of 520,000 waking hours per lifetime.

Weight = Mass x Gravity. Mass = how massive you are or are not. Gravity = that inescapable force that is always with you, for better or worse, as friend or foe.

I mentioned earlier that your spine spends its whole life fighting gravity, but I missed an important detail. It actually spends its life fighting gravity *multiplied by your mass*. And the greater your mass, the greater the fight. It is simple physics. I often see overweight clients who have been recommended disc surgery before even being given time to reduce their weight. This is crazy.

That said, and as you will learn in the coming chapters, your weight is not as big a problem as connection and location. A very overweight person can have a healthy spine, as long as they are not subluxated, and they have a good posture. As long as they befriend gravity. A very lightweight person will have a toxically degenerative spine, as long as they are subluxated and/or have poor posture. As long as they make gravity their enemy.

Befriend Gravity

We are guaranteed to succumb to two things in life. Gravity and death. The problem is that many of us succumb to gravity way before death, meaning decades of ill health and suffering before death. We can befriend gravity and work with it, rather than fight it. For as long as we stay upright, there is a commonsense way of doing this. We will all end up horizontal one day, the big question is how soon?

Locating Your Four Bones

Your spine has four main sections, each with their own curve, plus the tail bone. The base, called the *sacrum,* fuses during adulthood, from ages 18 to 30. The other three sections should have flexible curves of approximately 40 degrees and should line up directly above the section below. The vertical alignment of these four sections plus the curves between them determine your spinal health and ultimately your spinal age. Deviation from this state of balance is bad news. Gravity does not rest, so when you lose balance, you start to fight gravity. Your health depends on your making friends with gravity. This is just common sense.

There are many different ways to measure spinal curves, so don't be surprised if you have seen or heard measurements which don't match the above. The details are beyond the scope of this book, so I have included the reference to an online book chapter[18] which explains this topic in more detail.

C1. Your Atlas

So important is C1 that some chiropractors are dedicated *only* to the alignment of this one bone. Named "Atlas" after the Greek god who was said to hold up the world, this one little bone holds up your head, your brain, your own world. This, all while protecting the extension of your brainstem which runs inside it and ALL of the nerves to the rest of your body. This tiny little bone only weighs about 60 grams, or the weight of about two bags of tea! Yet, it supports about 5kg of head in the average adult. The alignment of C1 is the single most important anatomical alignment in your whole body.

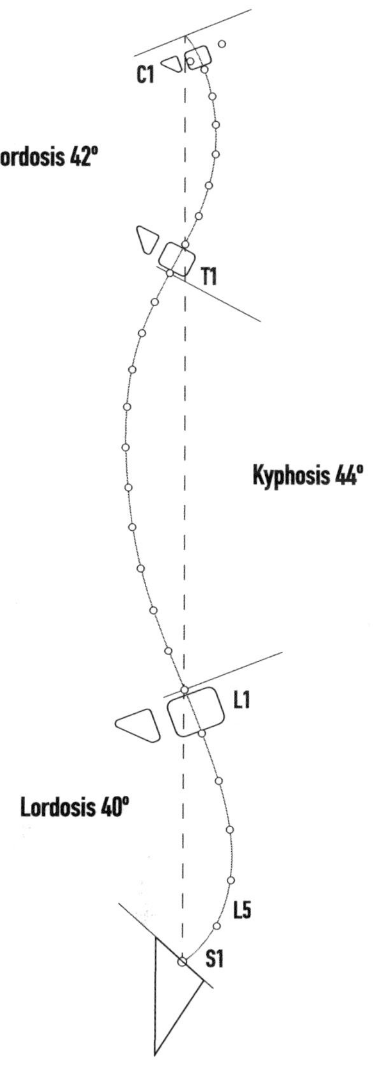

Figure 5. Your Four Bones. Stacking your spinal curves one on top of the other makes gravity your friend. Only in this posture can your body be at ease.[197] *It is just common sense.*

T1. Your breath depends on it.

T1 is at the top of the thoracic spine—your mid-back, at the level of your shoulders. Your thoracic spine holds your ribcage, so misalignment here changes the dynamics of your lungs, compressing them by up to a third. This is the only spinal curve which can be easily seen from the outside, even with your shirt on. You look older if you have a hunched back. This hunch is linked with bad long-term general health. But far more importantly, misalignment here can force your neck and head into bad postures, which can have severe consequences.

L1. Your discs depend on it.

The low back or lumbar section has five bones. These should sit in a relaxed curve, which allows L1, the first lumbar bone, to sit above the spinal base. If the base angle is off, or if the total lumbar curve is increased or decreased, then L1 will sit either in front of or behind its base, causing increased stress,[19] disc hernias, and degeneration.[20]

S1. The foundation of your spine

Your sacrum sits in your pelvis, like the

foundation of your spine. Having an increased angle at its uppermost section, called S1, can set up an excessive low back curve, causing your spine to compensate above.[21]

Not knowing the ideal can be dangerous

People who do not understand your spine and try to force your posture may make you look slightly better temporarily, but it is a dangerous practice. On too many occasions I have seen clients given spinal straightening exercises by their therapist or postural exercises by their personal trainer, which were *directly contraindicated.* Put another way, without understanding spinal mechanics, these “professionals” had given advice which would result in increased disc stress, ageing, injury, and suffering. The old adage of, “Pull your shoulders back and stand tall,” does have its place. For some people. For others, it is, “Push your pelvis back and relax your shoulders.” And others, “Tip your pelvis forward and lift your sternum.” There has been a free-for-all among insufficiently qualified professionals trying to change postures without understanding the individual needs of each client. In Chapter 12, we will go over some postural principals you can safely use, but if you really want to know your posture, you need to see a properly qualified professional.

Forcing Ideal can also be dangerous

Before we dive into the details, it’s worth noting that the world is not always ideal. Unfortunately, some people abandon and ignore their spines so badly that the degeneration and bony changes prohibit getting back to neutral. Ideally, a good doctor will move you towards the Ideal, coaxing and coaching your spine along the way and respecting your personal goals and circumstances. In Chapter 14 we look at how to choose your doctor.

Staying Curvy

Above I mentioned that each of your three mobile spinal curves should be *approximately* 40 degrees. This is subject to many different factors which we won't go into here, but why are these optimal curves so important? In fact, why do we even have these curves in the first place? Would our master designer not have solved a lot of problems had she simply given us a *straight tube* for a spine? Well certainly, a straight tube would be more rigid and certainly easier to balance upright, but how could it shock absorb? In the USA alone, 1.5 million people suffer spinal compression fractures every year.[22] And that is *with* the S-shape of these curves to protect us. The curves in your spine are designed to shock absorb and allow your spine to adapt to varying circumstances more easily.

There are some common themes to these curves, no matter which part of the spine you are talking about.

One quarter, or 25%, of your spine's height is made of cartilage. And there are two sets of cartilage at each level. One is the disc. Commonly talked about when people "slip their disc," this firm, cushion-like structure sits between each vertebra. The second, less talked about cartilages are the two facet joints, or "guiding joints" which sit behind the spinal cord. These joints are designed *to* carry up to 25% of the load. So the disc is designed mostly to sustain load, while the facets are designed to guide and support load.[23]

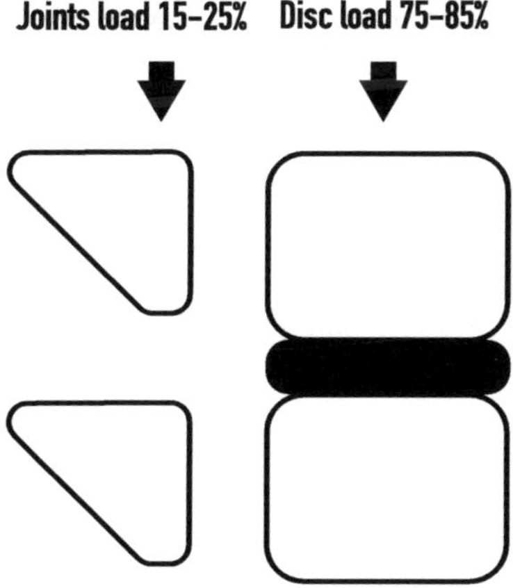

Figure 6. Neutral alignment means healthy spine and normal ageing.

Any spinal area which is *bent backwards* too far will increase the load on the facet joints, jamming them together and prematurely wearing them.[24] This phenomenon is far more common when you are younger and especially common at the base of your spine, at your belt-line. Characteristic are sudden sharp pains, which worsen when you lean back. And this often causes people to lean forwards subconsciously in order to unload the facets. For example, you rise from a chair and cannot straighten up for a few minutes. And then the pain lessens, often after a day or two, or perhaps a few weeks. It is common to think "it fixed itself." But it did not.

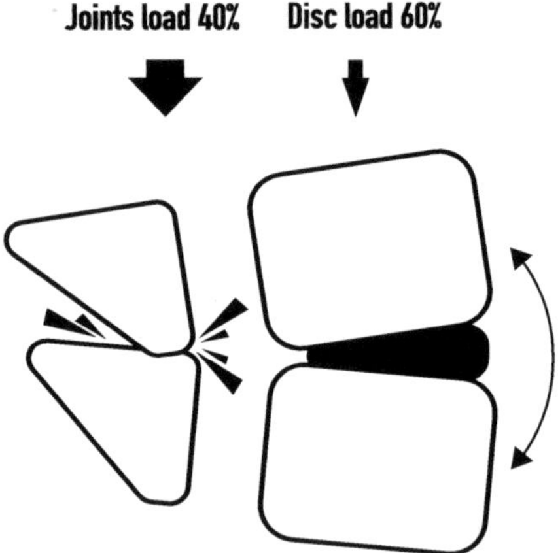

Figure 7. Too much curve overloads the guiding facet joints, often causing acute pain. Over time, this may cause arthrosis (arthritis), sometimes referred to as spondylosis.

Do this enough times, even very mildly, and the cumulative scarring in the facets forces you to *lose the natural curve* of that area, as your spine leans subtly forward. Your spine is literally leaning forward and away from the pain. Now enter phase two of the problem…

Any spinal area which is bent forward too far will increase the load on the disc,[25] pushing its content backwards into your spinal cord. And as the load in the disc increases, the facet joints get *unloaded,* and hence, *unstable*. So being bent forward not only increases the disc load and pushes the disc content out backwards, but the instability accelerates the discal degeneration. The disc loses height, loading the facet joints even further, and the cycle continues. This is all clearly bad news.

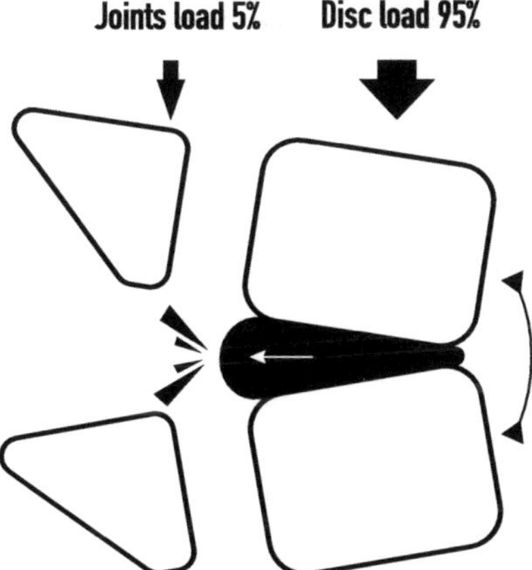

Figure 8. A loss or flattening of the curve overloads the discs and causes instability. This often progresses to disc hernias and degeneration.

I have seen literally thousands of cases like this in my career. These patients often described a history, perhaps years earlier, of sharp, sporadic back pains, which "self resolved" pretty quickly. But now, they have a disc hernia, and the problems have become chronic. These problems started when the original injuries were not treated properly, and the normal postural curves get lost as a result. *Any spinal curve* which is distorted from the normal position will degenerate prematurely, causing problems, disc degeneration, and eventual suffering.

Chapter 3 Checklist

- Your spine should stay upright with minimal effort, protecting it from overload or injury. This depends on (in order of importance):
    - Connection. A clear brain-body connection, which means an un-subluxated spine.
    - Alignment. Each of the four key bones sits vertically above the next.
    - Movement. Healthy, balanced movement, sharing the job between all levels.
    - Load. Your spine should normally only have to carry the load it was designed for.
- Befriending gravity involves stacking each of your "four bones" above each other to stay upright. Staying in this posture is easy; in fact, it feels like you are suddenly lighter.
- For your spine to shock absorb and be mobile, it needs to have healthy curves. Too little or too much curve predisposes you to degeneration in specific, predictable patterns.

Action Points

- Take stock: do your neck or shoulders feel tight, tired, or sore when driving, working on the PC, or near the end of the day? If you stand at a party for a while, does your low back start to ache? Does any part of your spine feel tired by the end of the day?
- Become conscious of your first to third "worst" postures. Perhaps on the mobile phone, perhaps on the PC. Try to line things up so that staying upright becomes easy.
- Insert:
- If you are near Marbella, Spain, go to www.duffyquiropractica.com to find out how to work with Dr Duffy.
- If elsewhere, go to www.chiroalliance.org or www.chiropractic.org to search for subluxation-reducing chiropractors.

Chapter 4

C1 and Neck Pain

"Not everyone can carry the weight of the world."

— REM

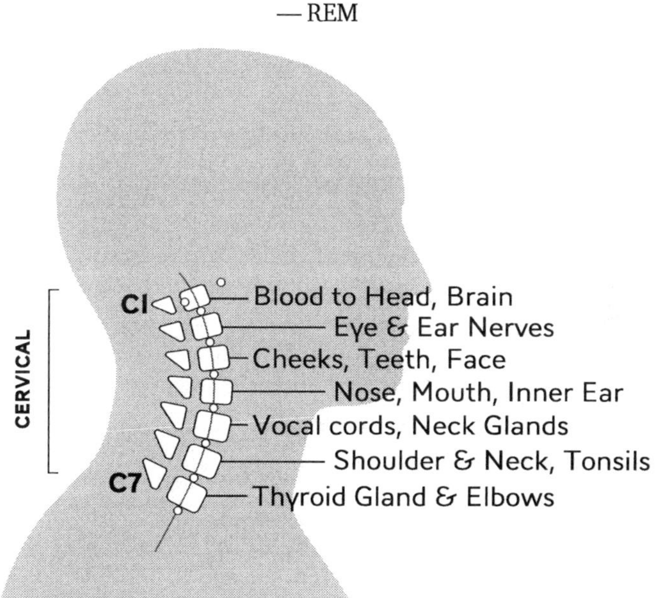

Figure 9. C1 & Your Cervical Curve. Every nerve to your body needs to pass through this gateway. Problems here can cause far-reaching effects—from thyroid problems to low back pain. All spinal exams should start with the neck.

C1 & Your Neck

C1, Forward Head Posture & Your Cervical Curve

Some people may have expected the "alignment" section to start with the pelvis, the base of the spine. And in a mechanistic world, that could make sense. Indeed, for much of my practice life, that was exactly what I did. I am not denying that the base you stand on makes a huge difference, but, as I said earlier, a clear brain-body connection trumps mechanics every time. So achieving a good neck alignment—a clear passageway for the nerves passing from your brain to your body—should be your primary goal, no matter what part of the spine you may have pain or symptoms. From lacking coordination to insomnia, from brain fog to fatigue, and from altered metabolism (thyroid function) to increased emotional stress, an unhealthy neck turns down the quality of anyone's life.[26] Research shows that the positioning of the top bone (atlas) can affect your blood pressure[27] and that degeneration in your neck is linked to abnormal heart beats called arrhythmia.[28] Some research even links neck health to longevity. Some chiropractors dedicate their whole career to nothing other than adjusting neck subluxations. Let us see why.

The Marvel of Engineering

The seven bones of your neck create a marvel of engineering. The top two bones, called the ATLAS and AXIS, have a special relationship and sit in a critical location. Here, the lower part of your brain, your *brainstem*, actually extends down into the top of your neck. Make note that your brainstem controls vital functions like your breathing and heart rate. The rest of the vertebrae have a soft disc between each one. The purpose of the discs is simply to leave space for the nerves which exit at each level. Think a moment of what you are asking your neck to do for you right now.

Hold the weight of your head (around 5kg!)

Support the weight of your shoulders and arms, which hang on your neck. When you lift a weight, so does your neck.

Contain and protect the supply of blood and the fluid irrigation (CSF) to your brain. We discuss CSF later in this chapter.

Pass every single nerve and its signals from your brain to your *body*

And still be able to move freely and look over both shoulders!

It is no wonder that injuries to this area can affect ANY part of your health and ruin your enjoyment of life.

Key to a Healthy Neck- A Healthy Curve & C1 Alignment

Your Neck Curve

This may be the most important yet overlooked part of neck health. It baffles me when I see medical radiologists commenting on "loss of neck lordosis" if the medical system currently has *no solution* to this problem. It is stated as a problem, as if it were a life sentence without any hope of recovery.

Your neck should *not be straight*. Depending on the angle of your upper back (T1), your neck should have a nice, relaxed curve of approximately 40 degrees.[29] This allows space for the spinal cord to relax without pressure and for the fluid which irrigates your brain (CSF) to flow freely, as we explore in the next section. It also means that the weight of your head is distributed *equally* between the discs and facet joints. Too much curve increases the joint wear and degeneration. Too little curve increases the disc load, wear, and degeneration.

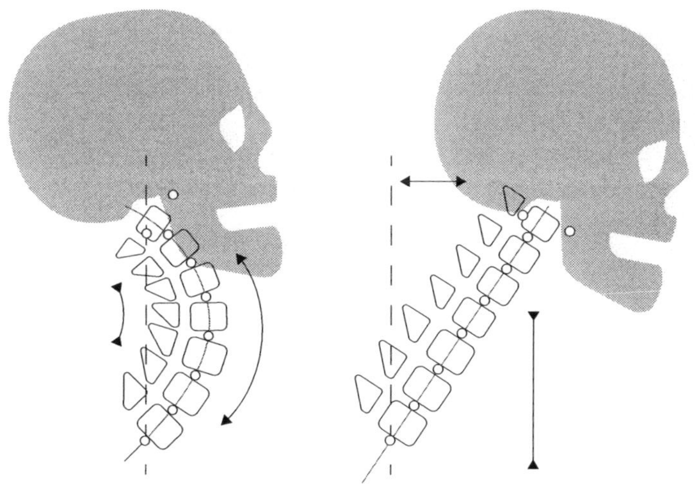

Figure 10. Cervical Curve. Your neck is designed to have a deep, relaxed curve. Loss of this curve changes the loads on the small bones and joints, triggering problems which can cause multiple health issues.

Your head should also sit directly *above* your shoulders. Tipping it forward just a little hugely increases the pressure on your neck and nerves, causing loss of curve and long-term problems. Think about all that time staring down at a mobile phone and imagine how those thousands of hours will affect your neck curve and ultimately your health. The resulting subluxations provoke premature degeneration. Yes, a loss of neck curve, in particular a curve reversal, will cause premature disc degeneration and hernias. And your neck is not a great place to get degeneration. Trust me, I know from experience! A youth full of rugby and contact sports, followed by way too much weight lifting, means that my own neck lives on "borrowed time." The degeneration levels mean that there is simply not so much space for all of the nerves any more. So what do I do? I get adjusted regularly, look after my alignment (more about this later), and make sure not to overload it. I know what I have done and know I will pay the price for my "misdemeanours," but the sad truth is that most people with this problem are walking around thinking their headaches or neck pains are normal. They are going to be shocked when they eventually get the bill.

C1 Alignment: Your Atlas, "The Mouth of God"

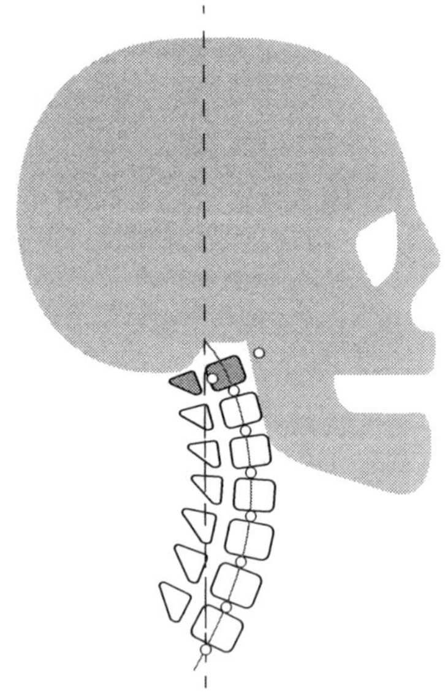

Figure 11. Your Atlas. C1, at the top of your spine, weighs just 60 grammes, but supports the 5 kg weight of your head.

The precise alignment of C1 is the most sensitive, yet important alignment in your body.

If your Atlas, the uppermost bone in your spine, at the base of your skull, has to sit on a neck that is already out of posture, it can never have a "relaxed" relationship to your skull. In spiritual practices, this space, where everything must enter and exit your skull is called "the Mouth of God[30]" Here are *some* of the reasons why it is so important:

The whole of your spinal cord (as thick as the base of your thumb) has to pass through this tiny gap.

Your brainstem, which controls your vital functions like heart rate and breathing, sits within this space.

Your vagus nerve, the most powerful nerve in your body, passes above C1 and down your neck, connecting your heart, lungs, and digestive system to your brain.

A ligament attaches your spinal cord to the base of your skull, so misalignment here causes tension in your whole spine.

As mentioned previously, some chiropractors dedicate their time to adjusting only this one bone. When my kids are not feeling well and ask for an adjustment, this is often the only bone I adjust. If it is "the Mouth of God," I would rather keep it open!

> I have had two chiropractic miracles which happened to me personally, and one has to do with C1. As a kid, I had two eye surgeries for strabismus ("squint" or "wandering eye"). The surgeries did not correct the problem, and for most of my life, I have worn glasses to read, use computers, etc. Except for one five-year period. During this period, I was blessed to have a very talented chiropractic associate in my practice. He adjusted my Atlas once a week for this whole period. I stopped wearing glasses altogether, unless I was very tired. To date there is very little research on this topic,[31] but I have seen many kids with strabismus in practice who have radically improved when their Atlas gets realigned. I always wonder if I would have had those surgeries had my parents taken me to a chiropractor.

The Two Main Types of Neck Damage

We mostly think of damage in terms of accidents—like car accidents or falls—and these are certainly important. However, we all suffer far more trauma from something far less accidental.

Chronic Postural Trauma

For every 3cm your head moves forward, the pressure on your neck increases by over 5kg! So bent over your mobile phone or even *reading this book,* your neck now supports up to a 30 kg weight! Now multiply this by the total hours you spend looking at screens per week, and you start to realise why we are seeing an epidemic of deep neck problems. I call them "deep" neck problems because they cannot be seen from the outside, but they have become a part of you and can be very serious.

The damage from this becomes permanent when your neck becomes subluxated, and although you return your head to an upright position, your neck stays subluxated. Over time, the nervous stress robs you of your health, eventually causing pain. It is no surprise that one in three office workers get neck and shoulder pain.

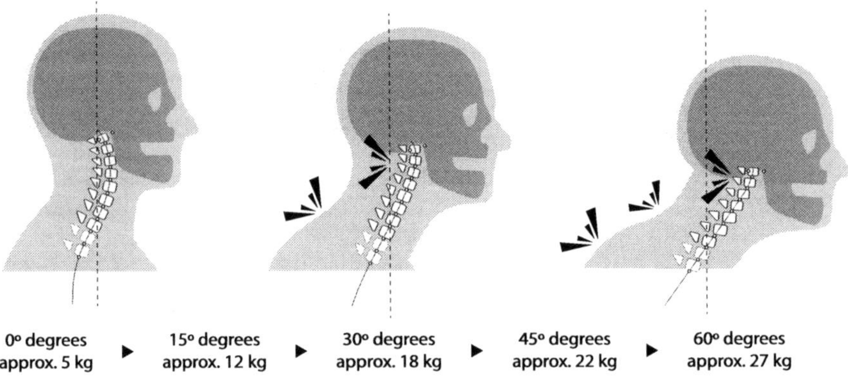

Figure 12. Forward head posture radically increases your effective head weight. This fatigues your neck muscles, and accelerates pain, degeneration, and ageing.

"Whiplash"

Even the smallest "whiplash" is a BIG DEAL! At only 8kph (fast walking speed), the forces on your neck can cause permanent damage. Think of falls playing sports, from the trampoline, or on the stairs throughout your life. The *longer ago* it was, the *bigger the problem*! If you had a whiplash yesterday, your neck has not had time to scar or get into the bad habit of subluxation. It is relatively easy to stay well with the correct treatment. If it was five, ten, twenty years ago, then that is a lot of scar tissue and habit to undo. It doesn't matter if it has been causing pain or not. In fact, some of the worst degeneration I have seen is when people have not had enough pain to act sooner!

More Time = More Scar = Bigger Problem = Slower to Heal Fully

"Visible" Symptoms of an Unhealthy Neck

It would be easy to assume that neck problems cause neck pain. But unfortunately, the problem is far bigger than that. The truth is that an unhealthy neck can cause such a wide range of symptoms and bad health. In many of these, it is not obvious that the neck is the cause.

Here are some of the problems caused by an unhealthy neck:

Headaches

The biggest headache category is "tension type headache" (TTH).[32] Much headache is called "cervicogenic," derived from the Latin, meaning "originating in the neck." You are more likely to suffer from all common forms of headache if you have a loss of curve in your neck.[33] And yet for most people, the only solution offered is regular use of painkillers, with all of the long-term side effects. Some try massage or similar therapy, which usually helps by giving temporary relief. In clinical practice, it is rare that headaches do not improve under care. And when your neck curve is recovered, that improvement is long-lasting.[34] It is nearing insanity to continue to suffer headaches or migraines without getting your neck properly checked.

Vertigo & Dizziness

Your upper neck is a key balance centre and can even affect how your ears and balance centres work. It is very common to experience some degree of dizziness when your neck is unhealthy. Research shows that improving the deep neck posture improves symptoms of dizziness,[35] and these improvements are long-term.[36] In reality, dizziness is often accompanied by headaches as symptoms of neck health issues.

Carpal Tunnel Syndrome

A huge percentage (30-75%) of people with carpal tunnel symptoms have a neck problem. The symptoms of aching, tingling, numbness or weakness in your hand be due to a neck problem. Research shows that, contrary to common belief, carpal tunnel syndrome (CTS) is not caused by keyboard use.[37] In fact, many "CTS sufferers" do not even have any wrist problem, with one study showing that 83% of diagnoses are not true CTS![38] This is even more probable if you are experiencing symptoms on *both* sides. Sleeping in an awkward posture, compressing the nerves at the base of your neck, will often cause compression of the nerves to your hands. 50% of people with CTS symptoms undergo surgery, of which up to 57% fail, with symptoms returning within 6 years.[39] Some estimates say that only 5% of all CTS cases are truly suitable for surgery. Remember that CTS surgery is normally followed by 4 weeks of proper rest.[40] Why not try those four weeks of proper rest *before the surgery*? It is essential to get a second opinion on the condition of your neck from someone who is *not a surgeon,* before having any irreversible surgery or procedures done to your wrists.

Tennis Elbow, Golfer's Elbow

Chronic elbow pains which feel, look, and behave like tennis or golfer's elbow may actually come from the neck and are called "false" tennis or "false" golfers' elbow. Research shows that up to 70% of people with neck nerve damage can have tennis elbow![41] In fact, if you experience it on BOTH sides, it is probably coming from your neck. If you have had tennis elbow which has lasted more than four weeks, there is a 90% probability that it will respond positively to neck care *without touching your elbow!* It just makes sense to check the neck first, as the healing of your arms depends on having a healthy neck. All people undergoing physiotherapy for tennis elbow should also have their necks checked and corrected as needed.[42] The issue is not that physiotherapy fails tennis elbows; the problem is that it often cannot work until the elbow is able to self heal properly. Freeing the nerves allows the physiotherapy to work optimally. This is obvious; this is easy; this is common sense.

Frozen Shoulder

90% of nerve compression in the neck will show as a shoulder or arm pain. In fact, there are many symptoms of the shoulder which originate in the neck.[43] Over 80% of frozen shoulder (adhesive capsulitis) which does not have a clear trauma, such as a fall as the cause, is due to neck health problems. If your shoulder problem lasts for more than four weeks, it makes sense to fix your neck *before* undergoing any unnecessary procedures.

Spondylosis or Neck Degeneration

Masking a deeper neck problem with painkillers or temporary relief from massage may be okay short-term. But even if the pain goes away, the deeper injury has to scar—deep tissue scars form around the ligaments and discs. The pain went away last year, but now your neck is quickly degenerating as calcium deposits into those scars. Your neck feels stiff, but that has become "normal." And then those calcium deposits start to stick together, and bony peaks start to occur around the discs. This is called neck disc degeneration or cervical spondylosis. *If you are lucky, this will cause you pain*, and you have the opportunity to seek treatment before it is too late. If you have no pain, you may not know it is happening. If you leave it too late, the bones form "bridges" over the joint space, basically fusing your neck together. This has to be one of the most compelling arguments for getting adjusted regularly for life. Once these levels have truly "stuck" together, the clock cannot be turned back again, and your lost youth cannot be restored.

Herniated Disc

Tipping your head forward multiplies the weight on the discs, way beyond the 5kg they were designed to support. Sitting hunched over a laptop or mobile phone gradually fatigues and wears your discs. Even without a previous fall or car accident, your discs now start to bulge into that limited space where your spinal cord and nerves sit. What you feel depends on what part of your nerve it touches. You could get shooting pain, or your hand could start to get slightly weaker. In some cases, you may feel nothing. Herniated discs are more likely to happen, even if while you are young, when you lose a healthy, deep neck curve.[44] Recovering the healthy curve and mobility and reducing the effective weight on your neck is critical to avoiding unnecessary degeneration, hernias, and even surgery.

I am often shocked to hear of people undergoing surgery for shoulder, elbow, or wrist complaints without having had proper assessment and correction of their neck. It makes sense to try correcting your neck first, as surgery carries considerable risks and is *never* fully reversible.

When Being Pain-free is a Curse

The sad reality is that many people have deep neck problems without ever being aware of it. The long-term effects of an unhealthy neck go far beyond physical injuries, striking to the very core of who you are and how you experience the world. Yes, the condition of your neck is a key factor in what people perceive as "your character." Let's look at how this happens.

Your Neck Feeds Your Brain

The only reason you have a heart is to feed your brain. The goal of every vital function in your body is to keep your brain alive. Your brain is the way that you experience the world: the connection between your essence and your earth suit! Electricity in your brain is the definition of your being alive. So let's take a look at how your brain "feeds" and "cleans" itself.

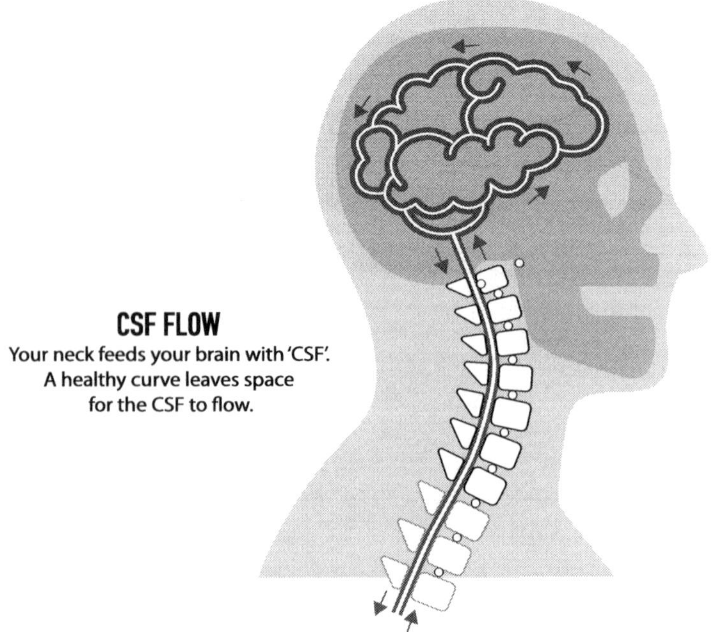

Figure 13. Cerebro-spinal fluid (CSF) constantly bathes, protects, cleans, and feeds your brain and spinal cord. It flows around your brain, down to your pelvis, and back up.

Brain Bath

Your brain sits in a bath of fluid—in a kind of "suspension"—which means that between the bony skull and your soft brain, there is always a cushion. This fluid absorbs shocks to your head to protect your brain but also irrigates (feeds) your brain and washes away toxic wastes. In fact, blood itself is *toxic* to your brain tissue. If you get blood in your brain, it is because you are bleeding, and this is called a stroke. This protective, irrigating fluid is called your *cerebro-spinal fluid*, or CSF.

Your brain itself is only about 2.5% of the total weight of your body, yet it consumes about 20% of the all oxygen you use. As you know, oxygen is transported in your blood, so there is a mechanism which "filters" this blood and prepares this special CSF "bath" for your brain. Your blood flows into an "exchange box" called the choroid plexus, which filters the blood into a straw-coloured fluid. This fluid then pulses slowly around your brain, down your spine to your tailbone, and back up again. The total volume of CSF is like a small bottle of water, between 90-200ml. And the system constantly regenerates about 20ml per hour. Most of the daily flow is caused by your moving around, passively pumping the fluid back up your spine.[45] But your brain can also actively "pump" the CSF across your brain, as it does during deep brainwave sleep (see Chapter 9). During these brainwaves, CSF is "flushed" across your brain, literally cleaning and regenerating your brain. You get the idea of how exquisitely balanced and designed this system is.

Now, like every single other thing in your body, when CSF cannot *flow*, then you cannot be healthy. Not only does a loss of neck curve affect your blood flow to your brain,[46] it also affects the CSF flow. And it is no surprise that decreased CSF flow can be associated with a host of nervous system disorders,[47] including memory loss, going on to dementia and even Alzheimers disease. We don't fully understand the mechanism behind this, but a brain affected by Alzheimer's has up to 66% decreased CSF clearance.[48] It seems that when the brain cannot be "washed" by the flow of CSF,[49] then the plaques which cause Alzheimers start to build up.[50] What is very clear is that to have a healthy brain, you must have healthy CSF flow.

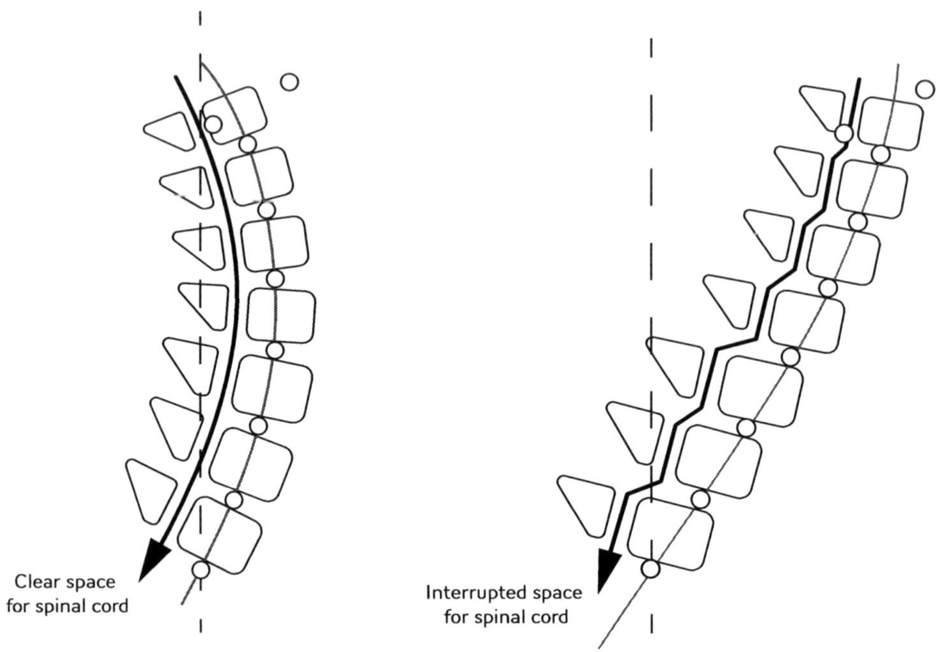

Figure 14. Loss of curve in your neck is followed by disc degeneration, narrowing the space for your spinal cord and its protective fluid.

In the image, you can see that you need space in your spinal cord for this fluid to circulate freely. Poor posture occludes that space, reducing the CSF flow. This neck posture also provokes disc degeneration. In this state, it is like someone has "thrown a boulder into the river which feeds your brain." The space is so reduced that the CSF struggles to flow freely. If left long enough, your neck would fuse through this degeneration. I have seen many cases of either nearly or totally fused neck. They always have one thing in common: they have some degree of lack of concentration, cognitive impairment, dementia, or Alzheimer's.

Research into loss of curve in your neck is starting to explain why this problem affects your body so profoundly and in such varied ways. One study measured the speed of the signals down the spinal cord in a group of people with neck pain. This "conduction velocity" is a measure of how fast the signals between your brain and body are traveling. It is effectively your nervous system's "reaction speed." Hear a truck coming your way and want to step back quickly? This speed affects it. Want to optimise your kidney or liver function? This speed affects it. Want to "catch yourself" before you fall over? This speed affects it. Want to win in your sport? This speed affects it. This is an absolutely critical measure of your core nervous system efficiency. This group was split into two groups, one control and one experimental. The control group received a sham treatment, while the experimental group received corrective chiropractic care, aimed at restoring their neck curve. The control group had no change in conduction velocity, while the experimental group had a an increased conduction velocity, in the region of 20% faster.[51] This is mind-blowing. Can you imagine the change in *every function* in your body if all the signals were 20% faster, without applying any more effort? This was not the first such study, with evidence building that a healthy neck curves increases your nervous system conduction speed.[52] Better still, another study looked at the same parameters in people *without neck pain*, and the improvement was still substantial, at around 10%.[53] Still a huge gain. Talk about bio-hacking... 10% faster nerve signals to my whole body? Yes please. The truth is, our understanding of this phenomenon continues to grow, but a subluxated, flattened neck curve is bad news for your *health, happiness, and performance*.

The start of this whole problem, the poor posture or the blockage of one or more vertebrae, tends to happen with absolutely no pain or symptoms. This is the primary subluxation. At this stage, it it easy to correct, but alas, most people only visit a chiropractor once the problem is more advanced.

It should be noted that you can have *neck problems* and never get *neck symptoms*. Your symptoms could be forgetfulness, poor sleep quality, headaches, dizziness, anxiety, or a sense of irritation. Or a combination of all of the above.

In fact, research shows that if you are suffering back pain and also have a loss of curve in your neck that restoring the curve in your neck resolves your back pain. It is not by mistake that I keep repeating this—connection trumps mechanics every time. You can see why the person who has pain is actually *lucky,* as they are more likely to seek care.

Scan this QR code now to watch a YouTube video of the CSF circulating in your brain. Like and Subscribe for more videos.

Unfortunately, there is no amount of stretching, massage, or even *manipulation* that will fix this. There are two keys to resolving this problem. Firstly, by getting specifically *adjusted* to address the problem levels. And second, restoring normal alignment to at least stop, but hopefully reverse, much of the problem. And speaking of reversing, the good news is there are protocols to specifically deal with this reversed neck curve. Using these protocols, for most people, even with significant degeneration[54] this problem can be improved or even "fixed".

Now, if your neck has been like this for years, even decades, but you only got neck pain or headaches last week, perhaps you may hope to be "fixed" within a week or so. But if you really want to be well again, to treat the cause instead of the symptoms, you should expect the changes to take at least months, perhaps years.

Is Your Neck Depressing You?

> Mayte was only 36 years old, but it felt that her life was over. For five years she had been suffering headaches, nausea, and general tiredness, alongside neck and spinal pains. But more importantly, over the past year, she had become depressed and extremely anxious. She left her job because of stress. She could not concentrate or

operate at the level she used to. She stopped going to the gym and became nervous to even leave her apartment. Her world seemed to be shrinking, getting darker and darker, and the future looked bleak.

Meanwhile, her husband organised tests and appointments with doctors and specialists, and Mayte had tried a number of different prescription medications, which only made her feel more disconnected, depressed, and lost. One surgeon even suggested she could have a spinal fusion...at the age of 36! She could not remember how long it had been since she last slept a whole night. One day, a surgeon said to her, "You have degeneration in your neck and the curve has gone, but nothing can be done about that. Continue on with your two physio appointments per week, and I will increase the dose of your pain and anxiety medications. Also, you can try taking these stronger sleeping pills.. I am sorry, but there is nothing else we can do." She felt dejected, desperate.

Thankfully, her husband heard of chiropractic and thought it was "worth a try." To be honest, at this stage, anything was worth a try.

Mayte was really suffering. She was very pain sensitive, and her whole, body, including her hands, were inflamed. She had put on ten kilos over the past six months and was undergoing testing for thyroid function. She brought in x-rays which showed a total loss of her neck curve. After examining her, I explained my recommendations, and we got started.

She was trusting as a client, and over the coming months, her pain and inflammation slowly disappeared. She started sleeping through the night, and eventually, she returned to sport. In fact, she started going to the gym every day to catch up on missed time! Five months later, she went back to the same surgeon who had told her that nothing could be done about the loss of her neck curve, and he took another x-ray. Mayte had recovered 75% of her normal curve.

But the biggest change was that she had recovered 100% of her life. She no longer feels the anxiety and depression which had affected her. She now sleeps well. And so is more relaxed, happier. Her relationships can bloom, and she can blossom.

Mayte's story—being written off and told that nothing can be done to help the condition of their neck—is not rare. When this happens, their life slowly shuts down around them. It is sad that, in the 21st century, people like Mayte are not offered alternatives to drugs and surgery, that they are not offered a chance to get their life back. Had Mayte's husband not kept trying, who knows where she would have ended up?

Research repeatedly links spinal posture to your psychological state.[55] Depression is, in my opinion, an almost inevitable side-effect of chronic subluxation and misalignment. Sooner or later, the "weight" of the subluxations gets too much. Reducing subluxation can be life-changing. For some, it is getting back to work and back to the gym. For others, it may be returning to being a happy, tolerant, fun mother or father. Or recovering the ability to concentrate, not forget names, to feel connected in your body.

I only wish that more people knew this and acted sooner. When is the best time to recover your happiness. In another five years' time? Ten years' time?

It Starts Young

Take any five teenagers today, and three of them will be suffering the same condition: damage to their neck. Half of all teenage girls suffer *regular* neck pain, often causing headaches and even arm weakness. 1 in 10 adolescents suffer from insomnia.[56] And about 55% of kids suffer from frequent headaches.[57] But all of these problems should be grouped as "growing pains" and ignored, right? Bullshit. Sorry, but it is total bullshit. Our "health" system fails in many ways, but when we write off the ill-health of our growing kids, I get angry.

When did it become normal for our adolescents to have chronic pain and headaches and eventual insomnia? This is the epidemic which our children, your children, nephews, nieces, and grandchildren are suffering silently right now. This problem is like a plague, not among grannies and bookkeepers, but among our *children*!

A well-hydrated kid, who has been adjusted for subluxations, and had their posture checked should not get pains, headaches, or insomnia. This is outrageous. I have even seen kids as young as 12 years old who have been taking painkillers and sleeping pills for four years. At best, this is negligence.

Bad neck posture causes not only pains, but poorer coordination—clumsiness, more difficulty concentrating, difficulty studying, fatigue, and increased sensitivity and grumpiness. And what are the hardest things in your teenage years? Clumsiness, concentration, getting out of bed, and grumpiness!

Digital devices and laptops are an inevitable fact of life now, but let us not allow this suffering to also become an inevitable fact. So common it is that they invented the term "text neck" to describe it.

I am not saying that a well adjusted neck "solves" the challenges of adolescence, but it definitely makes them far easier to navigate. As I write this, I am currently caring for over a dozen teenagers whose main complaint is concentration challenges with resulting difficulties at school and in exams. You know what percentage of these kids improve? There is no scientific study (yet), but I will tell you that my experience is nearly 100%. That is not an exaggeration. Unless there is something else going on, these kids will always improve with a pretty simple and extremely safe intervention.

Scan this QR code now to watch a YouTube video showing neck damage in teenagers. Like and Subscribe for more videos.

And if they do not get care sooner? Well, they mess up in exams, drop out of school, or just take a different career path. I have seen this happen. Or they continue to succeed in exams, but at the cost of their sleep and their mental health. They are teenaged, nervous wrecks. I have seen this happen. Few things make me much angrier than this total failure to give these kids a proper chance in life. It is not for lack of money or time or energy. It is nearly always a simple lack of awareness, education, and care options. The medical system cannot help these kids. It is not an emergency and so should not be a medical problem.

Our kids will face many problems in the future: climate change, repaying huge public debts, the list goes on. They will mostly face them together. But this deep neck damage, caused from a young age, will be something they will face on their own: in the morning when they feel hungover even though they didn't drink any alcohol; when they lie awake worrying at night, because their nervous system will not relax; when they pop another pill because neck pain and headaches is just a part of life.

We can do better.

Changing Your Neck Curve

Once you understand the need to improve your neck, there are some pretty obvious questions. How much can it change, how long will it take, and will the change last?

Your age, degenerative changes, and habits all affect the answer. The older the neck damage, the longer it will take to recover. But I can tell you the averages. Remember, though, neither you nor I are *the* average!

Under these protocols, the average rectified cervical curve recovers in the region of 50-60% of normal over three to four months of intensive care. Ongoing care in the region of nine months is needed to bring people to near normal, or as good as they are likely to get.[58]

If *no more care* is received, at one year follow up (after intensive phase), you are still expected to maintain 50% overall improvement, which means that the improvements are stable and very long-lasting. But, a bit like eating well, once you start a healthy habit, you tend to carry on for life. After how many healthy meals is "the job done?" When do you return to eating McDonalds every day?

I strongly recommend that everyone, symptoms or no symptoms, gets checked regularly for subluxation, which means that these changes should become lifelong improvements.

Compare this to other manual therapy methods, including manipulation (more about this in Chapter 9), physiotherapy, and massage, which show mild but temporary objective improvements after care, with nearly all of the benefit lost a year later, and you realise why this is such a popular technique in the USA and other developed countries.

If you follow these protocols, you should get results. But it might require some patience and commitment.

> When I worked mostly with professional athletes, a young professional soccer player was sent in for a second opinion. He had a torn disc in his low back. His physio and coaching team described his movement as harsh and "forced." At just 17 years old, he was an England hopeful, but his back could not tolerate the jumping needed for training, hence the career-threatening disc hernia. His tests showed poor balance and coordination, especially for a full-time athlete. It transpired that a whiplash injury, sustained a few years prior, had reversed his neck curve. His brain could not clearly "hear" how he was moving, so rather than landing with grace and efficiency, he was using brute strength, jarring his spine. He was paying the price, damaging his whole body. It was unsustainable. As we started care, and his neck improved, he felt like his whiplash was "coming back." His neck was going from having a *reversed* curve to having a normal curve. This was healthy, to feel discomfort as he healed. Imagine you injure your elbow, and keep it bent to avoid pain. Over the following years it gets tighter, and you cannot get your elbow straight any more. When you go to remove that injury, to free up your elbow, it may hurt. But this is not the injury "coming back." It is the injury *finally healing fully.* This is another reason why "treatments" aimed at just removing your discomfort do not make sense. He returned to playing a full professional career, but with a healthy neck curve and a fully connected body sense.

Chapter 4 Checklist

- Your neck should not be straight. Its deep curve leaves a clear space for your spinal cord to relax in.
- The space where your whole spinal cord leaves your skull, through the C1 vertebra, has been called "the mouth of God." This the most important alignment in your body.
- Even minor trauma to your neck causes scarring and possible loss of this curve, not to mention postural stresses, such as digital devices and poor neck health results.

- Neck damage can start young, and with the digital revolution, it is set to become one of the world's chronic illness epidemics. Visit this QR code to learn more about the damage being done to teenagers' necks.

- Poor neck health can damage any and all parts of your health. From the obvious "local" pains to head, neck, and shoulders, affecting all of your arms, but also extending to your whole nervous system.
- This damage eventually affects what you consider to be "your character," causing you to become more irritable, intolerant, anxious, and depressed.
- There are well-researched protocols to reduce subluxations and recover a peaceful curve in your neck. They require time and effort, but the rewards are literally life-saving.

Action Points

- What habits do you have today, which are causing, sustaining, or worsening neck damage? Look first at your mobile phone and/or computer postures. Bringing your phone and all screens to slightly above your eye height will radically decrease subluxation stress.
- Visit Chapter 12 for more sitting posture advice.
- Traumas and injuries that happened is the past are just that…in the past. Often, the past starts to define us, our pain levels, even our personality. Reducing subluxations reduces the grip that your past has on your neck health, freeing up new possibilities for health and happiness.

If you are near Marbella, Spain, go to www.duffyquiropractica.com to find out how to work with Dr Duffy.

If elsewhere, go to www.chiroalliance.org or www.chiropractic.org to search for subluxation reducing Chiropractors.

Chapter 5

T1. The Hunchback

"Life shrinks or expands in proportion to one's courage. "

— Anaïs Nin

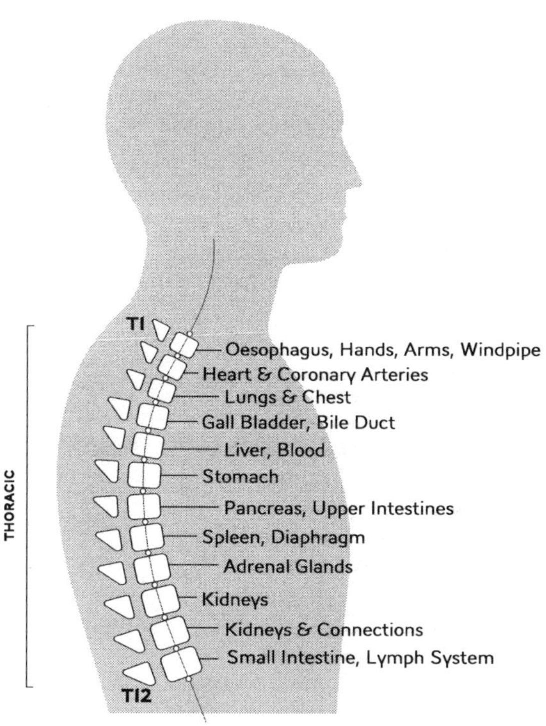

Figure 15. T1 & Your Thoracic Curve. Nerves from this region supply your chest and most of your abdomen. Problems in this area are often "hidden", producing referred pains or symptoms elsewhere.

T1 & The Hunchback

In the last section, we established that poor neck alignment is extremely dangerous for your health. But your neck may not always be the culprit. In fact, your "ideal" neck curve should always be measured as a function of the slope of T1, the angle at the top of your upper back. If this is stooped forwards, your neck needs a different shape than if this is totally upright. It is common for a client to come in with a herniated disc in their low back or neck but for their biggest problem to be in their upper back alignment, their "thoracic kyphosis." This is because your thoracic kyphosis is a "hidden" factor in many other spinal problems.

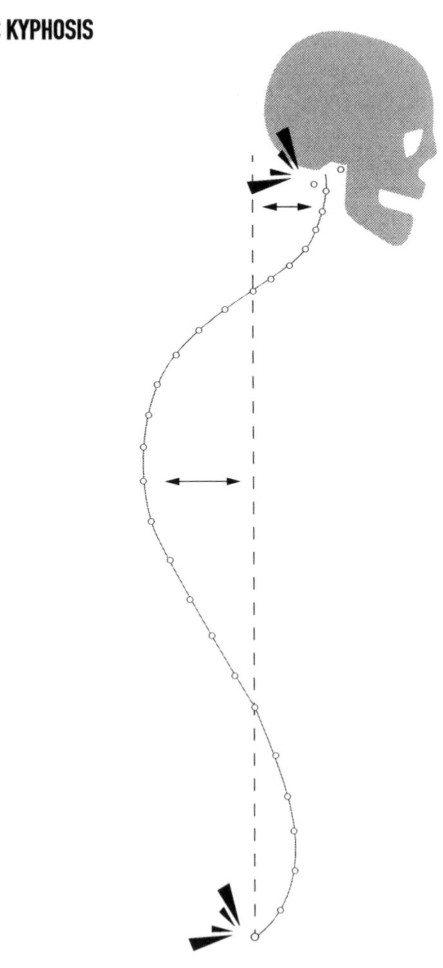

Figure 16. Hyper-kyphosis increases the stress on your neck and lower back, eventually triggering a cascade of ill health and pains.

A pretty solid structure

Think about your chest area for a moment. Pretty solid, right? Someone thought to design us with a *flexible* bony cage which protects our heart and lungs. We have 12 rib pairs, of which 10 pairs unite at the front through cartilage and into the sternum, your chest bone. The other two "floating" rib pairs protect your kidneys at the back, but don't make it around to the sternum at the front. They maximise the flexibility of the area, while partially protecting your liver, spleen, and kidneys. This flexibility is necessary for breathing and, obviously, movement. And ALL of these structures literally "hang" off your thoracic spine.

> You will hear the terms "thoracic" and "dorsal" used interchangeably to describe your midback area. "Dorsal" is more commonly used in the USA, but in Latin it simply means "of the back," so I prefer to call this area your *thoracic spine*.

That's a lot of structure hanging off your 12 thoracic bones! To complicate matters further, most of the individual ribs connect to *three places* on your spine, plus the vertebral disc itself! Each of these junctions has its own ligaments with its own nerves, controlling muscles, and ability to get injured. This means that when I, or any other doctor, pushes on just one thoracic spinal level, we are directly moving 16 or more joints. Which point I contact, which direction, and how far I push changes everything. You start to get the idea of why *untrained manipulation is a bad idea.*

And the muscles travelling between these ribs, the intercostal muscles, contain their own nerve *inside the muscle.* I would call this a "design flaw," if only I could come up with a better solution (which I cannot!). It means that just a little displacement of any of these joints can cause muscle spasm and a nerve pain which takes your breath away. Many people call this "popping a rib," but you start to understand that it's a little more complex than that.

Here are some of the tasks your thoracic spine is doing for you right now:

1. Supporting the weight of your heart, lungs, head, chest area, and both arms—about half of your overall weight.
2. Fully taking the weight of anything you lift in your hands.

3. Constantly "pulsing" in movement to allow breathing and heart contractions.
4. Protecting your spinal cord, including the nerves going all the way to your toes.
5. Protecting the nerves to your chest cavity and abdomen, plus some ascending nerves which return up to your head area.

And despite this, it is one of the least *symptomatic* areas of your spine. By that, I mean it mostly tends to "suffer in silence." Despite consisting of half your intervertebral discs, the thoracic region accounts for under 5% of all diagnosed disc injuries.[59]

Thoracic Curve and Alignment

Just like the rest of your spinal curves, the thoracic curve, or "kyphosis," should be in the region of 40 degrees, allowing T1 to sit directly above the base of your spine.[60] This is the most "visible" of spinal curves. This is because the lordosis postures of your neck and low back arch inwards, "hiding" what is going on, while the kyphosis arches outwards, showing itself far more readily. There is one big warning though, and one which many self-proclaimed "posture experts" should heed: your shoulder posture can both mask a hyper (excessive) kyphosis, just as poor shoulder posture can make a healthy spine appear hyper-kyphotic. Rounded shoulders and hyper-kyphosis are *related, but not the same thing.* And they have very different treatment solutions.

> "Kyphosis" is simply a type of outward-bending spinal curve, totally natural and normal in your mid-back. "Hyper-kyphosis" is an abnormal curve. When your doctor said, "You have kyphosis," they probably meant to say "hyper-kyphosis."

In this section, we will concentrate on excessive curve of your mid-back, *hyper-kyphosis.* I do not mean to infer that *loss of curve, or hypo-kyphosis,* is not a problem. It is a very big problem indeed. In fact, a loss of thoracic curve removes much of the stability in your mid-back, making you prone to *scoliosis* (as we discuss in Chapter 8). Hypo-kyphosis is more rare, and, in truth, far more complicated to treat.

It is simple logic that the top and bottom of your thoracic curve should sit in a vertical line, above your sacrum and below your head. But in reality, a majority of hyper-kyphosis is accompanied by what we call "posterior translation." This is often a symptom of a "swayback posture." Posterior translation means that your mid-back is situated behind that vertical axis. And this is where we really run into problems, pain, and degeneration. And they do not tend to be pains in your mid-back, but instead, problems in your neck and lower back.[61] If your thoracic spine is displaced backwards, it reduces your overall height and radically increases the stresses on your neck and low back.

> I mentioned in the previous chapter that I have experienced two personal chiropractic miracles. The second has to do with with asthma and my thoracic spine. At nine years old, and a few years after being admitted to intensive care in hospital, intubated and ventilated with pneumonia, I was diagnosed with asthma. From about age nine through 29, I "survived" on a concoction of asthma drugs, which opened my airways enough to compete in sports and avoid being overloaded with the symptoms of allergies. Now, a few decades later, I know what to do when I start to get "wheezy" lungs. I know that I am subluxated in my upper thoracic spine and am overdue an adjustment. Research proves that chiropractic helps asthma sufferers,[62] yet we do not fully understand the mechanism. I now consider myself "not asthmatic," but instead I know that I have "sensitive airways." Chiropractic adjustments have not rid me of this sensitivity, but I have not owned an asthma inhaler for well over a decade.

History of Hunchbacks

Before we go any further, let's take a quick look at the "history" of hyper-kyphosis, or hunched back. The evolution of our workplace postures radically affects our upper back curve.

Not new, but very "in fashion"

When I started in practice about 20 years ago, every now and then I would see a condition we once knew as "accountants posture" or "draughtsman's neck," because these professions spent a lot of time leaning over papers, and so ended up looking like this…

HUNCHBACK POSTURE

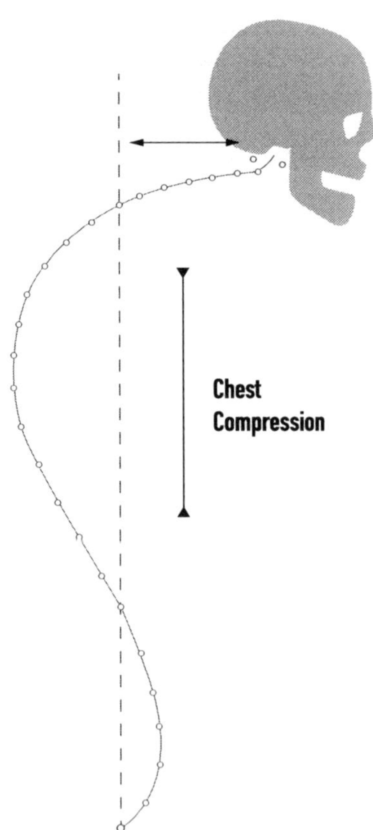

Figure 17. Hyper-kyphosis compresses your lung capacity, making you feel and look older than your years.

This was once an exceptional thing to see, perhaps one case every month or two. But now, I see two or three similar cases every week. In fact, you may have heard of the new phrase "text neck," where someone's head is poking forwards, making them look gangly and un-athletic. But here is the thing, don't be too quick to blame your neck. Because your neck position is largely set up by the angle of your upper back, so this hunched posture causes a huge number of neck problems.

The deformed figure "Quasimodo" in the famous 19th century novel *The Hunchback of Notre Dame* made this posture famous, and our millennial generations seem committed to doing Quasimodo proud. Because never before has a generation spent so much time staring downwards at digital devices. From abnormal eye development to difficulties socialising, this digital generation will clearly pay a high price. But this postural deformity hides a whole host of bad health news for the person who has it. Up to 10% of teenagers suffer with hyperkyphosis.[63] A mostly avoidable and treatable condition. So what will these kids' postures be like when they are 40 years old? Or 80 years old?

A kid's posture is far more important than *most* of the educational worries we place on them daily. Your exam results when you are 14 years old are not going to determine your future health and happiness, but your posture will. How has society gotten so wrapped up in exam results that we are tempted to forget our most important responsibilities as parents? Let us prioritise our kids' health and happiness. We all hope for our kids to have an education which gives them choice and flexibility in life, but that should always be secondary to their health and happiness. How does the average government, school, or family spend their resources on our childrens' health and happiness, as compared to education? It doesn't have to be this way.

What happens as these poor postures age? It has become an accepted *"normal"* thing for older people to hunch over forwards. Well, this is certainly an option as our lifestyles get more sedentary, but it sure makes us look a lot older a lot sooner. Up to 40% of over 60 year-olds suffer from hyperkyphosis.[64] Again, this is a collective and individual choice. It does not have to be like this.

Try this for a moment. Hold your breath for 20 seconds. Then return to breathing normally for 40 seconds. Then stop breathing again for 20 and return to breath for 40. Repeat this every minute, again and again all day long. When you are doing sport, when you are watching TV, even when you are *making love*. An excessive curve in your mid-back reduces your lung capacity by about one third. This is *big news* for, er, well everyone who…likes oxygen… Read on for more shocking statistics.

The Unhealthy Trend

Hyper-kyphosis has been making the medical press. The ageing populations of many countries have prompted the research, not because big corporations and governments are kind, loving people, but because healthcare for old people is expensive. And so figuring out *which old people have more health risks* is becoming a more interesting topic from an economic perspective. The research is very clear.

A slumped or hunched posture turns gravity into your enemy. As a recent research review put it, *"The data on these issues is quite compelling".*[65]If you have a slumped posture, I advise you sit up and take a deep breath before reading this next passage, because here are some *research-proven links between hyper-kyphosis and poor health.*

Hunchbacks Are Never Healthy

This posture increases your all-cause mortality by 44%.[66] In older adults, the risk of bad posture is as bad for your health as the risk of smoking. Many of us would never consider smoking because of the obvious health risks, yet our poor posture is equally as dangerous.

Poor lumbo-thoracic posture **can provoke gastro-oesophageal reflux disease**[67] also known as GERD, for which 10 billion dollars worth of antacids are consumed yearly. The out-of-pocket cost pales against the health cost associated with kidney problems, Vitamin B12 deficiency, and other malabsorption syndromes that are also high on the list. We visit this topic more in chapter 13, when we discuss drugs and surgery.

Multiple research studies associate this slouching posture with **loss of muscle strength, drop in activity levels, increased fatigue, lower walking speed,**[68] **and increased fall risk.**[69] It increases vertebral **fracture risk** two- to three-fold.[70] Furthermore, it predicts **future disability, depression, and poorer quality of life.**[71] Be it for yourself or for an ageing relative, these are all ominous signs.

Not only does hyper-kyphosis radically **complicate osteoporosis**, but evidence suggests it may also *worsen or even cause* this bone-weakening disease.[72] In one study, over a 4-year timespan, those with severe hunched backs were **3.5x more likely to become disabled.**[73] A Japanese study showed that *even untrained, non-medical raters* could accurately predict the likelihood of a group of people becoming disabled within 4.5 years, simply by *looking at the people* and scoring their "hunchback" posture! They proved that you don't need a medical degree to understand how big a problem a hunched back is.

Speaking of big, here is another big one. Most of us want to care for our lungs and heart, especially as we age. We already mentioned the **reduction in vital lung capacity** by about a third, a similar effect to **chronic cigarette smoking.**[74] Knowing that chronic lung disease is the third leading cause of death in the over 65 year-olds, would it not be nice to reduce these statistics with a simple, safe, low-cost intervention?[75]

Every week a new research paper is released, showing how dangerous this posture type is for you. Making gravity your enemy is dangerous. The very week that this book goes into final edit, another study shows that a forward posture is **predictive of cognitive decline**—in other words, **losing your memory** and mental clarity.[76] I, for one, need no more convincing. Let us look at how we can reverse this scary trend.

> I very fondly remember a family I cared for in my main practice near London, England. I looked after the whole family over the course of more than a decade. By the time I left England, their two sons towered over me, both of them over 1.9m (6ft 3in) tall, with beautiful, upright postures. One had started university, the other a career as a personal trainer. They were both flourishing. They came to the practice to say goodbye, and in a moving speech in front of a packed waiting room, their mother declared, "Thank you for your work, Doctor Duffy. My sons may not have had cello lessons, or play multiple instruments, but at least I made sure they have great posture, and I think that is a good start." The real credit goes to the conscious mother for so cleverly investing the time, money, and effort in giving her kids a real head-start.

How to Change a Hunchback

By this point, you have realised that changing the alignment of your thoracic spine not only affects your neck and lower back, but also vice-versa. Although it is not rocket science, identifying the "key" in this equation is a professional skill possessed by few. The truth is that each case is different, yet I can make some general recommendations.

The first two techniques people tend to reach for in order to improve their hunchback posture are "shoulders back" and "strengthen your back." Let's be clear. Rounded shoulders are more common in hyperkyphosis, but rounded shoulders can *neither cause nor fix your thoracic posture*. If your back needs strengthening to hold your thorax upright, it is already too far out of balance.

I have seen people with flatback syndrome (loss of curve) being told to "pull their shoulders back" by other "professionals." They get more and more injured by this bad advice. I also see people with scarred, rigid thoracic spines, hiding this problem under their retracted shoulders and strengthening their backs till the cows come home. Only suffering lies ahead for these poor clients. If you have ever tried to "sit up totally straight," you probably already know that forced postural changes are *not sustainable*. In fact, they often cause more harm than good. Sustaining a good posture should be a *balancing act*.

Take a moment to do this simple exercise:

- Stand with your back to the wall so that your heels, bottom, upper back, and head all touch the wall. If you struggle to do this, skip straight to point 1 below.
- Note how everything realigns. Your mid-back curve may have just decreased. Try to relax your spine.
- Now step away, and keeping that upright posture, note the weight on your heels. Staying relaxed but upright, go and look at yourself in the mirror.
- How much does this change how you look? What if this were your normal posture?

Steps to correct a hunchback

1. Your thoracic spine must be *mobile* enough to *reach neutral posture*. If it cannot get there, then why strengthen it or do anything else?! To achieve this mobility, spinal adjustments are needed, first and foremost. Stretches and traction also help with mobility.

2. If your brain-body connection is not fully alive, this area will never find a neutral posture. Not because it could not, but because it does not know what neutral is. The only way is to reduce subluxations, turn on your sixth sense of proprioception, and then change posture.
3. If a professional who understands your whole-spine balance is not adjusting your whole spine, it is unlikely that you will find this balance.
4. If you continue to stay in poor postures where you slouch, then you will constantly undo your own progress and never "make it."

Most older people with hyper-kyphosis need to start with point 1 above. As in, there is *no chance for health* until the mobility is restored. Many children, adolescents, and young adults have poor posture simply because their brain-body connection is switched off, and points 2 and 4 are most relevant. Switch on your proprioception, then look after your habits.

But for everyone, the best way to address the problem is to get clever, look at the whole system, and start with point 3. Addressing the problem postures (changing workstation height, etc.) is important, but if you are already stuck in a bad posture, it won't fix the problem on its own. I'm sorry to say there is no shortcut here.

Chapter 5 Checklist

- Although it causes fewer pains than your neck or low back, your thoracic spine is a key piece of your spinal "stack." When it is too curved, you look like an old "hunchback."
- Poor thoracic alignment puts you at risk of a cascade of health problems as you age.
- It also causes your neck and low back to take the strain, provoking a chain of other problems,

Action Points

- Take a moment to do the exercise in the last section. How much difference would that posture being *normal* make to your image? To your health? To how you age?
- Review points 1-4 and their explanation in the last section. Which most apply to you?
- Resolve to look after your mid-back posture. Look after it as much as your teeth, diet, exercise, or any other part of your health routine. Your older self will thank you for it.

If you are near Marbella, Spain, go to www.duffyquiropractica.com to find out how to work with Dr Duffy.

If elsewhere, go to www.chiroalliance.org or www.chiropractic.org to search for subluxation reducing Chiropractors.

Chapter 6

L1 & Slipping discs

"Paingry: A state of anger caused by long term pain."

— Unknown

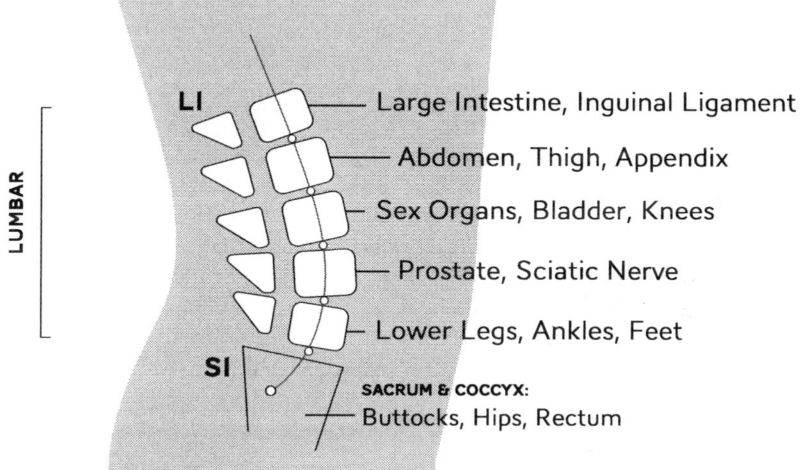

Figure 18. L1 and your low back. Transferring your whole upper body weight to your pelvis, your low back also needs to protect the nerves to your abdomen, pelvis, and legs. Chronic degeneration and pain is the normal price for not looking after this area.

L1 & Keys to Lumbar Health

Alan was 53 years old and had never had any back problems, according to him. His wife booked his appointment to come and see us.

"I don't have back problems," said Alan, sitting in front of me with his arms crossed.

"That's great," I responded, "So you're here to improve your health, right?"

"Well no, I mean I have very good health. I mean, I want you to fix my back pain, but it's just these last two weeks. It was picking up that

> pen. I never had back problems before that pen."
>
> "OK, so if I had met you, say three years ago, you would have said you never had any back pain?"
>
> "Correct, no problems at all, except for, you know, the normal aches everyone gets..."
>
> "Normal aches everyone gets?"
>
> "Yes, well, you know, when you get out of a chair or off the toilet, your back is stiff. You know, what everyone has, just aches and pains from ageing." At this point, I got irritated because Alan just used the "A" word... "ageing."
>
> "Okay, so when you get out of a chair, your back hurts?"
>
> "Well yes, but my leg mostly, and sometimes, it's just tingling in my foot, but I have a strong back, you know? I go to the gym. It's just that darned pen which somehow got me"
>
> "So say I had met you a decade ago...You say here you used to play tennis. At that time, you had no back pains or complaints at all?"
>
> "No, none at all. I was fit as a fiddle. I mean, I used to miss the occasional week or two of tennis, because my back got stiff, but it was nothing really."
>
> "And how about when you were a teenager? Your back was strong and healthy then, too?"
>
> "Yes, I was a very sporty teenager. I competed at a high level. I mean, I used to take a lot of Ibuprofen, and sometimes wore a back support, but it didn't stop me."

Alan sounds like quite a character, but his replies and views represent a big section of society. We have normalised having back pain so much that I gave up having conversations like that with clients a long time ago. Alan's spine, just like your spine, does not lie, so instead of asking his opinion, I can just ask his spine for the truth. In any case, what happened in the past does not matter so much as how his spine is today and how to get it healthy again. Don't take it personally if your doctor is not interested in the details of every injury you have had in the past—it is probably a good sign.

Alan's story of on and off episodes of back pain over the years is also a very common one. These problems appear to "fix themselves," but the scar tissue remains. Unfortunately, your spine and your nervous system remember every trauma. Eventually this "background stiffness" will make us grumpy and even snappy. And unless we are "lucky," we soon become the stereotypical "grumpy old fart." It can erode and define us a person we are not before we even realise why. And sadly, most people think it is normal, or worse still, "just ageing."

For others, however, this pain becomes a show-stopper. What was an aching back starts to refer into your hip and buttocks. In fact, you may well start to wonder if you have a problem in your hip. And when it becomes acute, it makes you wince. It is hard to find words to describe it. I have never given birth, but I have heard many women say that they would give birth time and again rather than have acute low back pain.

The way I see it, ALL (not some, but ALL) of what I have described above are symptoms of a *loss of health* in your back. Not of injury or illness, but a *loss of health*. Put another way, the darkness is not the problem, it is the lack of light. Rather than focus on the darkness, let's look at shining some light again. Let's look at the keys to recovering a healthy, strong, flexible back.

Anatomy

I am no art critic, so I shall not call any one part of your spine more artistically beautiful than another. But if your spine were a work of art (and it is), then while your neck would be a masterpiece watercolour, your low back would have to be some sort of concrete or steel sculpture, bordering on architectural, because the loads your low back endures are mind-boggling.

We hear a lot of talk of the discs of your low back. They are super-strong "cushions" with a tough layered skin (Annulus Fibrosus) and a softer "toothpaste-like" core (Nucleus Pulposus).

They shock absorb, allow mobility, but most importantly, keep the space between the bones so that your spinal nerves can exit between each vertebra without getting pinched. These nerves are the lifeline from your body to your brain.

Any pressure on them and the communication to your sex organs, blood circulation, or muscle coordination could be in danger. Pain is only the tip of the iceberg.

No matter the state of your back, here are some things that you ask of it everyday:

1. Hold most of your body weight and a lot more. In a seated posture, the peak compressive force in your low back may be over 100kg, and in some gym "abdominal" exercises, these forces rocket to near 340kg[77]— a third of a tonne, passing through a disc about the size of a car key. Imagine dropping 340kg on your car key. What would happen?
2. While carrying this load, it shock-absorbs when you move, supporting any extra weight you decide to pick up.
3. Protect and pass the nerves and their signals to your lower digestive system, sex organs, legs and circulation.
4. Be able to move freely and flexibly.

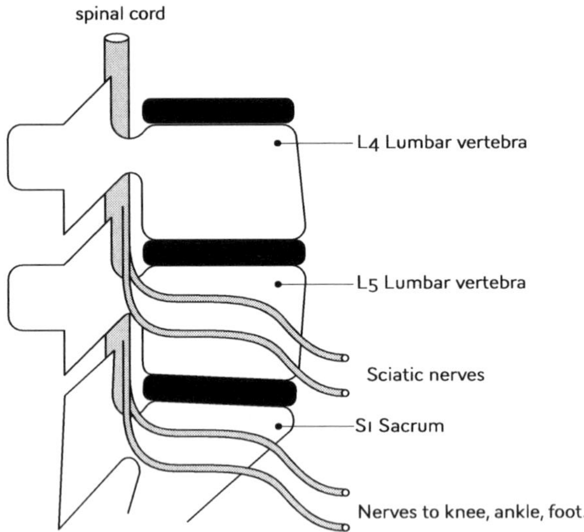

Figure 19. The base of your back. Your lumbar spine copes with huge compressive loads while protecting the nerves that supply your pelvic area and legs.

It is no wonder that injuries to this area quickly become chronic and life-changing, limiting our activities and making us feel old. You can only blame your age if every other joint in your body is in the same condition. If you have left hip arthritis, but not in the right hip, can it be because of age? Are they not both the same age? When you unpick it, age is a ridiculous, cop-out excuse. Nearly all spinal problems are due to *premature ageing* of one area more than the others. So what makes one part of your spine age faster than the rest? Subluxation, imbalance, loss of health.

Keys to a healthy lower back

There are FOUR KEYS to having a healthy lower back. Everything else follows:

1. Connection

The simplicity of having a subluxation-free spine means that your spine will constantly seek a good posture. Clients who have done years of stretching and strengthening will suddenly improve their posture when they are subluxation-free. Obvious it may not be, but every low back "treatment" should start at the top of your neck.

2. Alignment

As mentioned before, this is one of the **most important**, **yet overlooked** parts of spinal health. Why would a surgeon order MRIs but no postural x-rays? MRIs only show, slice by slice, the *pathology* of your spine. They show how bad the damage is. I love looking at MRIs, but they give us no information about *how* it got like that—we don't find out *how* it got damaged. Postural x-rays or images show *why* your spine is overloaded in certain areas. They show *how* to change your spine to get it healthy again. Only taking MRIs is like already settling on surgery as the only option. I don't think surgeons do this on purpose; this is simply how they have been taught. It is not the surgeon's fault, but it is still very bad news for you, their patient.

Your lower back should share your weight between the discs and the joints at the back (the facets). In order to do this, your lower back needs an optimal curve, again in the region of 40 degrees. Changing the angle of the sacrum, low back, or both, can shift the weight all onto the disc or one side of the disc. Being bent too far forward or even slightly to the side spikes the stresses inside the disc, making disc hernias more likely.[78]

L1 sits at the top of this curve. Misalignment in this area becomes magnified further up your spine. If **L1** is tipped backwards, you are doomed to have a swayback posture, most probably with a hunchback. And resulting neck problems. Think about all that time bent over a computer or mobile phone, and imagine how those thousands of hours of "abuse" will affect your lower back discs and ultimately your health. You may not feel this abuse at the beginning but often decades after you started the damage...

3. Movement

Your lower back should allow you to touch your toes, lean back, tip side to side and rotate, *without pain or restriction*. The mobility needs to come from ALL levels of your back. This is the key. If you could never touch your toes, even as a kid, it is possible that you have had damage in your back from a very young age.

But touching your toes is a misleading measure of back health. I often see clients who have certain areas which are heavily subluxated. They don't move well and may be degenerated, and the nerves are under stress. But they have other areas which are hypermobile. For example, they can still touch their toes, because their hips and a few spinal levels are still flexible (a common problem among yoga practitioners). They think their spine is fine, as they appear flexible. In fact, no amount of core or strengthening work can fix this until the underlying subluxations are corrected. The problem is not their overall flexibility, but the *quality* of the movement. It's a real bummer to spend decades doing yoga, pilates, strengthening, and stretching, only to find out you have chronic, degenerative subluxations. In Chapter 2, I referred you to our online subluxation self-test. It is a good guide to see how severe your subluxation stress is. But there is only one way to reliably check this. It is just like looking at tooth decay. The dentist cannot assess his own tooth decay. I cannot assess my own deeper subluxation levels. I see another chiropractor for that.

Being flexible and/or strong does not guarantee a healthy spine. Each level needs to do its bit. Without quality mobility, you cannot have good blood supply and good tissue drainage. Your spine literally becomes malnourished. And the discs suffer first.

4. Light Load

There is simply no escaping that the more weight your low back has to carry, the more likely it will have problems.[79] This goes for being overweight as much as it does carrying loads or working out in the gym, with one big caveat: the strength work done in the gym involves huge amounts of rest (between each session), whereas being overweight means your spine and discs *never get to rest*.

But it may surprise you to hear that a **light person in a bad posture** can have far **more spinal stress** than an **overweight person in a good posture**.

This is because certain bad postures (such as sitting) can increase the internal pressure by 3 to 4 times. So while weight counts, alignment is still far more important. The perfect storm, of course, is the person who already has bad posture and then puts on weight. This happens to a lot of us as our activity levels nose-dive in our middle age. Blame the kids or the mortgage—it doesn't matter—poor posture plus increasing body weight spells future disaster.

Some people may be surprised that core stability or core strength is not on this list of the most important things for a healthy lower back. It is very, very important, especially if you are asking a lot of your spine. But with good alignment and healthy mobility, it is unlikely that your core should be weak. If it is, it is either because you just don't move enough (i.e., you sit too much), or more probably, because a previous injury did not recover, causing subluxation and abnormal nervous control of the area. Research shows that just one episode of acute back pain switches off your core stabilisers, and *they do not automatically switch back on*[80] The problem is not the muscles but the control mechanism. In any case, core training without clear brain-body connection, or with a poorly aligned spine, can only help so much. Tightening things around an unstable structure with poor feedback may stop pains, but longer term problems will arise again. In fact, doing core stability work when you have reduced your subluxations becomes far easier, as the feedback is restored.

How to Slip a Disc

The Two Ways to Hurt Your Lower Back and Herniate Discs

We mostly think of damage in terms of accidents, like slips or falls (or in Alan's case, picking up a pen), and these are certainly important. However, we all suffer far more trauma from something far less accidental.

1. Chronic Postural Trauma – by far the most common cause of back injury

Sitting

You may think that you are "resting" while sitting on the sofa or reading a book, however, your back can only rest when you are lying down. And even then, as many night time back pain sufferers know, not always. As already mentioned, sitting in a flexed posture (the way we mostly sit) will commonly produce pressure of over 100kg compression in your lumbar discs. This is because the natural curve, which shares weight between the back of the spine and the discs, is flattened. In some people this factor will rise up to threefold your weight. Meaning that a 70kg person has 210kg of compressive forces on their discs! Humans are simply not designed to sit for long periods of time. So modifying your sitting posture and getting up regularly *radically* reduces risks not just for back pain, sciatica, and disc hernias, but also for a number of other health conditions, including heart disease. Put simply, sitting too much is extremely bad for you.

Sleeping

Although sleeping should be a time of rest, too often our low back ends up in a twisted or compressed position, meaning that it cannot recover overnight. In fact, the discs in your back literally "feed" overnight in a process called imbibition, where the disc "imbibes" or "sucks" fluid and nutrients from the vertebrae above and below. This means that it literally swells overnight, causing you to wake 1 to 2cm taller than you went to bed. The adage "measure height in the morning, shoe size in the evening" is really true.

Scan this code now to watch a YouTube video of a sleep posture which can help your discs to recover. Like and Subscribe for more videos.

Tightness and poor postures means the pressure overnight is not even. Leaving some parts of your back recovered, but other parts "malnourished." This means that as you wake in the morning, your low back feels anything but refreshed. It makes you feel a hundred years old and takes 30 to 90 minutes before you warm into your day. This is a likely sign that your discs are suffering, and you may even have disc instability. A good sleeping posture, plus knowing how to decompress your spine as you lie down, can make a big difference.

Car

It is no surprise that car seats are a big culprit for causing back problems. It's not that manufacturers have not tried. It is that sitting with your feet near the height of your bum is pretty difficult. Not only do seats force you into a very flexed position, often for prolonged periods, but the additional road vibrations into your spine have been shown to increase the load and fatigue on your low back. The less "car-like" your driving posture, the better. For example, a more "van-like" or upright posture often helps people who are suffering from back pain while driving. Either way, apart from trying to improve your posture, the best solution is taking regular breaks. Planning longer journeys to include a walk, lunch stop, etc., can really help to lessen the fatigue.

Digital Devices (Phones, Laptops, and Tablets)

If you read my articles or watch my Youtube channel, you will quickly realise that "digital devices" are one of my pet hates. They are one of the greatest threats to our spinal health. Regular laptop use is *totally incompatible* with a healthy spine. They are designed for short-term use only. Working from a laptop long-term guarantees spinal stress and problems!

Mobile phones are at least as dangerous, as we don't realise how long we are using them. "Text neck" (dealt with in Chapter 4) is a known neck injury from using the phone, but it extends to your low back too. We commonly see clients who have lumbar disc problems including hernias, hunched over their phone. Being conscious and changing these postures is important if you want to be healthy and well.

Standing

Unlike lounging on a sofa, standing and walking are our natural evolutionary states. And so should be friendly to our low backs, right? Well yes, but any activity with poor alignment, poor mobility, or excess weight can still be bad for our backs. In particular, standing still for a long time can cause what we call "Cocktail Party Syndrome," where a poorly aligned back forces you to "hang on your ligaments." The muscles cannot support you upright, your back cannot balance in neutral, aso your spine ends up "clinging on" as you try to enjoy your evening. This results in increasing pain and discomfort, and you find yourself looking for a chair. If standing for a period causes you back pain, it is possible that you have deeper alignment issues, a lost sixth sense, and subluxations.

2. Lifting, Falls and Slips

Lifting, falls, and slips are often the "final straw" on a back which is already struggling.

When people think of "trauma," this is what usually comes to mind: a slip on a wet floor or icy path, a fall down some stairs, or lifting something awkward and/or heavy. But the chronic trauma listed above is far more common. So when we do get unlucky, is it really bad luck, or was this "accident" waiting to happen?

If you are fit and playing a sport, and someone lands on you, that is bad luck. But this type of bad luck is extremely rare.

The truth is that so many of us have **fragile** backs from chronic postures, that even small loads have us on the edge. We already lost our spinal health a long time ago. The pen that "caused" Alan a forty year history of back problems is a comical, but real, example. As I write this chapter, this very week I saw an aspiring professional golfer as a new client. He was *adamant* that he has a strong back, yet spent his teenage years with chronic back pain and regularly suffers acute episodes. Worse still, he has been seeing a physiotherapist who has been manipulating it when he is in pain. He actually said the words "but my physio fixes it every time." It is true that he has good flexibility and even strength. He is extremely talented; it appears he will go far. But maybe not, because his back is a total mess. A postural mess, a neurological mess, a spine full of subluxations. And yet, he is a clever athlete, convinced that he is fit and strong. I delivered the bad news, gently but honestly. I suspect he needs another few years of inhibited performance, re-injury, and struggle, before he will be ready to face the music.

It is certainly possible to tear a muscle from overloading your back. And if indeed it is muscular, it should recover within a few weeks, *and not recur*. If it lasts beyond that, or recurs, then it is *not* "just muscular." Although you may finally feel your "back go" when you pick up a pen from the floor, or slip slightly, the reality is that a healthy back should be "immune" to all but the greatest slips and falls. Don't be like Alan.

Although very common, it is *not normal* to go around "protecting" our back from loads. That is just a sign that we need to act now. The accident, like picking something heavy, may be the final straw for a struggling lumbar disc. The overload causes it to rupture its walls, herniating its nucleus and bulging into the spinal canal. With luck there is enough flexibility and space for it to not fully compress a nerve. If not, then you might end up dealing with sciatic or leg pain.

Many people like Alan and this golfer "get past" these episodes with pain medication or rest. But the scarring continues inside. In fact, some of the worst degeneration I see is when people have not had enough pain to act sooner. Sometimes the "show stopper" pain can be a great gift.

More Time = More Scar = Bigger Problem = Slower to Heal Fully

It should be noted that if you have a fall which results in sudden radiating pain, especially if it causes changes in your bladder or bowel habits, you may have had an acute disc rupture and should seek emergency medical assessment as soon as possible.

A quick note on Physiotherapy.

Don't think that I don't like physiotherapy. In the UK I always had Physiotherapists working in my teams, many of whom are still close friends. It is an essential service, and it is under-valued and under-utilised. I believe that no patient should ever leave *any* surgical ward without seeing a Physio first. But chiropractic and physiotherapy serve very different purposes. I often recommend that clients return to see their Physio for treatment of an elbow, hand, or knee injury which seemed "not to improve" previously. Once the client's subluxations are reduced and their spine is more healthy, many such injuries quickly improve under physiotherapy. Chiropractic works on the master system- the spine and nervous system, so that any part of your body can heal better. It is not condition-dependent. Indeed the best time to get chiropractic care is when you do not yet have any injuries, pains, or illnesses. Chiropractic and physiotherapy work brilliantly together.

Exploding Discs

So we have looked at how your lumbar spine should "stack," how the curve should "shock absorb and bend," and how subluxations and abnormal postures can damage the spine. But what do all of these things mean in the medicalised, "symptom-centric" world? After all, that is why many people will pick up this book. Not to improve their quality of life or their flow of life-force, Chi, or Prana, but simply to get rid of pain…

Most people assume that lower back problems cause…lower back pain. Hopefully, this book highlights that lower back problems really cause an *unfulfilled life*. It does not have to be that way. The truth is that an unhealthy back can cause a wide range of symptoms and bad health. In many of these, it is not obvious that your back could even be related.

Here are some of the more obvious problems caused by an unhealthy back:

Chronic Back Pain with Stiffness

When your back is "just" stiff and painful, it is often a symptom of vertebral subluxation—insufficient movement at one or many levels. This tends to be worst "post-static," i.e., after you have not moved for a while. Pain on getting out of the car, sitting in a cinema or theatre seat, or first thing in the morning are common signs. When left unchecked, this progresses to degenerative changes such as spondylosis and osteoarthritis. Static stretching will generally alleviate the pains, as will massage. However, it feels like you just need to stretch more and more, and eventually, that is not enough. Unfortunately, excessive static stretching (such as too much yoga or stretching too hard) can accentuate movement imbalances, resulting in more irritation and an overall worsening of things. These positive stretching practices can actually mask the underlying cause. The only solution is to reestablish normal movement through adjusting the subluxations. Then, once reconnected, you can effectively strengthen and stretch the area.

Muscle Strain & Muscle Spasm

This must be the most misdiagnosed back condition. Excuse your doctor if they sigh when you tell them that your problem is "just muscular." Sure, you can partially tear (strain) a muscle by overloading your spine, but in practice, healthy spines do not tear muscles unless something truly unexpected occurs, such as catching a load (like a falling child) or slipping. Although much back pain is caused by muscle guarding, stiffness, and spasm, this is almost always a reaction to a deeper problem. Think about a chronically bad posture. If you are risking damage to your spinal nerves, of course your muscles will stay in contraction to try to protect it. Is the solution to relax the muscle? Think about a degenerating disc, where certain movements risk herniation or further rupture. Of course your back muscles will spasm! The small joints at the back of your spine (facet joints) are also highly sensitive and cause *acute spasm* when overloaded.

Are any of these muscular problems? Do muscle relaxants, which turn off this protective mechanism, make sense? They may make you feel better temporarily, but now that you have removed the protective spasm, what happens next? Trying to numb muscular symptoms in your lower back mostly causes more damage and longer-term problems. If you have had ongoing treatment for tight, stiff, muscles or spasms, it is very likely that something deeper has been missed. I cannot tell you how many clients I see who have excellent global flexibility and still think they need to stretch more to fix their problem. Stretching has its place, but with rare exception, you cannot stretch your way out of an unhealthy back.

Pinched Nerve

The sensation of a "pinched nerve," with shooting pain, is a horrible one. It can provoke all of that muscle spasm we just mentioned. If you are younger and you have an increased curve in your low back, this may be the facet joints screaming, *"Get off me."* But if you have had ongoing back problems and a loss of the curve, the disc may be bulging and compressing one or more nerves. The truth is that most "nerve pinching" tends to happen a lot more slowly than it feels, with either a herniated disc or bad posture gradually pressuring the area. People often feel they have a pinched nerve, because the pain is sharp and comes and goes quickly. But this is a healthy sign, where your back is trying to tell you that it is in danger. Your body is very literally shouting "STOP!" at you. Is the solution painkillers or anti-inflammatory drugs to shut it up? Again, it makes more sense to ask *why* it is doing this and then look for a long-term solution to a healthier back.

Osteoporosis

The topic of osteoporosis is a big one. Is it a symptom or a cause? Is it dietary, genetic, or activity-related, or all of these? But osteoporosis in itself is not dangerous. It is the resulting fractures which are dangerous.

One thing is for sure. If you have poor spinal alignment, you radically increase your risk of osteoporotic vertebral fracture. That is, the bone weakening and *collapsing*. This creates lots of severe, toothache-type pain and is extremely difficult to treat. Bad posture makes it *nearly three times more likely* for this to happen to you. In fact, a bad postural curve or scoliosis can become life-threatening when osteoporosis advances. This is yet another reason to aim for *optimal spinal alignment* as young as possible and to keep it as long as possible. You may have to live with osteoporosis, but it need not be a life sentence.

Spondylosis, Osteoarthritis & Degenerative Disease

Doctors love fancy names which make us feel smarter than everyone else. Spondylosis is a fancy medical way of saying "unwell spine" or degenerating spine. Osteoarthritis (inflamed joints) or osteoarthrosis (unwell joints) are basically different ways of saying the same thing. In different countries, we use different terms. Some people even call it "wear and tear," and sometimes they are correct! If you visit a medical doctor as you age, you are almost guaranteed the gift of at least one of these "diagnoses."

So if it is "wear and tear," it will be evenly distributed throughout your whole body, correct? If this degeneration is evenly distributed throughout your whole body, then let us blame age. Your body is not designed to wear out quickly in some areas, and slowly in others. You are better designed than that. If it is just one area or level, then injury, postural imbalance, or something else is to blame, and blaming age is just a soft excuse.

So while spondylosis, osteoarthritis, osteoarthrosis, and degenerative disease are all interesting names, what is far more interesting is *why* that particular part of your body is suffering and degenerating faster than other parts and *how* to offload that area and look after it so that it (and you) can have a longer, healthier, happier life. With good alignment, mobility, and normal load, your spine should degenerate uniformly, with no focal "problem areas." So you should never feel "written off" by the *misdiagnosis* of "it's just your age" or "it's just wear and tear." Look to the cause. Every year, millions of people with spondylosis, osteoarthritis, and degenerative disc disease get brilliant results simply by reducing subluxations and improving alignment, without drugs or surgery.

Bulging Disc, Herniated Disc & "Slipped disc"

Finally, we arrive at the diagnosis you have heard your family and friends talk of and may even have received from your own doctor. If you have seen a doctor who said you had a "slipped disc," either it was over thirty years ago or they are not a real doctor!

No disc has ever "slipped." The discs are so well "glued" to the bone that the bone would always break first. But discs do bulge, herniate, and more. As mentioned earlier, your discs are made up of a soft toothpaste-like core (the Nucleus Pulposus), contained within tougher layers of fibrous "skin-wall" (the Annulus Fibrosus). They suck nutrients and fluid from the vertebrae overnight. Their job is to shock-absorb, move freely, and protect the spinal nerve roots which are sending life-critical messages to and from your brain and body. And as we have discussed, we obliviously abuse them for decades on end, without love or thought. What on earth could go wrong?!?!

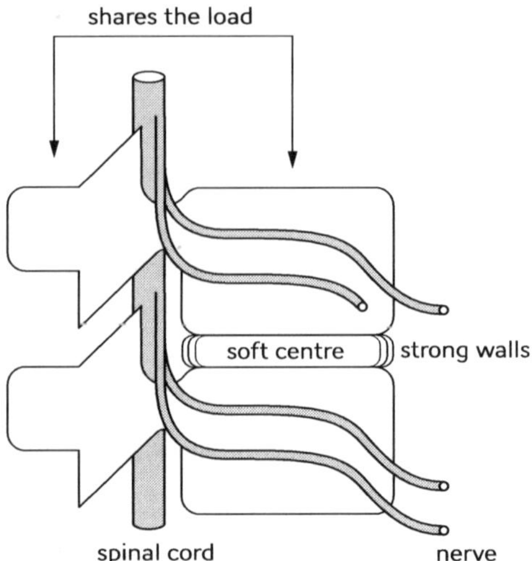

Figure 20. When your spinal curves are neutral, the load is shared between the joints and the disc. Deviation either way from neutral causes inevitable stress and eventual problems.

Well, you could have a small back injury, which limits the mobility in an area. You feel okay, so you return to normal activity. No big deal. But the vertebral subluxation – the abnormal movement and scarring – persists. And so, that level moves abnormally, placing too much pressure on the disc and soft tissues, until one day, some seemingly small thing causes it to become a very big deal.

It could be a long journey where you sit stressed, and after getting off a flight, you pick up your suitcase and…*big deal!*

Or you could sit way too much on a long journey, pressuring just one part of the disc, fatiguing the wall, and altering its shape. And then lean over to pick something up…*big deal!*

Or you could have an athletic childhood, then stop sport and movement, denying the discs their normal nutrition, and letting them slowly degenerate…*big deal!*

Or you might always be in a poor posture (no big deal), which forces all of the disc material (nucleus) either forward or backward, or even to the side (for example in a scoliosis). Then, this material pushes on the disc wall (annulus) until one day it gives way…*big deal!*

Or you could be very flexible, stretching regularly, and therefore not notice a small injury developing at one vertebral level. You feel fine, so no big deal. Over time, the adjacent levels stretch more and more, as the damaged level struggles to keep up, and the disc weakens rapidly. At a young age, you already have advanced disc degeneration, despite being super-flexible and apparently very healthy...*very big deal!*

Or you could be overweight for many years, simply asking too much load-wise from your discs, so the nucleus bulges through the walls until they cannot hold back any longer...*big deal!*

Or it could be any combination of the above, plus a thousand other things! We ask so much of our low backs every day that it is no surprise that so many things can go wrong.

So now you have a disc bulge. A bulge and even a hernia can happen *quietly* without hitting the part of the nerve which causes pain. In fact, around *one in three disc hernias cause no obvious pains*. You can be "less lucky", and the hernia can hit the nerve directly and send you into a breathless cycle of pain. The pain can stay in the low back area or radiate into your buttocks or even all the way down to your feet.

This all sounds very negative, so let me be clear: your body is more than capable of healing. In fact it wants and is trying to heal the whole time. Give it a real chance, and it will surprise you.

A disc **hernia** refers to an abnormal bulging of the disc, beyond its normal size. It is graded into three "severities." **Protrusions** are still contained, meaning the disc has spread, but the wall is still intact. This is the most common type of disc hernia, as it is still a "bulge" and may cause no pain or symptoms. In an **extrusion**, the wall is breached, and the material exits into the spinal canal. This may cause huge levels of pain and even become a surgical emergency. But it also has the possibility of being reabsorbed and broken down by enzymes, so may not be as bad as feared if you allow it time. Finally, a **sequestration** occurs when the disc fragment separates from the main disc and can migrate up or down your spinal canal. It sounds very dramatic, but because it is mobile, it may actually move into a place which reduces pressure on your spinal cord. Each case is different. You are not an MRI or an x-ray.

When you have pain and a disc hernia is diagnosed, too often, surgery is offered as if it were the *only* option. This is simply not true. For example, there is evidence that up to 90% of spinal fusion surgery can be deemed as unnecessary.[81] The same goes for multiple other surgeries. And that is without going into the associated risks. See Chapter 13 for more information on when to choose surgery.

Every year, hundreds of thousands of people suffering from disc hernias recover naturally. Getting to the root cause of the problem means improving the mobility of that level and the alignment of the area. The right care sets the foundation for a healthier, stronger back, and a natural recovery. When it comes to healing your spine, you can do it!

Pain in the Arse

Do you have a hip problem or a back problem? It is often not an easy question to answer. MRIs and x-rays can be misleading. They are only part of the picture. Logic says fix your spine first. Fix your brain-body connection first, and then see what else needs clearing up. I cannot tell you how many of my clients were on the list for hip surgery, who never needed hip surgery. I did not fix their hip but restored their brain-body connection, allowing their hip to heal itself.

Hip and leg tightness and pains often stem from nerve stress in your lower back.

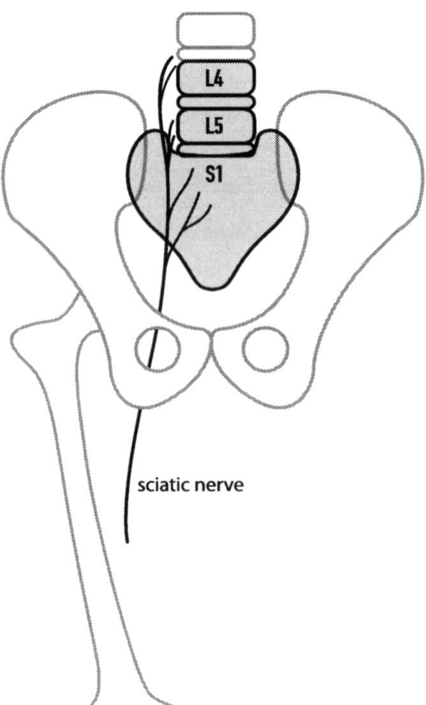

Figure 21. Your lumbar nerves combine to form the sciatic nerve, a thick nerve which runs down the back of your leg, all the way to your foot. Irritation at any point in the nerve can cause inflammation from your low back to your foot.

Sciatica

True sciatica is not just buttocks or leg pain but pain in the distribution of the sciatic nerve, down the back of your leg and normally past your knee. So while someone may have called your leg pain "sciatica," that may not necessarily be the case. The sciatic nerve is mainly made up of the nerve roots of L4, L5, and S1. These are near the base of your spine, coming out at the level of your belt. The discs in this area are under huge amounts of stress. When one or all of these nerves are inflamed, they may inflame the sciatic nerve.

Characterised by pain in the back of the leg, true sciatica often makes it hard to sit without lifting that leg slightly. Any pressure on the back of your leg causes pain and often cramping. The sciatic nerve can also be irritated as it passes through the pelvis, in what some call a "piriformis syndrome." It is unfortunate that the sciatic nerve passes through muscles which have the same nerve supply as itself! This means, for example, that an L5 injury can cause inflammation in the sciatic nerve but also send the piriformis into spasm, often compressing the sciatic nerve as it passes through! So you end up with a vicious cycle. This is one of the reasons why sciatic pains so often become life-changing and chronic. All parts of the cycle (the cause and the effects) need to be relieved to experience health again.

A lot of energy is spent stretching piriformis muscles and gluteals (buttocks) for people with sciatic pain. While these things are important, they are the effect. The tightness and spasm will keep coming back until the pressure is removed from the cause: the nerve itself. That might take time—most sciatica cases are preceded by years of back stiffness! Sciatica does not need to be the "sentence" which so many people get used to.

When I worked in the UK, these problems were routinely sent for chiropractic care, in accordance with the national guidelines.[82] Yes, a lot of medications to "numb" the symptoms were prescribed, but most medical doctors knew that they needed to refer these cases. Where I live in Spain, I routinely see clients who regularly attend their hospital emergency department to get anti-spasmodic injections for this problem. They return for the same injection another six or twelve months later. Again and again they get these injections as if they might solve something. Year after year. Symptom relief with no proper treatment causes a negative spiral into illness and disability. As the injury and scar tissue mounts up, treating your body this way makes you a prime candidate for future surgery. I don't think that the medical system was designed to do this, but what other choice does an emergency room doctor have they see someone crying with pain? The doctors don't want you to suffer, so they use the tools they have to hand. This is, in my opinion, neglectful *use* of the medical system. It is a sorry fact that if you or a family member want to get out of this negative spiral, *you* have to take it on yourself to do something different.

A quick note on stretching. We already discussed this in chapter 3, but I should reiterate that stretching is great. Use it to gain flexibility, or to help with recovery after a workout. Use dynamic stretching to warm up pre-sport. Use yoga poses to add strength in a challenged or stretched position. Stretch gently as part of your wake-up routine. All of these types of stretching are great. But regularly *needing to stretch for pain relief* is a warning sign. It may give temporary relief, but the constant *need to stretch* just *to relieve pain and stress* is not normal. Either you have altered nerve stress—which should be addressed, or you are holding a fatiguing posture—which should be addressed. You cannot stretch your way out of a subluxated or misaligned spine.

Tight or Torn Hamstrings or Calves

Many, many athletes have their careers spoiled by gluteal, hamstring, calf, or achilles injuries which become persistent. They get orthotic insoles, change how they run, do strength training, stretch, and rest. These are all good ideas, but these injuries just keep coming back. So they just learn to live with it through regular massage, and loads of stretching. Their sporting career is, at best, painful, and at worst, ruined.

Then one day they have back pain, and they get adjusted by a chiropractor. And within weeks, a decade-old injury clears up. The tone and function of all of your leg muscles is set by the nerves which exit your lower back. Relieving pressure in your lower back can result in what look like miraculous healings, but the "miracle" is that your brain is back in control and can relax your low back when needed. If a muscle group in your leg keeps getting tight, it is time to ask why.

90% of professional athletes in the USA use chiropractic care to stay injury-free and enhance performance:[83] to avoid getting injuries and improve their results. Athletes who compete without chiropractic care are at a disadvantage. Life does not have to be a constant fight with tight muscles!

Playing with Your Sex Organs

Back in 2002, as with many new graduate doctors, I was blissfully unaware of what I was missing in many of my clients. And so, like anyone destined to become a good doctor, I had more listening than learning to do. I remember very early in my career a series of three cases which caught my attention and made me listen.

All three had a lot in common. Three career women. Two in their thirties. One had just turned forty. Two of them told me that they had been trying for a baby but had been unable to conceive. They had been through multiple rounds of IVF with no joy. The other just told me that she had been on a career break and was returning to focus on her career. All three had lumbar spine problems. But for only one of them was this significant, causing her actual pain. Another one was suffering from headaches, and the other had neck pain after a car accident. In my new graduate, bumbling way, I adjusted them to the best of my abilities over a few months. And they all came back to me with the same accusation.

"You got me pregnant!" As if I was not already sufficiently awkward and nervous, this sort of news did not help to settle my nerves. But no, I had not had any romantic relationship with any of them. I had simply (and pretty unskillfully) freed up the nerve stress in their spines. I had changed the balance of their nervous system, allowing their bodies to do what they had wanted to do—to procreate.

The funny thing was, in all three cases, they were more certain that the adjustment had allowed them to get pregnant than I was myself! This is because they had been through so many attempts, hurdles, moments of hope, and moments of despair. And the only thing which had changed in their life was getting adjusted.

I will never forget this phase of my career. Sure, there were plenty of embarrassing, awkward moments, but I lived in a constant state of *surprise* at what spinal adjustments could change in someones body.

In Chapter 9, we look at the balance in your nervous system. This global balance surely has a lot to do with the "miracles" we routinely see in practice. But look at the chart below, and it becomes clear that reducing nerve pressure from your low back can have major effects on other parts of your health.

Knowing that you have digestive problems, food intolerance, poor bladder control, erectile dysfunction, abnormally painful or heavy periods, poor leg circulation, or difficulty conceiving should not change the plan when you see a good doctor. I have seen so many people have these problems clear up partly or entirely under care, I could not count them.

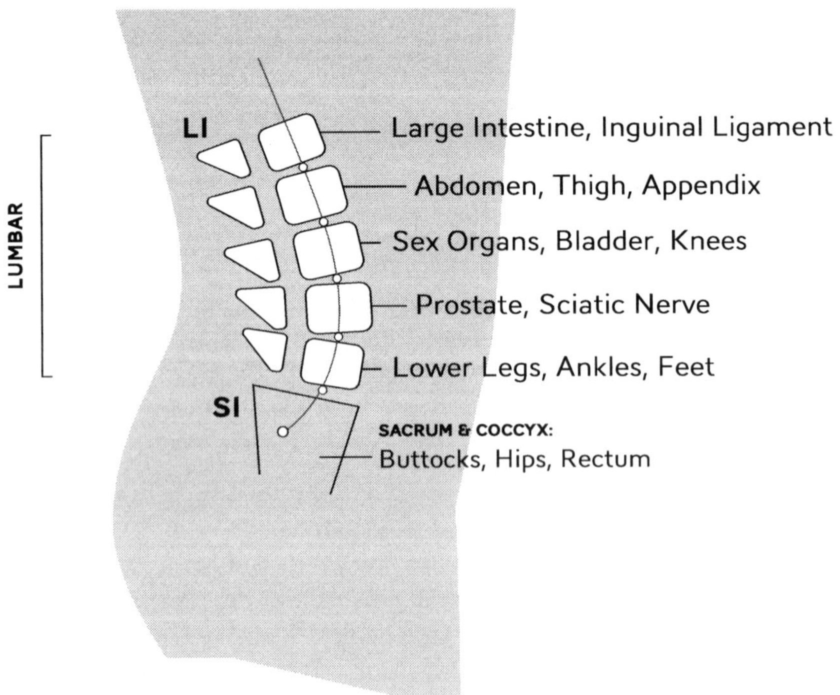

Figure 22. Each nerve root supplies one or many organs. Though they overlap, these are the principal organs supplied by nerve root level.

As mentioned in Chapter 2, when *all* of the focus is on reducing subluxation and clearing the brain/body connection, *then and only then* can these "miracle healings" occur.

Chapter Summary

- The way in which we have normalised low back pain is absurd. Back pain which "goes away" without care often leaves scarring, subluxations, and future degeneration.
- It is rare to see a low back problem which did not start years ago, even if you only felt it start last week.
- Our discs are amazing but predictable. Too much load or an uneven load due to poor spinal posture, and you will pay the price.
- Sitting spikes the loads in your low back discs and causes more damage than falls or other injuries.
- Low back nerve pressure often manifests as hip pain or sciatica. But it also puts pressure on the nerves controlling the digestive system and sex organs.

Action Points:

- When was the first time you ever damaged your low back? And before that? And before that?
- If you have old injuries and scars in your low back, set a plan to rebuild it not over days or weeks, but over months and years. Then plan to keep it strong, for life.
- Visit Chapter 12 for postural tips, and minimise how much you sit!

If you are near Marbella, Spain, go to www.duffyquiropractica.com to find out how to work with Dr Duffy.

If elsewhere, go to www.chiroalliance.org or www.chiropractic.org to search for subluxation reducing Chiropractors.

Chapter 7

S1, Your Sacrum, and Pelvis

"What humans can't engineer, evolution can."

— Kevin Kelly

The Healthy Pelvis

And so we get to the foundation of the spine. S1, your first sacral bone, is the top of your sacrum. Your sacrum fuses between ages 18 to 30, so its shape may be formed and influenced earlier in life.

Anatomy

Your sacrum is a wedge-like structure which is literally "forced" down between your pelvic bones, pushing them apart. These junctions, the sacroiliac joints (SIJs) are magnificent structures. The ligaments here have to be strong; otherwise, your sacrum would literally separate your pelvis and fall out through your bottom! This unique construction, called force-form closure means that SIJs behave like no other joint in your body. In essence, they are totally stable with a few exceptions. In fact, it has long been argued that they do not move at all. And this remains an area of some debate. If they did not move at all, we would have evolved with them fused, and they would not degenerate from wear and tear (as they do). The fact is that they do move, but in some cases, this movement is well under one degree, so it is difficult to perceive.[84] Most healthy SIJs move about three degrees forward and back and even less in rotation and side-bending. This is a tiny movement. But these are big joints. A tiny movement in a big joint which transfers half your body weight into your leg and sets up the alignment of the rest of your spine can be very significant.

Furthermore, the SIJs themselves have no "active" muscular control. What? That cannot be right. Yet, it is. There are no muscles to be massaged, strengthened, or stretched. I guess our exquisite engineer knew better than to try to build muscles to "fight" this battle. Perhaps, too, this is why the joint is so structurally stable. Build it bomb-proof so that it is too hard to break. And to be fair, it does a pretty good job of that.

Here are some of the things which you ask your sacrum and pelvis to do every day:

1. Transfer your whole upper body weight from the centre (at S1), around the bony ring of your pelvis, and down into one individual leg.
2. While doing that, pull up on your other leg, so that you do not fall over! The act of standing on one leg involves huge conflicting forces at S1, your sacrum, and your whole pelvic ring.
3. Pump your CSF. Within the sacrum, you have a small reservoir of fluid called CSF.[85] This "brain and spine irrigation" is pumped from your sacrum, up your spine, and into your brain (see Chapter 4: Your Neck Feeds Your Brain).
4. Protect your lower digestive system, bladder, and reproductive organs.
5. And act as a rock-solid anchor for your enormously powerful leg muscles.

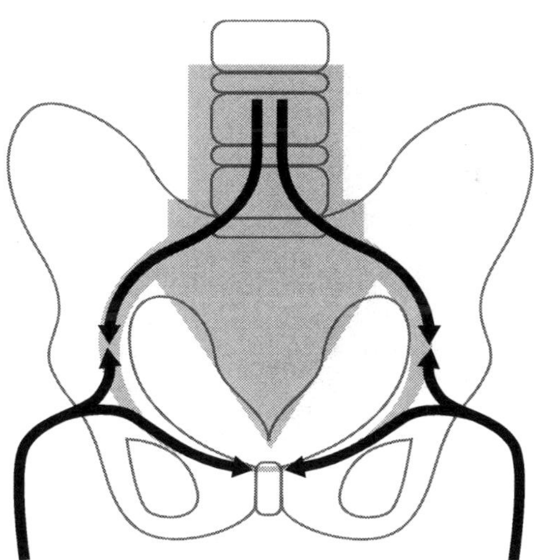

Figure 23. The pelvis performs the mammoth task of transferring many times your body weight and power from one leg into your lumbar spine, all whilst protecting your fragile pelvic organs and occasionally offering safe-house to another living being for nine months.

As in the base of your spine, small misalignments can become magnified higher up. It is common to see a small imbalance in this area provoke a major scoliosis higher up.

4 Keys to a Healthy Sacrum and Pelvis:

1. Connection

First and foremost in any spinal health is having a subluxation-free spine. All the good alignment in the world cannot keep your pelvis healthy if your brain cannot communicate clearly with it. If your brain is not clearly connected, injury will come sooner or later. This means being connected to your pelvic floor muscles and a lot more. In other words, a healthy pelvis actually starts with a healthy C1! Many are the clients who have huge relief of pelvic problems and pains after only having their neck adjusted for subluxation.

2. Alignment

Two legs of equal length make a good start here. If one is longer, something has to compensate. Not only this, but how the pelvis and sacrum tips forward and backwards on the tops of your femurs can radically affect the weight bearing and curves into the rest of your spine.

3. Movement

The fact that the joints of your pelvis only move a small amount, makes the balance of that movement even more important. Not only that, but the mobility of the adjacent joints (hips and low back) can radically change the stresses on your pelvis.

4. Peace

A bit difficult to describe, the organs within your pelvis need to be at peace in order to keep your pelvis healthy. Irritable bowel problems, painful periods, haemorrhoids, and other pelvic organ issues may not only be caused by nerve pressure problems, but themselves will cause pelvic problems. This is because the deep muscles of your pelvis respond with tightness or spasm. This, in turn, compresses the joints and nerves, and the cycle then worsens. The net result is a person being unable to tell if they have back pain, menstrual problems, IBS, or a combination of these. Reducing subluxation stress is the logical place to start.

In some ways, the pelvis has "fewer moving parts" than the rest of the spine, and so should be easier to look after. My experience is that pelvic and SIJ problems are often the result of the long-term ignoring of the subtle signs. This is because the signs are pretty confusing. Who, with bladder control issues, constipation, or problem periods, instantly thinks, "I need to get my spine checked?" Often, by the time the spine is identified as the problem, the problem already has a 5 to 10 year head-start.

The Twisted Pelvis- A Ticking Time Bomb

How to "Twist" your SIJs and Pelvis

If the pelvis is such a robust structure, how does it get damaged and why do so many people have pelvic pain? Indeed "hip" complaints are more often pelvic problems with the hip joints—by that I mean the ball-and-socket joints—only tending to cause problems later in life. In such cases, someone may eventually tell you that you have a "twisted pelvis." So what are all of these problems, then?

While there are two principal causes of pelvic and SIJ problems, in reality most problems have multiple causes.

Sitting

What supports you when sitting? Your sit bones! These bony bumps, called your ischial tuberosities, are located relatively far back in your pelvis. They are not nice and flat, to hold you steady in a good posture. Instead you have to "balance" on your ischial tuberosities, and therein is the problem. Were we to have evolved to sit as much as we do, no doubt we would have flat bums, but this is not so!

So as you sit on them, your pelvis has a tendency to "tip back." This instantly causes flexion through your sacrum and lower back. Indeed, this causes much of the disc pressure which damages so many lower backs, as described in Chapter 6. But it also "jams" your SIJs into an extreme posture, and then leaves them there. For how long? You tell me. Do that with your legs crossed and the problem, the stress in your SIJs, is multiplied tenfold.

The hip flexor muscles act indirectly across your pelvis, then gradually get shorter and shorter. Your SIJs don't move at all when you are sitting. So you jam them into a fully flexed posture, perhaps cross your legs, and leave them there for hours and hours. Days and days. Years and years. You get the picture. Sitting, especially prolonged sitting, is bad for your back and evil for your poor pelvis. When you go to get up, your sacrum is blocked and your hip flexors are tight. The cycle of problems has begun. And when you get "injured" years later, it seems that the problem only started at the moment of that injury.

Falls

Whereas lifting, falls, and slips are most often the final straw in lower back problems, they are often the *first straw*, the *original cause*, of pelvic problems. This is because of that "force-form closure" I mentioned earlier.

Let me demonstrate this with two real examples. When I worked in England, we sponsored and looked after many professional and elite cyclists and triathletes. Steve and Jay were both top Ironmen for their age groups. Steve came in regularly for wellness care. He got adjusted about every two weeks, with or without injury. Before races he increased this frequency to ensure he was ready and on top form. Jay came in from time to time, when he had pains or symptoms. He was actually more competitive than Stu, always placing above him in races. They were preparing for the South Africa Ironman race the following April. With the race so early in the calendar, it required a lot of winter preparation. So in January, they were out on a club bicycle ride together on a Sunday morning. It was freezing cold, and as they entered a corner, they both slipped on black ice and landed on their side. They slid to a halt, got up, pulled themselves together, and after checking their bikes, rejoined the ride. A few grazes and bruises don't stop cyclists.

The following Monday, Steve came in, bruised and battered. He was achey but had no specific problems that he could identify. But on checking him, he had lost 30% of the power in one leg. The fall had damaged his right SIJ, which was now literally "blocked out of place." I adjusted him twice that week, and true to form, he was back to full strength and training the following week.

Jay, with similar injuries, carried on training as usual. In March, nearly two months after the fall, and with four weeks until the race, he came in to see me. He was suffering groin pain during long rides, had constant pain in the outside of his knee, and felt weak in his whole right leg. Jay had exactly the same SIJ subluxation that Steve had also suffered some two months prior. The difference now was two months of scarring and about 200 hours of training. The anchor for all of his muscles was ever so slightly out of position and locked up. The nerves were under pressure. It was provoking a cascade of problems into his leg. He started intensive adjustments and physiotherapy. His subluxations improved, but despite all that our physiotherapists could do for his knee, they could not get it ready in time for the race. He pulled out of the race. A whole winter of training and the whole season had been thrown away because he didn't make a few quick visits to get himself checked after that original fall. This is the difference between the less talented athlete who wins and the more talented athlete who fails. Their health philosophy.

Now let's imagine that Jay had *not come to see us at that point*, late as it was, but instead stopped racing due to his ongoing knee problems and then left it another ten or fifteen years before coming into us with a herniated lumbar disc. This is not at all uncommon. You start to see how "minor" falls on the pelvis can do far-reaching damage to your health.

A twisted pelvis is like a ticking time bomb.

"Leg" Injuries

Which came first, the chicken or the egg, the pelvis or the leg?

It is pretty obvious how pelvic misalignments can cause leg problems. But the opposite is also true. Misalignments in your feet, leg length inequalities, or untreated sports injuries will inevitably cause pelvic compensations. So you get the leg problem treated, and it recovers. But now your pelvis and low back are the problem. And pelvis and low back problems cause, among other things, leg problems.

Again, it becomes pretty obvious that proactive care for your whole body is the only thing that makes sense. Any problem which causes subluxation will eventually cause other problems. This is why 100% of American football NFL teams use a resident chiropractor in their medical team, as do 72% of PGA Golfers (including all of the greats), and most other professional sportspeople. Obviously, these people put extraordinary stresses on their bodies and rapidly pay the price for any misalignments. But everyone, including you and I, will eventually pay the same price, albeit more slowly and chronically. If you want to ensure a long, vital life, with strong legs and mobility, only you can take the action to stay subluxation-free.

> Tiger Woods has famously used chiropractic care to not just keep him playing, but to keep him performing with fewer injuries over the years. **"I've been going to chiropractors for as long as I can remember. It's as important to my training as practicing my swing." – Tiger Woods**[86]

Hip Pain

Your Hip Bone is Connected to Your...Back Bone.

The hip joint is the ball-and-socket joint at the top of your thigh, connecting into your pelvis. Many people describe everything from their low back to the top of their leg as their hip. In fact, people complaining of "hip pain" can have anything from low back problems to uterine fibroids, and the pain many look the same. Someone with "hip pain" presents to an orthopaedic surgeon, who takes x-rays to see the condition of the ball and socket joint. If there is wear and tear, hip resurfacing or replacement surgery is recommended. We go into this theme more in Chapter 13, but the joint replacement surgery industry is worth $20 billion in the USA alone.[87] Research estimates that $8.3 billion of this surgery is not necessary, with clients getting equally good results without surgery. In fact, despite this evidence, hip surgery rates have soared, and according to the International Congress for Joint Reconstruction, are expected to more than triple in the coming 40 years.[88] Moreover, revision surgeries – meaning having the same hip done for the second time – are expected to increase four-fold. This is big business, with big money on the agenda. Your personal health is not on the same agenda.

Over the years, I have seen many clients who now proclaim that I "fixed their hip" so that they didn't need hip surgery. I even once had an orthopaedic hip surgeon who I bumped into in a restaurant ask me what I had "done to the hip" of a friend of his, whom he had recommended for surgery and who never needed hip surgery. To be precise, I did nothing to any of these hips, nor do most chiropractors work directly on the hip joint itself. But the hip joint forms a part of a bigger system—that system which transmits the *central* load of your spine through your sacrum, into your pelvis, around the bony ring, and into the hip joint, out to the *side of the body*, before passing that load down your leg. It all sounds pretty obvious, but when you consider that dynamic, it becomes clear that the ball-and-socket hip joint itself is only one part of the big equation. Squeeze all of your walking and jumping muscles, the blood supply to your legs, your reproductive organs, bladder, rectum, and a whole network of controlling nerves into that same space, and it should be clear that your hip area is a whole lot more than a ball-and-socket joint.

To recap, the sacroiliac joints (SIJs) connect your sacrum to your pelvis. They bear ALL of your weight, and as you stand on one leg, are responsible for sending your upper body weight out to the side and down your leg. They are big, solid, fibrous joints. Their alignment is critical, and any irritation to them or the nerve supply passing through them can cause pain not only in those joints, but in the ball-and-socket joint itself. It is just common sense to get your hips and pelvis healthy *before ever considering* any surgery. Best case scenario, you avoid becoming one of those 2 in 5 unnecessary surgeries and gain all sorts of better health in the process. Worst case scenario, you still have surgery, but you know that you really needed it, and you are far healthier, recovering better, and returning to full activity afterwards.

In 2007, an orthopaedic surgeon and cyclist friend of mine came to our practice. At the time, he was operating mostly on hips...and ironically he was getting hip pain while cycling. We did his full spinal analysis, set up a course of chiropractic spinal care, prescribed him orthotic insoles for his cycling shoes, and recommended physiotherapy to strengthen his knee imbalances and improve his alignment. At the end of his report, he sat still and speechless. He was staring slightly blankly into space, as if he had received very bad news. As a friend, I felt a little bad, and said, "Come on, it's not all bad news—you'll still be able to ride your bike!" He apologised, and said "No, no, you don't understand. I have just never seen anything like it before. When I look at a hip, it is a hip." He held his hands one above the other, like two shelves above and below his hip. "I mean that's it," he continued," a hip, nothing above or below. I have never

> before seen anyone look at the whole body just to figure out what was going on in one joint." He was being dead serious. Needless to say, within about six weeks, he no longer suffered hip pain and is still a club cyclist today. Note that we never treated his ball-and-socket hip joint, just his connection and alignment, and the hip took care of itself. Good holistic practitioners will refuse to treat you like a single joint. If you meet someone who is only interested in where you have pain, alarm bells should sound.

Sex and Melons

Since the Victorian times introduced the "privatisation of sex," talking about what is inside your pelvis has almost become taboo. But I want to highlight two important factors relevant to making babies. One relates to the necessary ingredients for procreation — sex. The other relates to a healthy pregnancy and birth.

Sex

When I say the ingredients for procreation, I am not just talking about an egg and a sperm cell. It is important to understand the neurology of our two greatest instincts. The two greatest instincts of all living things are self-preservation/survival and reproduction. In particular, it is important to understand that their neurologies are *mutually exclusive.* We will cover this more in Chapter 9, but here is a quick summary. Survival is a *sympathetic* nervous system function. Reproduction is a *parasympathetic* nervous system function. Each nervous system function "shuts down" the other system. If your nervous system perceives a survival threat, be it a real tiger or just a modern-day, digital equivalent, you will not reproduce. With too much parasympathetic stimulus, you will not get out of bed to run away from the tiger. These are evolutionary facts, which come back to haunt us in our current lifestyles.

About 1 in 7 couples have fertility challenges.[89] We live in a world of perceived threats, from mortgage repayments and work assignments to wars in other countries and your mother-in-law. Many perceived "tigers" culminate in a nervous system primed for survival. If your nervous system is busy protecting you from death, it will not spend energy on making a baby. It is pretty obvious, but chronic stress and healthy procreation are mutually exclusive. The first step for any want-to-be parents is to simply get themselves healthier and happier. Get your spine and nervous system balanced. Allow your body to bathe in parasympathetic hormones as often as it likes. Relax. Have fun. Have wild sex. This should come long before counting your ovulation cycles and longer still before looking into in-vitro fertilisation (IVF) or other "treatments."

Pregnancy and Birth

So you have reset, sorted out your spine, gotten healthy and happy in yourself, and you are now pregnant. *Congratulations!* You know that pregnancy is a job for your *parasympathetic* nervous system. In you go to the medical centre to have your dating scan, which tells you when your baby should arrive. It's like your wedding date or your final exam date, so you now have something to worry about, despite the fact that fewer than one in 20 babies comply and actually come out on that exact date.[90] A nice little dose of survival stress. Now, after one of your routine scans, you are asked to come back in to do it again.

In the UK, 15% of 20-week "anomaly scans" are repeated,[91] because they could not see all they needed to. That is 15% of prospective parents who have to spend a few weeks with their hearts in their mouths, scared there is a problematic anomaly with their baby. What happens to their nervous systems during this time? Another big dose of *sympathetic* survival stress. About 1 in 300 of these will go on to find some sort of abnormality,[92] often not significant, but 100% of them will have increased worry and stress.

And if you, in the final trimester, are the one in every three women who are told that their baby is "too big," what then? "Too big" for what?! Having been told this, you are now far more likely to elect a caesarian section, irrespective of your baby's actual birth weight.[93] This is despite the evidence showing that this "diagnosis" is often incorrect.[94]

The inaccuracy of ultrasound weight calculation is 15-20%, or around 550g.[95] So an expected 4kg "big" baby could easily come out below average, at 3.2kg. In fact, only 1.3% of non-diabetic mothers really have big babies, weighing 4.5kg or more.[96] But how are your stress levels now? Studies show that baby positioning is far more important than baby size when it comes to the ease of a natural birth. All of this stress means that, when the big day arrives, your body may be trying too hard to survive, to even consider letting the baby out. Would mother nature have you deliver your baby while you are being chased by a tiger? Even if the tiger is virtual, it is real to your nervous system. The risk-managing medicalisation of pregnancy is a modern tragedy, robbing so many women from a relaxed, natural, beautiful childbirth.

Perhaps you can hear me hopping up and down with frustration on this topic. The medical system is geared for crisis. They work in a high-risk environment, and risk reduction is the name of the game. I understand. But this energy of risk-management totally forgets to trust in your innate ability to do the most magnificent of things imaginable. To create and deliver another human being to the world. You were born with an innate capacity. Your body is made for this. You, your body, and your miraculous intelligence run the show far better than any medical doctor or midwife ever could. While it is nice to have support in the case of crisis, why not assume that your pregnancy will not have any crisis? Be prepared should there be a crisis, for sure. Plan your birth as if a crisis were inevitable? Not such a good idea. It is time to reconnect with your inner power, your inner ability to do this. This comes out of trusting your body, letting go of doubts, trusting that nature knows best. It is the greatest moment in your baby's life. It may be the greatest moment in your life, where all of your innate power shines through. Let it shine!

Rock Your Pelvis

This might be a good time to mention that not all pelvises are made equal! Indeed the female pelvis is designed differently, to have the marvellous privilege of bringing new life into this world. And that inevitably comes with its own challenges. Please excuse my humour when I use the melon reference. Because when you look at a baby's head, it does look impossible that a melon is going to fit through that lemon-sized hole. In reality, the melon-sized baby head distorts radically, literally shrinking to fit through your pelvis. And your pelvis does some magical work too. Here is how the female pelvis differs from the male:[97]

1. The overall shape is quite different. It is lighter, wider, more shallow. And importantly, the "pelvic inlet" is wider, allowing easier passage for the baby.

2. Your coccyx is shaped differently and is more mobile, meaning it is more "out of the way" of a baby. Women with a history of coccyx damage can still have healthy, natural births.
3. There are extra ligaments, most notably those which attach to the uterus. These are called the uterine ligaments and play an important role in holding the uterus when it is, well…full.
4. The pubis, the joint right at the front between your legs, is smaller and far more mobile than a man's, allowing it to pivot.
5. The sacroiliac joints are oriented differently, and "nod" up to 11 degrees during the birthing process…*if they are mobile.*

What a magnificent structural design! If all of these structures are flexible and balanced, an easy birth should occur. But what if there is a history of falls, trauma, or simply sitting too much? Having a healthy pelvis in the run up to and during pregnancy can be a game-changer.

Studies show that imbalance between SIJ mobility causes more pain during pregnancy.[98] But that is kind of the obvious part.

Consider this as a common example: one set of ligaments, which hold the uterus in place, are called the "round ligaments." When not pregnant, these are normally 10 to 12cm long. They should be difficult or even impossible to find, even though they are 1cm wide. As the baby and placenta grow, the uterus migrates upwards. These ligaments get stretched up and outwards,[99] reaching a maximum of 40cm length! To describe it crudely, they hold the uterus back, so that the baby does not "fall out." Now, what happens if you have an uneven pelvis, and the right ligament has more tension on it than the left? Rather than migrate up evenly, the uterine sac has to twist slightly. This twist puts tension into different parts of the uterine sac. The baby no longer sits in a balanced uterine sac. What happens when the baby needs to turn, as it should do multiple times before birth? And what happens when the baby is supposed to "present" head down, facing the back of your pelvis? It is not hard to understand how balancing these ligaments throughout pregnancy can lead to an easier birth. In the USA, one in 16 women see a chiropractor to help with their pregnancy.[100] Women under chiropractic care have between 24-39% shorter labour times,[101] presumably because of the "ease" of the process in a more relaxed, well-balanced mother.

There was once controversy when clients in the USA started attending chiropractors for what expecting mothers were calling "The breech turn technique." Breech presentation is when a baby is aligned feet-first before birth, and this can complicate the birth process. After receiving the chiropractic technique, correctly called the "Webster Protocol," 82% of breech babies turned to the correct presentation.[102] Obstetricians in the USA were quick to point out that this was the practice of obstetrics. But the babies had never been touched, because that *would* be obstetrics. The Webster Protocol is aimed at restoring balance of the pelvic and uterine ligaments. When the ligaments are better balanced, the baby may more freely assume the correct position. Again, when we simply focus on restoring a natural balance, then the "miracles" occur. More often than not, I have seen such a "miracle" occur when I have used Webster Protocol with my pregnant clients.

Getting your nervous system and pelvis balanced *before* getting pregnant, and then maintaining that health through to your healthy birth, is just common sense.

Realign Your Pelvis

If you have a pelvic misalignment, it behooves you to see a chiropractor who is trained to adjust your pelvis specifically.

This is a very clear example where *manipulation* (as opposed to trained adjustment) is a very *bad idea*. Understanding SIJ biomechanics and knowing what to do is simply not covered in a weekend "manipulation" course. Chiropractic doctors spend at least five years at university studying this, plus post-graduate studies. If the position of your SIJs is so important, and someone keeps manipulating it in whichever direction allows it to "click" or move, you are bound to keep worsening the SIJ position. Every year I see countless clients who have been manipulated for years without care for their alignment. See Chapter 10 for a greater understanding of why manipulation can be a bad idea.

Chapter 7 Checklist

- Although your triangular sacrum is wedged pretty firmly within your pelvis, a small misalignment here can provoke problems, including scoliosis, further up.
- Again, sitting is a big problem, but your pelvic joints are particularly vulnerable to falls onto the side of your hips. This is especially evident in athletes.
- "Hip" pain can often come from pelvis problems, and before undergoing any hip surgery, you should aim to improve your pelvis mobility and health.
- Your pelvic health is most needed during pregnancy and birth. Balanced ligaments, free movement, and a clear brain-body connection improves the chance of a healthy, happy pregnancy and a peaceful birth process.
- Less skilled pelvic manipulation is a bad idea. Always ensure to see someone who is highly qualified at adjusting your pelvis.

Action Points

- Don't cross your legs when sitting! Or if you do, ensure to cross them the same amount each side.
- If you have a fall or slip onto the side of your hip, ensure to get your alignment checked and, if needed, adjusted soon after. It may save you many problems at a later date.
- If you are planning to get pregnant or are already pregnant, find someone who is suitably qualified to adjust and keep you balanced all the way through to the birth. Don't wait until someone tells you, "The baby is breach," to panic and get adjusted!

If you are near Marbella, Spain, go to www.duffyquiropractica.com to find out how to work with Dr Duffy.

If elsewhere, go to www.chiroalliance.org or www.chiropractic.org to search for subluxation reducing Chiropractors.

Chapter 8

Scoliosis

"Just as the twig is bent the tree's inclined."

— Alexander Pope

Scoliosis Matters

Scoliosis has long been a subject of special interest and study for me. Many consider me to be a scoliosis expert, but I believe this to be an exaggeration. I am an expert at simply envisioning your optimal spinal health and using a commonsense approach to get you there. If you or a family member might have a spinal curvature, I suggest you search for a copy of my book on scoliosis at the website link below. In this section, I am going to fly through the essentials so you know why and when to check for scoliosis. You can perhaps point a suffering friend to a healthy alternative for improving their spinal health.

Scoliosis can be a big problem. It ruins some people's lives. And one in three scolioses have not even been diagnosed. It can be a huge risk to your child's health, performance, and happiness. But the majority of scoliosis causes *no pain or symptoms* until adulthood. The investment a parent makes repays itself when the "child" is over 25 years old and can live a healthy, pain-free life.

Like most fields in medicine, there is a lot more opinion than there is research. But one point of consensus is this: big curves start small.[103] Scoliosis always worsens.[104] It either worsens quickly during childhood or slowly during adulthood.[105] But it always worsens. Get it checked and, if needed, reduced before a small curve becomes a big problem.[106]

Scoliosis Ages with You

"But I am 35, have had a scoliosis since I was a teenager, and don't have any pain or symptoms at all," you may hear that from a friend or family member. And they may be right. Only they missed one word from their sentence: "yet." They don't have any pain or symptoms *yet.*

We start life with young, soft, and adaptable bones and then grow quickly until we reach "skeletal maturity." Although this is formally between 16 to 19 years old, in reality, some people complete their skeletal growth as late as 25 years old. The soft bones of youth can be seen as the first severe "risk window" for scoliosis. Most people then forget about the process of growth, thinking it is all over. But your bone constantly replaces itself through life. And it regrows in response to the stress it is under. Put simply, a scoliosis can continue to "remould" your bones through life, advancing as fast as 1-2.5 degrees per annum.[107] So a pain-free 20-degree curve at 40 years old can easily start to cause pain as a 40-degree curve for your 50th birthday surprise. But then we start to lose bone density. Our bones get weaker. If you have really healthy spinal alignment, this softening of your bones should not affect things, as you bear weight evenly across each bone. But if you have poor spinal health and alignment? This is the second severe risk window, when a milder scoliosis can simply "collapse" parts of your spine, doubling you over and affecting your health as described above.

What Causes Scoliosis

The full scoliosis classification system is extremely complex and includes many rare disorders, which we will not mention here. 90% of scoliosis is diagnosed as "idiopathic."[108] This means the scoliosis is "self-making of unknown cause." My view of the human body is that problems don't magically sprout from nowhere and then sustain themselves to become a huge problem in that person's life. Call me naive or wishful, but I believe our bodies want to be healthy and that a trained eye can find the cause of such problems. When I examine such cases, there is often a very clear cause, which often can be improved.

The first and most common is a lack of a clear brain-body connection. We discussed this in Chapter 3, where we described the sense of proprioception. Without an accurate feedback system, your brain cannot keep up with the corrections needed in the rapidly-growing spine. If you are older and have a more minor curve, the switching off of these sensors allows that curve to progress as it wishes—it lets gravity win a lot sooner than you might wish. The simple act of getting adjusted, of getting the subluxations reduced, and then keeping your spine moving, can allow you to make peace with gravity. Befriending gravity can have a radical impact in such cases.

> I was once chatting with an older client, when he said, "I can see why they call you the White Witch." Taken aback, I asked what he referred to. He had been referred by a friend, a mother who had brought in Nuria, her 8 year-old daughter with a 25 degree scoliosis. After taking postural photos on the posture stand, I adjusted her and then stood her on the posture stand again. Her mother and sister were watching in disbelief. Not two minutes had passed, but it appeared that her scoliosis had magically disappeared. Countless medical appointments and worries, all gone in a moment. All I had really done was reduced her subluxations, switched on her proprioceptors again, and her body had voluntarily self-corrected. Her brain-body connection was so shut off that it could not protect her from this awful posture. This effect was temporary. We needed to "retrain" these sensors to work properly by reducing subluxations in order to get long-term results. And there was nothing unique about her—this is quite common. But I still giggle to myself when I think of the "White Witch" reference. I was doing no magic here. The only magic was the will of her body to self-correct when allowed a clear connection.

Scan this QR code with your phone to watch a young girl's spinal curve "magically" disappearing just by turning on the spine's proprioceptors. Like and Subscribe for more videos.

The second and more common cause of adult degenerative scoliosis is an unrecovered injury. One or more injuries result in small "antalgic" postures (antalgic means "away from pain"), where you lean away from a painful hip or low back. The pain soon settles, but the posture continues. This is where it is normal to say "it healed" or "it went away on its own." But by not getting this fully corrected at the source, this small episode of pain now triggers what eventually becomes a significant scoliosis. It scars, and eventually causes degeneration. Add in age-related reduction in activity levels, and eventually weakening bones, to cause life-shortening problems.[109] You can see how an apparently innocuous episode of low back pain, when left to scar, can provoke major issues later in life.

I already mentioned a third cause in the previous chapter about S1 alignment. Your sacral alignment is critical in all of your spinal alignment. A small imbalance here can amplify higher up your spine.

> I have cared for many professional golfers over the years. One PGA golfer stands out because he could not stand straight. He was in his mid-twenties, early in his PGA career. He had a trapped nerve which was affecting the sensation into one leg. Despite all of the biomechanical analysis, spine x-rays, physiotherapy, and other coaching he had received, no one had ever looked at x-rays of his pelvis in standing posture. Those x-rays showed a 28mm (over an inch) leg length difference! It was like he was playing every shot, including teeing off, out of the bunker!!! Sometimes the simplest things, like a short leg, are missed. Sometimes, the solution, like a heel-lift, can be so simple!

If you, a friend, or family member has been told you have a spinal curvature or possible scoliosis, make it your mission to get good quality care and advice. Visit the link below to get a copy of my book on Scoliosis, but most of all, take a proactive approach to living fully, such that scoliosis need not cast a shadow on your life.

Chapter 8 Checklist

- Scoliosis can have devastating health consequences, yet 2 in 3 scolioses have not yet been diagnosed. They rarely cause symptoms in children, when it is easier to manage them.
- Simply improving a kid's general spinal health can dramatically impact a spinal curve.
- Some cases of scoliosis are caused by simple, correctable causes. Get a second opinion early to assess options.

- It often has a "quiet" period as an adult but starts to cause pain when the degeneration sets in.
- Scoliosis always tends to worsen. Big curves start small. Improving a small curve is easier than improving a big one. Act sooner.

  Insert:

Go to my website www.glennduffy.com to check for my short book on scoliosis. It includes home-tests which can help you decide when you or your kids need a professional opinion.

Action Points

- Every now and then, check your kids spinal alignment, with their t-shirt off. Or routinely have them see someone qualified to check them. Catching things early makes a huge difference.
- If you have *any* family history of scoliosis, ensure to get all your kids checked *at least every two years until adulthood,* in case something is missed.
- If you are told that a spinal curve is "no big deal" or to "just go swimming" or to come back for a review in six months, get a second opinion. Looking for a cause and an action plan early on can make a huge difference.

  Insert:

If you are near Marbella, Spain, go to www.duffyquiropractica.com to find out how to work with Dr Duffy.

If elsewhere, go to www.chiroalliance.org or www.chiropractic.org to search for subluxation reducing Chiropractors.

Chapter 9

New Spine, New Personality

"You are not your past, not your habits, not your compulsions. When you get to know who you are, anything becomes possible."

— Geneen Roth

The Automatic You

Although we have spent a lot of time on your optimal spinal structure and how this allows a state of peace and healing to prevail in your body, we have barely touched on the most impactful changes which happen when your spine is subluxation-free. By now you understand how so many illnesses can be the side effects of a loss of spinal health. But the real life impact of living subluxation-free is beyond the scope of this text, and hence, the topic of my second book. Here, I briefly introduce two important things that happen to the very essence of *YOU* when you reduce subluxations.

Autonomic Activity and Balance

The most primitive part of your nervous system is called the Autonomic Nervous System (ANS). Every animal has this nervous system, only yours is more evolved. You have heard lots about your ANS throughout life, only not by this name. When people talk of the "fight-flight" or "freeze" responses, they are referring to the most basic "survival" state of this system. We call this the sympathetic nervous response. Thankfully, we evolved first and foremost to survive. This defence system is more active in the average modern adult than it was in our ancestors, when it developed to save us from being eaten by predators. This defence mechanism shunts your body's resources into vital functions, survival mode. Your brain receives more blood flow to its "instinct" centres, so you respond more emotionally. Your adrenal glands are stimulated, giving you a hyper-alert "high." Your reaction times quicken, as does your muscle tension. But this state was designed to be temporary. After the threat had gone, we were designed to return to a state of recovery and healing.

This state, the opposite side of the ANS, is less Hollywood and less spoken of. This is not about how to survive. Known as the "rest-digest," or "feed and breed" system—this is about how to *thrive*. Each part of your body has nerves from each of these two systems. They compete for the same energy resources, based mostly on your brain's *perceived survival threat.* When your brain thinks you are safe, the blood flow can shunt back into the prefrontal cortex, the rational, thinking centre, and your decisions become more considered. Your adrenal glands relax, and growth and happiness hormones can be released. Your muscle tension can relax and your digestive system receives full blood flow to properly digest food. Most importantly, your immune system has free reign to use all of your resources to fight any infections you may encounter.

But our nervous system did not evolve with cars and traffic, with work and deadlines, with bills and mortgages, with caffeine and alcohol. And it is unable to distinguish from perceived and actual threats. A newspaper article, school exam, TV programme, or even well-meaning mother-in-law can all subconsciously prime your survival system. Although there is no actual survival threat, your nervous system initiates a cascade of changes, ready to protect you. If this were an isolated incident, that would be no problem, but the stress levels with which we live in our modern society do not allow this survival response to rest.

It shuts off your digestion, runs down your immune system, makes you react less rationally and more emotionally, tenses your muscles, makes you frustrated, provokes abnormal fat metabolism, fatigues you, and eventually causes you a host of chronic illnesses. From cancer to diabetes to heart disease, all of the modern "big killers" are, at least in part, due to this chronic survival state.

But here is where your spine and nervous system health come in. Even when the threats have long gone, even if you have "let go," and moved to some blissful paradise like Marbella, your nervous system may not let go of them. A subluxated spine, especially neck subluxation, literally blocks your ability to release these stressors. So, despite healthy lifestyle habits, despite a good diet and exercise, you still feel a deep tension, a state of unease, in your body.

When you start to live subluxation-free, these stresses may release. This "discharge" can even be uncomfortable at first, but it is soon followed by relaxed, restful sleep. It is soon followed by improved tolerance, not getting stressed by little things anymore. It is followed by a greater capacity for gratitude, for growth, for love.

> Carla was a 32-year-old mother of two beautiful kids, three and eight years old at the time of writing. She came in with neck pain and headaches. She confessed that she would never have come in, but her lack of sleep was making life impossible. She said that she was "stressed by the kids." She was lucky to come in sooner, as although she was severely subluxated, her spine had not yet started degenerating. To me, she was clearly in chronic survival mode, most probably from long before she even had the kids. We started care, aimed at reducing subluxations of her spine and restoring a state of peace. Four weeks later, at her first review, she started sobbing uncontrollably. After many tissues and way too much snot, and between the sobs, she managed to say, "Doctor....The kids.... My babies....We are in love again." Then she carried on crying and crying. She later explained how she had spent the past years "fighting" to parent the kids, thinking that it was normal or that her kids were just being difficult. "But it was always me," she said. She had been in chronic survival mode, and now that was released, her parenting could be through tolerance, patience, and love. No matter if you are a parent, lover, spouse, boss, or sibling, living subluxation-free opens you to tolerance, patience, and love.

Flexible Brainwaves, Happy Life

Let's briefly look at your brainwaves and their flexibility so that you can harness the power of this change when it happens to you.

Your brain holds different "waveforms," based on your state of wakefulness, relaxation, or stress. The brain wave pattern for sleep is radically different to that for studying for an exam, for example. A healthy brain easily flows between different states. From excited studying state, it can drop into a relaxed meditation state, or even into sleep, without any challenge or resistance. We call this brainwave flexibility. It is essential for your inner health and happiness. Without it, you are not in control. Without this flexibility, you cannot decide when to relax and how much, because your brainwaves may be blocked in the wrong pattern.

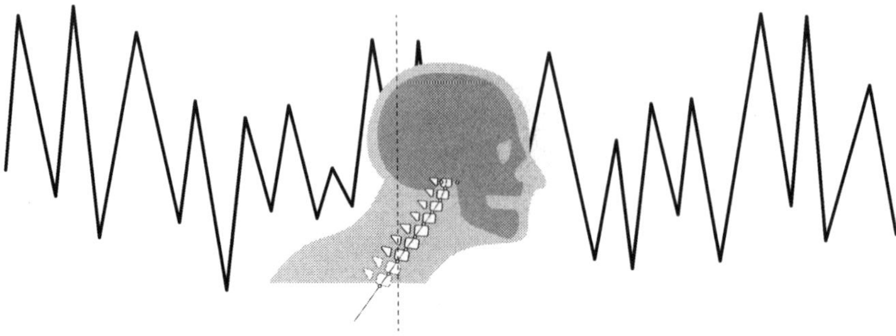

Figure 24. Brain in stress. Inflexible brainwaves are related to anxiety, stress, intolerance, and even overwhelm.

Inflexible brainwaves are bad news, as different states of blockage happen in different disorders. Inability to relax your brainwaves is linked to depression, "stubborn thinking patterns," anxiety, and an inability to relax and sleep.[110] Alcoholics and addicts struggle to achieve relaxed brainwaves, resulting in an impulse to "soothe" the brain by drinking or other substance abuse.[111] Inability to excite your brainwaves can produce difficulty concentrating, resulting in attention deficit hyperactivity disorder (ADHD).[112] And an excess of certain waveforms is associated with Tourette's Syndrome,[113] chronic fatigue, and even Fibromyalgia.[114]

We still do not understand the full picture of why your spine influences your brainwaves so much, but the science does make two things clear. Research has shown that chiropractic adjustments improve brainwave flexibility.[115] In clinic this is very obvious. Every day we see clients who have been "stuck in a rut" for years and even decades. They think that they are simply "an anxious person" or have "short concentration." Often, they say, "That is how I am. I have always been this way." The adjustments relieve the blocked state, simply opening the door for them to shift brainwave pattern and start to encounter a new version of themselves. Many people gradually emerge from deep and long-lasting depression.[116] Research also shows that after an adjustment, your brain instantly drops into a more relaxed, meditative state.[117] Getting adjusted normalises and balances your brainwaves.[118]

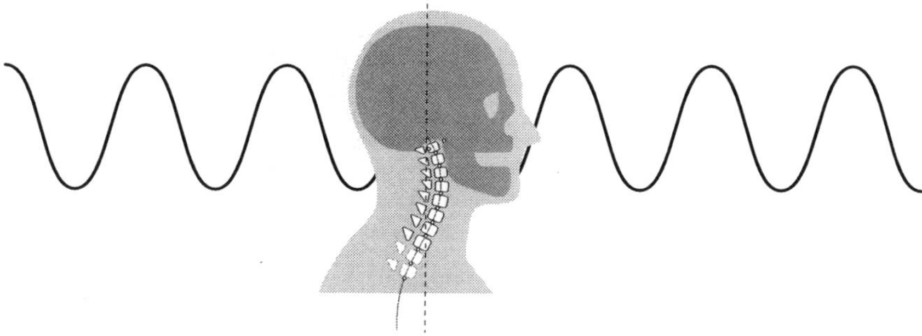

Figure 25. Brain at peace. Flexible brainwaves induce a state of peace, relaxation, tolerance, appreciation, and abundance.

If you want to make changes in YOU—in your sense of ease, your anxiety levels, your self-image—it is far easier to do that when your nervous system is out of survival mode, and you feel safe inside. Then your brainwaves are flexible, and you are at peace, in a relaxed state. Many clients go from being "stress heads" to successful meditators, on starting chiropractic care. A chiropractor does not change your life circumstances, but skilful adjustments open the door to a new way of being… a new you.

Chapter 9 Checklist

- The core of all your health is managed by your automatic nervous system, your ANS. This has two "competing" sides: the fight-flight and the rest-digest responses.
- A balance between the two sides of this system is vital for health, relaxation, peace, and happiness.
- Getting adjusted allows your body to re-balance between these two systems, allowing you to move out of survival and into a thriving state.
- Your brain is designed to flow flexibly between different levels of excitement. A poor flexibility is associated with various neurological disorders and even illnesses.
- When you get your spine adjusted, you improve the flexibility and ability for your brain to relax. Many conditions can improve, sometimes unexpectedly, when your nervous system is at peace.

My second book is all about this topic, the inner peace and happiness which comes when your nervous system and spine are set free. Go to www.glennduffy.com to sign up for updates.

Action Points

If you identify as an "anxious person," a "poor sleeper," or "easily irritable," ask if that is really you or just nervous system pressure?

Could getting adjusted free you from this nervous system pressure, allowing you to express the real you?

If you are getting adjusted, observe how you respond to things. Do you notice a sense of "space" or "ease" in situations which used to stress you? How can you harness this freedom to react and be more in alignment with the best version of yourself?

If you are near Marbella, Spain, go to www.duffyquiropractica.com to find out how to work with Dr Duffy.

If elsewhere, go to www.chiroalliance.org or www.chiropractic.org to search for subluxation reducing Chiropractors.

PART III

Making the Most of your Healing

"It's when we start working together that the real healing takes place."

— David Hume

Chapter 10

Reducing Subluxation: The Spinal Adjustment

"The wound is the place where the light enters you."

— Rumi

Reducing Interference

I have talked a lot about adjustment, the way a good chiropractic doctor will remove stress and restore health to your spine. But what is an adjustment, really?

The spinal adjustment is so alien in our pill-popping society that we have to take a moment to understand what it is and is not. Bear with me here, as I try to condense five years of university study into just a few pages in this book.

One of the challenges here is that we do not fully understand the myriad effects of the adjustment. Another challenge is that the adjustment is delivered and used in different ways by different people.[119] An adjustment is definitely not just cracking joints to give a gratifying release. So let's start with a definition:

> *An adjustment is a specific input into the neurospinal system, aimed at reducing subluxation and restoring balance.*

1. When I say specific input, this means that certain tissue pressure or hold may be used. An adjusting instrument such as an *activator* or a special *drop-table* may be used. Gentle, specific vertebral movement on the tip of my finger is my personally preferred method, but in some cases, I use non-manual techniques, and these too are adjustments. The adjustment each client gets depends on their needs and on their state on that given day. There is no "one size fits all" for clients. There is not even a "one size fits all" for your different vertebrae. An experienced chiropractor constantly changes this input.

2. This input is to the neurospinal system. This means that there is a purpose *beyond* the place the doctor is touching, which, in turn, means that the adjustment may be nowhere near the place you experience pain. The doctor must understand and respect your neuro(nerve)-spinal system and know how to positively affect that. It may look crazy when the doctor holds your ear, tummy, or other body part, but understand that they may be affecting the *tone* in the nerves from your spine, adjusting and rebalancing your whole system.
3. Reducing subluxation usually gives the immediate sensation of release, as it allows your brain and body to connect better. Indeed, you usually feel more relaxed and mobile. But the long term goal is restoring balance within your system. This may not occur on the day of that one adjustment, but as part of a longer-term plan. For example, with structural adjusting, which aims to change your long-term posture, you may even ache afterwards. You feel as if you have gone to the gym, as your posture gradually improves. The aim is not to make you feel better on that one day but to bring your system back to a place where it is in balance with gravity and can self-heal so that you are more healthy and connected forever.

Did you note that I talk of *reducing* instead of *removing* subluxation? Understand that the effects of some subluxation may never be fully removed. If your spine is restricted and irritated and only a week has passed since a minor fall, that subluxation may quickly be removed. But if that same subluxation does not get adjusted for a further ten or twenty years, then all of that scar tissue could take a long time to become normal. If there is also degeneration and abnormal bony growth then 100% removal is wishful thinking.

Parents are shocked to learn that most newborn babies (nearly 90%) show signs of subluxation at the top of their neck.[120] Commonly called KISS (kinematic imbalance due to suboccipital strain) Syndrome, it is believed to happen because of the stress in the birth canal, yet it also occurs in caesarian-born babies.[121] Even natural, unforced labours without drugs or forceps or other intervention will cause subluxation in some babies. KISS does not stop your baby from breathing, or feeding, or pooing. Research is ongoing to understand its contribution to dyspraxia and dyslexia. Because your newborn now has to do everything with stress.

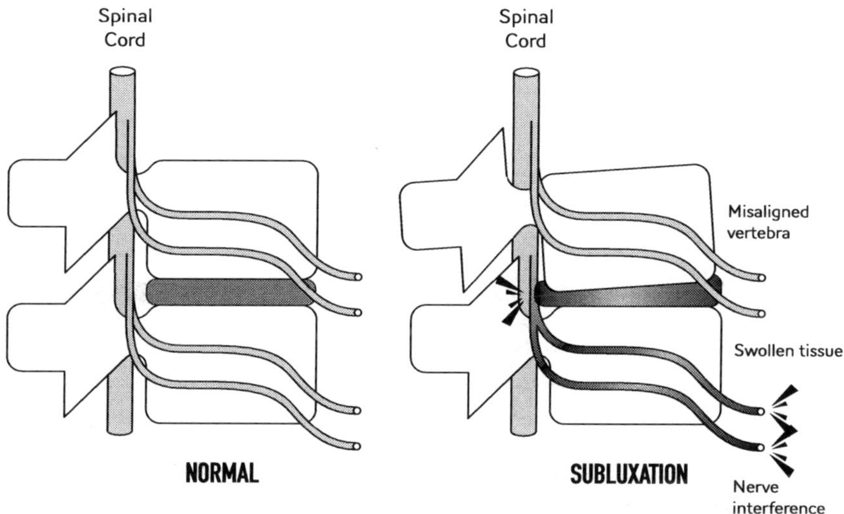

Figure 26. Normal vs subluxated spine. Subluxation is caused by multiple factors, produces multiple effects, and can be reduced by various specific techniques. This is the unique role of the Chiropractor in healthcare.

Everything is just harder than it would otherwise be.[122] This subluxation, if left unaddressed, can persist for life. Yes, at 60 years old, you may be adjusted for a subluxation you have had for 60 years. Can a 60 year-old subluxation be removed? Probably not. But reducing it and continuing to reduce it as long as it tries to recur can open up health, emotional, and other possibilities which you may have considered impossible for the past 60 years.

What is also true is that you and I are constantly under subluxation stress. As long as we are alive, we will always live with some subluxation stress. Whether it's postural, nutritional, or emotional is not relevant. Your nervous system stores it all. It may look and feel different, but physical, chemical, and mental stress can all store in your spine. Yes, you are literally an evolving set of subluxations. Or put differently, you are constantly adapting to your environment, and as you make all of those adaptations, you become subluxated. Getting adjusted reduces the maladaptations. So you can opt to wait until those subluxations cause pain, or be proactive and get adjusted to reduce that interference sooner.

Feeding Your Brain

"Get high on your own supply"- Wim Hof

Imagine that you have gone through your corrective care programme, and your posture and spinal curves have improved. Your subluxations have reduced, and you are feeling so much better. If your spine is now so much healthier, why would you continue to get adjusted?

Part of this answer lies above: we all have ongoing subluxation stress, and it's better catch those earlier than later. But for me personally, there is another compelling reason to get my spine adjusted regularly.

Not only does getting your neck adjusted increase the blood flow to your brain,[123] it also feeds your brain in another, very profound way. In Chapter 3, I mentioned proprioception. We learnt how these sensors feed back to your brain to keep your spine balanced. Nobel Prize winner Dr. Roger Sperry stated that 90% of the stimulation and nutrition to your brain is generated by spinal movement, mostly by your proprioceptors.[124] This means that a spinal adjustment is like a three-course meal for your brain.

The most mysterious part of your brain, your cerebellum, sits at the top of your neck and controls your balance and *automations.* When you talk, pick up a glass of water, or catch a ball, the cerebellum is doing all that work automatically. Although it is only 10% of the size of your brain, it is estimated to contain 50-80% of all of your brain's nerves and use 90% of your brain's electrical power.[125] 50-80% sounds like a big range, no? That is because we know so little of the cerebellum. In fact, this "black box" in your brain is perhaps the least understood part of the universe.[126] No, that is not a typo. For decades, many physicists have postulated that we know more about the universe than our own brains,[127] and this part, the cerebellum, is the least understood part of your brain.

What we do know is that spinal movement "feeds" this part of your brain. We also know that stimulating this part of your brain with movement short-circuits your stress cycle. This means that, rather than get stuck in the emotions of a stress, your body can exit that cycle and move on. In so doing, it also releases a load of natural feel-good endorphin (exercise-high), and opiate painkiller (heroin-like) hormones,[128] putting you into a naturally more relaxed state. Better still, the adjustment spikes your oxytocin (love hormone) levels.[129] restoring a state of happiness and peace in your body. These feel-good hormones are your own happy drug supply. Yes, this is getting high, on your own supply!

Chiropractors at conferences often get adjusted not once but many times over a few days. When you have been getting adjusted regularly, you really start to reap the rewards. It's very much like driving a car with a clean windscreen. You can drive four hours on the motorway and still see fine. But when you stop and clean the windscreen, suddenly the eye strain is removed, and you can see everything with more clarity. You could brake faster or respond faster to an accident. You have effectively had an upgrade. This, in chiropractic terms, we call being reconnected. Reconnected to 100% of that intelligence which flows from your brain to your body.

Your Body, Not You, Chooses

We revisit this topic in Chapter 14, but it is important to understand that neither you nor the doctor should choose what adjustment your body gets. Only your body can choose most wisely. The doctor's job is to have an overall plan, and then listen to your body on the day. Imagine that you have "hip pain," around your SIJs and pelvis. "Click my pelvis back in, Doc!" "Straighten my pelvis up." These are things people say. You may want to have your hip clicked, but your buttocks are in spasm, locking up the area. Neurologically, you are subluxated at L5-S1, the base of your spine, which controls the tension and healing in your buttocks and hips. The doctor may jump to adjust this level to help your hip area heal. But taking a step back, the doctor listens to your whole body. C1, at the top of your neck, is very subluxated. Your whole body is in a state of high alert, ready to defend anything, including a well-meant adjustment at L5. Your body is saying "adjust C1." The most experienced, connected practitioners seem to have an intuition. This is simply their listening to your body's call. Your body says more than you can ever know about it. The best doctors have trained to listen to your body, not what you consciously feel. And to react to its needs while bringing you towards your long-term health goals.

> Freddy was a dynamic and successful entrepreneur, traveling between various countries for work and spending precious little time at home with his family, where his mother helped his wife to look after his young daughter. Only 38 years old, he had been suffering from sciatica for nearly six months. Over the previous three months, his leg pain had become unbearable. It was affecting his whole life; he was struggling to concentrate or sleep properly. When home, he would argue with his wife and mother, and shout at his daughter. He was now booked for spinal surgery in two weeks time. His mother heard of a foreign doctor who may be able to help and booked him to come to see me. He did not want to come in, and rescheduled twice. Finally, his mother brought him in to see us on a Tuesday. His surgery was scheduled for that Thursday. The pain medications were of little use, as so often they are with severe nerve pain. He was sweating with the pain level. He wanted me to do something to his leg to relieve the pain. Logically, I may have adjusted L5, the level where the nerve was pinched. But his body called for me to adjust his upper neck. I adjusted C1. The top of his neck. For a few moments he was "in shock." We shook hands, and he left. He came back in the next day, smiling, excited, emotional. He had already called to cancel the surgery. His leg pain had totally gone after one adjustment at the top of his spine. This may sound like something magical, but it is not at all. His body was in such a state of fight or flight, such a state of defensiveness, that nothing could heal, let alone a nerve injury like sciatica. The simple act of reducing such a severe subluxation at the top of his neck allowed a huge release of tension. A huge outflow of healing. Had I listened to his symptoms, where it hurt, or even the nerve which was causing that, he would probably have had spine surgery at just 38 years old. His greatest gain, in my opinion, was not the relief of pain in his leg, but the reconnection with who he was as a grateful son, a caring husband, a loving father. His body knew better, and thankfully, I was able to listen.

Adjusting symptoms is like a dog chasing its tail. A lot of excitement, a lot of action, but you will never get anywhere long-term. Your body knows best.

Manipulation v. Adjustment

Spinal adjustment is not the same as spinal manipulation.[130]

Spinal manipulation is simply moving joints to release them into movement, generally aimed at "cracking" them and hoping to reduce pain.

As we already said, spinal adjustment is a specific input into the neurospinal system, aimed at reducing subluxation and restoring balance. The adjustment may or may not include the "crack" associated with manipulation. It may use tools or specialised mechanisms in a purpose-built table. The intention, specificity, and training level needed for the adjustment is totally different.

This topic could make me unpopular with some physiotherapists or osteopaths. I have close friends who are physiotherapists and who occasionally manipulate people. I take no issue with the great job they do, but I take issue with the "M word." I have a big issue with manipulation.

I'll give you an example. I am hard to adjust. I have quite a flexible spine, and at 188cm (6ft2) and 90kg (over 14st), am big and awkward. My neck is flexible but severely subluxated at the top (base of my skull), possibly since childhood, and at the bottom (junction with my shoulders) from lifting weights in the past. Plus, I have disc hernias at the base of my neck. The top and bottom of my neck are the two areas which are severely subluxated and need specific adjustments to move better. In the past, I have seen a friend who *manipulated* me. They turned my neck into rotation (the easiest way to crack a joint) and rotated it further, quickly and hard. My *middle* neck cracked. Phew. To be honest, I felt a lot better and more relaxed. But a few days later my neck was even worse than before. If had done this repeatedly, I would end up with more problems.

You see, manipulation is easy. I mean I could teach you to manipulate the spine in a few hours. Indeed, that is why massage therapists, karate instructors, and in some countries, even hairdressers include manipulation as part of their package. Many people even do it to themselves by "cracking their necks or backs." It feels nice, for a few minutes. But manipulation makes the flexible areas more flexible and the blocked areas more blocked. This "kicks the can down the road" in that you will still have problems, and even more problems, even though you feel temporary relief. Is it more natural than pain medication? For sure. Is it more safe than pain medication? Even in unskilled hands, manipulation is still far safer than drugs. But does it “fix” the problem? Absolutely not.

Manipulation is like a cheap, imported copy of a high-quality Italian handbag. It looks the same. And the price and availability is attractive. When you buy, it makes you feel good for a while. But after a while of use, something is not right. It starts to fray and the fake “leather” dries and cracks. Later, the lining tears, and you realise that it is really just junk. So you throw it away and move onto another rip-off, cheap handbag.

But the difference is that you cannot throw away your spine and buy another cheap one. You can get another therapist, but you still need to live with your spine!

The adjustment seeks not to “poke the pain” but to achieve all that we have set out in this book. Reduce interference. Feed your brain. Improve your spinal alignment. And do all of that while respecting where your body is and where it can go. Holding a vision for a clearer, lighter, more vital you. That means that, although you are the same person with the same spinal curves, the best way of adjusting you may change between Monday and Thursday. Which means that while I have a plan of how to get my clients from illness and into health, the technique I use *today* has to respond to you *today*. A good doctor is constantly listening to your body. And that requires constant attention.

So you can understand that the skill of adjustment grows over years of training and revision. These are techniques which have been developed and refined over 120 years. I will never know all of the chiropractic techniques available, nor would I want to. I want to master skilfully the ones which I feel get the best results for my clients. It is a lifetime commitment to mastery. Would I have space to massage, tape, or do physiotherapy whilst becoming such a master? Of course not. Perhaps someone else could mix these things and still adjust like a master, but they would be a unicorn. I have yet to meet a unicorn, let alone to be adjusted by one.

But if adjustments and manipulation look the same, feel similar, and can be done respectively by highly- and poorly-qualified people, then how can you, the client, know what you are getting? We return to this in the “choosing your doctor” section, but here are a few tips.

There are a few giveaway signs that you are buying a cheap copy of that handbag.

1. The practitioner talks about manipulation instead of adjustment. This is an easy giveaway.
2. They ask you where it hurts and treat that spot. Adjusting subluxations is not just poking the sore spots.
3. They are chatting about other things *as* they adjust you. I am not saying when they meet you, but *as* they adjust you. Adjustments require "listening carefully" to your body, so in the moment of the adjustment, the master can do *nothing else* than adjust you.
4. After the manipulation, they want you to feel better immediately and ask how you feel. Adjusting severely subluxated areas like my lower neck does not make you feel better instantly, so how you feel instantly is no measure of an adjustment. If the only goal is "poking the sore spot," again, that is manipulation.
5. They do multiple therapies, like massage, taping of your joints, injections, or prescribe drugs. Specific adjustments are a skill which take phenomenal training and concentration. If I see a heart surgeon, I want them to specialise in heart surgery, not to do a bit of everything.
6. Their hands are not certain. If you "listen" to the practitioner's hands, you can hear how certain they are. If their hands are certain, then you can relax and forget where you are, and trust in the adjustment.

What is the "best" technique? A chiropractor who says that they have the best adjustment technique is like a chess player who says that they have the best chess move in the world. No such thing exists. Just the best thing for your body and your needs, having considered many unique factors. We discuss this more in "Choosing Your Doctor," in Chapter 14.

Chapter 10 Checklist

- Reducing subluxation is done by specific adjustment, the greatest effect of which is not just on your spinal bones, but on your nervous system.
- Subluxations are a life-long issue. From childbirth to death, we all experience ongoing subluxation stresses. The majority of these cause no pain or discomfort but do cause nerve stress. Some people live great lifestyles, but are actually putting up with subluxations. Life could be better.
- The adjustment not only reduces subluxations, but "feeds" your brain with healthy messages and resets your stress cycle. This allows you to live and perform in a higher state of connection.
- Unlike manipulation, which just aims to crack you, the adjustment is skilful, precise, and with a specific goal. It is not about "poking the pain," but reducing subluxation, improving posture, and ultimately restoring peace and balance in your body.

Action Points:

- Read through Chapter 14 for advice on how to choose your doctor.
- If you have had injuries and niggles, even in the past, find and get checked by a chiropractor.
- If you have not had injuries or niggles, but want to live life to the max, find and get checked by a chiropractor!
- Find someone who is happy to check and adjust you and your family regularly, for as long as you want in order to live a healthy, happy life!

If you are near Marbella, Spain, go to www.duffyquiropractica.com to find out how to work with Dr Duffy.

If elsewhere, go to www.chiroalliance.org or www.chiropractic.org to search for subluxation reducing Chiropractors.

Chapter 11

The Road to Recovery

"Healing is an inside job."

— BJ Palmer

Spinal Care v Dental Care

How did people used to look after their teeth 80 or 100 years ago? Did they brush and floss every day? No. Did they visit the dentist regularly? Nope. And what happened to their teeth? Exactly. It wasn't pretty. People didn't know to look after their teeth and that was the result. Nowadays, only 2% of people do not brush their teeth daily. And those people most probably have no friends.

But most people you know are making the same mistake that people used to make with their teeth, only they are doing it with their spine, right now!

How do we look after our teeth today? We brush at least twice a day, we floss, and we get regular dental checkups. Knowing what you do, would you consider stopping looking after your teeth today? Of course not! Do you feel sorry for the people who did not or could not look after their teeth in the past? Of course, because they had bad dental health.

Now skip forward 80 years from now, to the year 2100, and everyone is looking after their spine, knowing how important it is to their health. In 80 years people will probably feel sorry for people who today, did not look after their spines, and hence suffered poor health. Our goal is to spread the message, that just like dental care stops tooth decay, so chiropractic care stops spinal decay.

And, because they are on the front of your face, it is far easier to see neglected teeth than it is to see a neglected spine. But it is also far easier to fix neglected teeth than it is to fix a neglected spine.

When should your family start looking after their teeth? And stop looking after them?

When should they start looking after their spines? And stop looking after them?

Time for Braces

In Chapters 3 to 9, we discussed the ideal spine and how alignment of your four key bones will affect your spinal and general health. In any corrective care plan, it is worth remembering that changing postures can take time, and may ache. Imagine you have braces for your teeth. They are designed to gradually pull your teeth and gums into a different shape. At certain points they will ache. Think of corrective care as being the same, gradually pulling your spine and body into a different shape. This can only happen gradually and with repetitive adjustments. Spinal remodelling research shows that a *baseline* of care takes place over a *minimum* of 36 adjustments. Of course this can vary for different people. The intensive corrective care is typically over 8 to 12 weeks. This is important, as you cannot gain momentum if you do not "push" a frequency. Getting adjusted once a week over 36 weeks is better than nothing, but do not expect the same change as if you "push harder" to gain momentum. Would you get the same results wearing your braces occasionally as wearing them as recommended?

During this time, there may be times when your body aches as if you had just done a hard gym workout. This is temporary, only lasting a few days. It is no different from having your braces adjusted by the orthodontist. The extra stress is felt as discomfort, but as long as you carry on, it will pass. If you suddenly take the braces out every time they cause discomfort, how likely is it that your teeth will straighten? It is the same with your spine. For some people, there will be periods of discomfort, which are a totally natural healing process.

Remember, that in many if not most cases, poor spinal alignment exists long before any pains. Many such cases end up getting recommended for surgery. The relative discomfort and inconvenience of realigning your spine is minor in comparison to surgery. Realigning your spine is not just for pain relief, but for long-term health.

Marathon v. Sprint

This does not mean that after the intensive period, all the work is done. Many people continue to improve well past the year mark. I have clients who experience huge breakthroughs two or more years after starting care, reaching new levels of freedom and health which they had forgotten decades earlier.

> Richard, only 45 years old, was on the list for lumbar disc surgery. He was overweight, as he had not been able to exercise for the past few years. His pain was not acute, but chronic and irritating. The sort of pain which makes you a grumpy old man. He had a *lot* of degeneration in his low back. After a few months of care, he had restarted exercise. He was smiling. He had changed. The colour had returned to his face. He felt like a new person, a happier, better father. But he still had pain. In fact, he refused the surgery, but continued to have milder pain for about two years after he started care. Had care not worked? Of course it had. But, for some reason, his body was not able to heal this pain level in his low back. About two years after starting care, he went on holidays. Nothing new or different. But on return, he felt like a different person in my hands. Something, I do not know what, had shifted in his nervous system. His lower back progressed rapidly, and his pain soon disappeared. What Richard had was rare. Not clinically, because this does happen sometimes, but his patience and belief in his own ability to heal was quite rare. Chiropractic aims to make you healthier and happier. Not just pain-free, but more connected. Just because a pain persists does not mean that a change has not happened. A clear connection is more than enough—it is everything.

So how long should you try a given therapy or doctor before deciding whether or not they work for you? If you want to upgrade your health, I would recommend giving care 12 to 18 months to really see its greatest benefits. Does that not sound like a ridiculously long time? Yes. But that does not mean you will not see many benefits meanwhile, it just means that the greatest health benefits occur later on in care.

Retracing & Resetting

Imagine you have neck pain and headaches. You start under chiropractic care. Things seem to be moving along nicely, and then, you suddenly have a bout of lower back pain, knee pain, rashes on your bum, or something else. This is one of the most fascinating and little understood healing phenomena. Retracing. Here is the theory.

Have you ever spent too long in one posture, perhaps holding a telephone to your ear? Then you realise that your elbow has gotten really tight and change hands. For a few moments, the tight elbow gets really sore, as the normal signals come back into it. Or you sat in the same position for too long, and when you get up, your leg had gone fizzy and numb. As it comes "back to life," it is actually sore. Nothing is wrong with it, but the act of "waking up" an area can cause discomfort.

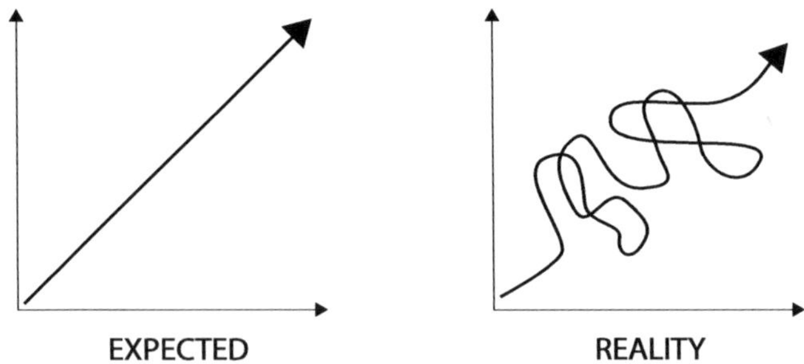

Figure 27. The average healing process goes nice and smoothly, but no one is average. Each healing journey is different. Sometimes blissful, other times turbulent. Patiently trusting your body always helps.

When you have your spine adjusted, you release the ability of your body to heal better. And suddenly, it is again healing an area which you thought had already fully healed. Thankfully, it is not every joint in every way, and normally, it is quite subtle. But when you get your neck adjusted, and later, your left shoulder suddenly starts to hurt, it may simply be that it is healing again. It is this passage back through the steps of healing that is called "retracing." Is it disconcerting? It can be. Is it a bad thing? Definitely not. In fact, it shows that the release of the nerve pressure is allowing your shoulder to communicate with your brain better, and hence, heal. Your shoulder was not injured by the adjustment. Instead, your chronically injured shoulder got *reconnected* by getting adjusted. Now it can genuinely heal.

It is important to note that retracing only happens with genuine healing. By that, I mean that when your body turns off symptoms, as with pain killers, electrical therapies, and sometimes even massage, it is unlikely that you will feel retracing. Only when there is an improved connection, leading to healing, does retracing occur. Retracing is seen as a very healthy process for you, as it signifies a deeper level of healing.

The Healing Reset: Not a Crisis

Changing anything in your body requires a process of re-adjustment. Getting fit requires a bit of aching after a hard gym session. As mentioned earlier, getting corrective braces on your teeth can cause pain. Chiropractic adjustments are extremely safe, just occasionally causing some aches as if you had been to the gym. But if your nervous system has been stuck for some time, even without your being aware, the process of liberating it can occasionally cause what feels like an over-correction.

Imagine your old car has a sticky brake pedal. You are used to pushing hard to brake. You bring the car to a garage, who free up the pedal but forget to tell you. You leave the garage and are driving along, you brake, pushing hard because you still expect the pedal to be sticky. But as it is now free, you effectively slam on the brakes, shocking yourself and those around you. After a few drives, you have gotten used to the right amount of pressure to use, and you are back to driving gently. You, your car, and those around you are healthier and safer for the future.

In Chapter 9 we looked at the balance between your fight-flight and your rest-digest nervous system. Imagine that the rest digest "brake" pedal has been sticky for many years. You get adjusted, and this system can now take back control. But rather than doing so gently, it goes to town. It slams on the brakes. And does any or all of the things the brake pedal does so well. You can suddenly feel as if you had the flu without having the flu. Or feel abnormally tired and lethargic. Some people even get nauseous, as this part of their nervous system is liberated. In healthcare we call this a "Healing Crisis," but I think the name is misleading. More accurate would be a "healing liberation," or I prefer a *"Healing Reset."* No matter what you call it, if you are one of those rare people who experience this, it can at first surprise you. Yet this is a really healthy sign that your nervous system is releasing and correcting. It may take a few weeks to pass this phase, but greater ease and healing lie ahead.

Setting Health Goals

In Chapter 1 we discussed the normal illness care model in our medicalised society. In Chapter 14 we will discuss how your doctor should help you set goals. But what affects your goal setting most is your personal philosophy of health. How do you really want to live? How much are you willing to invest in that vision? At the end of this chapter, you will find a short exercise, which helps you to take stock of your health investment. Once you have finished the chapter, I thoroughly recommend you get a pen and paper and take 15 minutes to go through the exercise in detail. Those 15 minutes could be the best-spent minutes of the rest of your life.

> A 65 year-old lady recently came in with hip and leg pain which had come on over three years. She had clearly never done anything to invest in her health. She was slightly overweight but had thought she was totally fine until she had started getting pain. The pain was now stopping her from sleeping. She had given up all activities and was now confined to her home. After her second review, about two months into her care, she was doing much better. She had returned to swimming and walking with her husband but still had aches and pains. She hit me with a fantastic comment. She said, "I feel like these last three years I've been paying for the previous 62 years of perfect health." Thankfully, she had a good sense of humour. Because I nearly fell off my chair, laughing. "Maria, my love," I said, "you are not paying for the previous 62 years of perfect health, but the previous 62 years of self-neglect!"

It literally dumbfounds me how people who do little or nothing to look after their health can think they should expect good ongoing health. Only when you invest in something should you expect a return. Create health, or expect illness.

Most people start care when they are low on the health spectrum. Even if you perceive yourself to have good health habits, it is quite possible that your spinal health is not so good. All care types start similarly. That means they start intensively. But your ultimate goal changes how this intensive care goes. If your goal is simply to get out of pain, then you are best off going to the pharmacy or getting a massage or even surgery. They will not add any health to you long-term, but they may temporarily remove some of your symptoms.

If this is your health goal, to get a quick-fix, then recognise it and embrace it, including its limitations. This will mean you do not get frustrated when the problem or something else recurs. This is easy-access illness care, and we have all used it at points in life. Most of us have used painkillers to get through a problem at some point. I can and do not judge people for doing this, as I have done it myself. I hope for something greater for everyone but acknowledge that some people are in a time or place where the illness care model is what suits them best, or indeed is all that is available. I wish it were different.

In a parallel universe, the health system is really about generating health. The government invests in real health generation, and this real health care is affordable, available, and expected by everyone. But for now, we need to deal with our reality in this universe.

Have you ever hear someone say that chiropractic "did not work?" The question is what did it not work for. Removing a pain that had been there for 12 months in just three visits? Restoring a 20 year-old postural problem to neutral in four weeks? Good quality chiropractic care will always help your nervous system and spine. Whether or not you achieve your own goals does not depend on chiropractic, as much as whether or not your goals are realistic and aligned.

If you hope for more health, more health stability, and more wellness, you need to go through this intensive phase a little differently. As you look to add health to your body and life, the process may take a little longer and even involve some corrective aches or even retracing . The main goals in this phase are opening up old patterns, freeing your spine and nervous system, and gaining momentum.

As you come through this, there will be a period of reorganisation that needs to occur. I call this the stabilisation phase. During this time, adjustments will change in nature. Things start to come together.

Although you may have already seen many obvious changes, your measurable postural gains really start to show. During this phase, we make this improved posture, mobility, nervous system peace *normal*. Remember that body map that your brain holds? That has to change. If your improved posture and health does not become normal to your brain, then the moment you stop getting adjusted, your nervous system will want to return to the old normal again.

Maintenance, Prevention, or Wellness?

So you have gotten through the intensive period of correction. You have stabilised and normalised a new level of neurospinal health. In the past, we would talk about maintenance care at this stage, yet there are three very distinctive goals you can have in the longer term. Making your goals a conscious choice will totally change your health in 5, 10, and 20 years time.

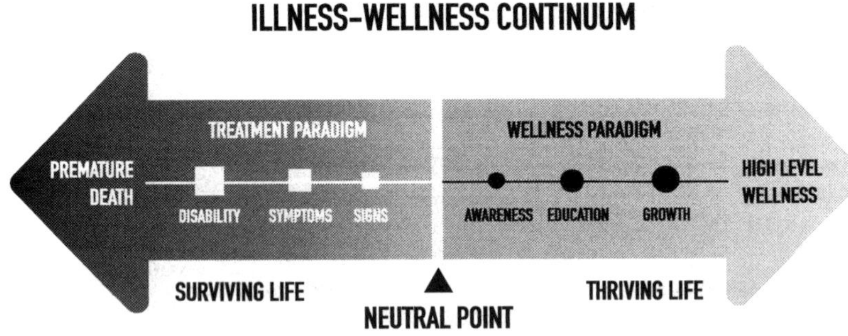

Figure 28. A reminder of the Illness-Wellness Continuum. All the way to the left is 0% life, also called death. All the way to the right is 100% life. Blissful wellness. Your healthcare philosophy drives your position on this spectrum.

The first goal is to maintain your progress. If you go to a chiropractor just once a month, it is probably called **maintenance care**. All you are doing is slowing your deterioration, not really maintaining a good level of health—too many things happen in a month! Consider, how long did you have those subluxations before you started care? If you have had a herniated disc and degeneration, does your body ever fully forget? How many times in a month might you sleep awkwardly? How many times can you step on an uneven surface? How many times can you get stressed or think negative thoughts? How many toxins are you exposed to in a month? It is hard, I would argue impossible, to keep a new normal with just one adjustment per month.

The second goal is **preventive care**. This is something that even the medical system is becoming more aware of. The goal is not just to prevent relapse of previous problems, but also to avoid future problems, and no doubt, this is a part of lifelong care. Important are also lessening the probability of future problems, removing yourself from those horrible statistics, and avoiding a fate like John's in Chapter 1. Although preventive care is part and parcel of ongoing care, I personally find it a very negative focus. It means that you are metaphorically walking backwards through life. Backing away from the things you *do not* want instead of moving *towards* the things that *you do* want. This may sound semantic, but it is energetically and psychologically profound. Many a great guru has said, *"Where your attention goes, your energy flows."* So rather than place your energy on prevention, why not place it on your vision?

The third and greatest goal is **wellness care**. This, for me, is the greatest motivation to keep your spine well adjusted. This means knowing that life in your body is the electricity passing from your brain to each cell. It involves recognising that 100% clarity means 100% brain-body connection and 100% capacity for your nervous system to heal you. It means that you acknowledge that subluxation, pressure in your spine, reduces that clarity. Knowing this, what percentage of clarity, what percentage of *life* do you want in your body? 50%? 75%? Wellness happens when you are closer to 100%. Yes, less illness happens too, but more wellness happens! As we discussed in Chapter 1, this is where *salutogenesis,* health-generation, occurs. Holding the vision of doing what you want without restriction, no matter what age you are, means moving *towards* wellness for *life.*

> Kaye and her husband had been under care for about 16 months. They both originally had many symptoms. He had previous herniated discs in his lower back, which had been operated on. The chronic back pain had now gone. She had a combination of headaches, hip pains, and digestive problems. Over the past year, these had all disappeared. At the beginning of January, she sent me a photo on

> Whatsapp. It was of a filing cabinet with one of the drawers open. That drawer had all of the usual folders with titles. They were all empty, except you could see the green report folder which we give to our clients when they start care. Her message read, "No more doctor or hospital visits!" I assumed she had mistakenly sent the message, but she explained when she next came in. Every new year, she would go through the filing cabinet and empty unneeded papers, putting them into an archive filing system. Normally, this drawer was full of papers from doctors and hospital visits, including tests, etc. Since starting chiropractic care, she and her husband had been in such good general health that they had totally stopped all such visits. The folder was empty. The message was a bit obscure, but the meaning was profound for their health, happiness, and future. This is true health, living the "undoctored life."

Your choice of health care model affects you and those around you. This is most evident as we eventually become elderly. I do not mean old, but elderly. One day, all of us will become weak, vulnerable, and frail. This is the natural course towards death. We have a lot of control over how soon that day will come. We can proclaim, "I just want to live my life, and when illness comes, will deal with it," or "I have never had any pains or symptoms; I am perfectly healthy, so do not need to do anything proactive." I believe that these are both selfish choices. Who has to look after people who do not look after themselves? Almost invariably it falls to your closest family to "pick up the pieces" from your bad health decisions. We all have examples of this in our own family. Someone who did not invest in their health and became ill and disabled prematurely. So one or more family members have to commit perhaps years of their life to caring for someone who *could have chosen differently.* This is a painful experience for everyone involved. As this is a family member, such sacrifice is made without question, but what is clear is that not caring for yourself so that you age healthily is *a very selfish decision.*

> Insurance statistics show that people under chiropractic care have 60% fewer hospital admissions, 62% fewer outpatient surgeries, and 85% lower medication costs.[131] Investing in health means you save on illness.

When you live a conscious life, you make a selfless choice. Choosing to invest in your own health is one of the greatest gifts you can give to your family. It will affect your current and your future health and happiness, making you a different person to be around. It will save your closest family from the suffering of having to care for someone who did not care for themselves. But most of all, it will ripple through your friends and your family, making them, in turn, make better health decisions. When you *live* the wellness model, you do not need to convince friends and family to follow. Your friends and family are naturally pulled in this direction. Do you want your kids, your grandchildren, to make positive health choices? Then lead by example. Making this simple, conscious choice can change not only your life but your impact on the world.

Chapter 11 Checklist

- Just like dental care was backward and reactive 80 years ago, so spinal care is today.
- As your spinal alignment improves, you may have aches, just as if dental braces were improving your tooth alignment.
- The greatest benefits of improved posture and spinal hygiene are really seen over 12 to 18 months and beyond.
- Though the average person feels great through their progress, you are not likely to be "average." Ups and downs are not a cause for concern. Certain body areas may "wake up" as they heal properly, which is called "retracing." As your nervous system rebalances and resets, it may "overreact" temporarily. These are all perfectly healthy healing processes.
- Judging your progress by how you feel short-term misses the point.
- "Maintenance care" slows an inevitable physical decline. "Preventive care" deals with problems at source and is more positive but is still illness-centric. "Wellness care" involves looking to how good it could be and staying focused on that, generating genuine health and resilience.

Exercise:

- Get a pen and paper. Briefly review your personal health habits.
- On the top line, write down the things that you invest most in. Is it your teeth? Your skin? The gym? Your diet? Meditating? Learning? Your spine and brain health? The investment could be time, energy, money or all of these. You should have a list of 3-6 things, side by side.
- Below that, write what each one mostly relates to. Is it how your body feels, how you look and feel about yourself, how happy you are, or how healthy you are inside? Is it all of these, or something else?
- Now write down, how do you invest in each of these? Is it time? Money? Energy?
- Below that, again, consider if each these habits are *maintaining* your current status, *preventing* illness, or truly *generating* wellness?
- Now close your eyes, and take a few minutes to visualise the "best you" as you generate more wellness. Imagine how you look, feel inside, how happy you are, and how your future health will be. What is missing to make this picture come true? Where do you feel you can invest more and in what way?
- This exercise can be eye-opening, so quickly write down any thoughts and commitments. Set a date in your diary to check in in three months, to see how you are doing. Repeat this exercise a few times per year, for example before your birthday, or around the new year.

If you are near Marbella, Spain, go to www.duffyquiropractica.com to find out how to work with Dr Duffy.

If elsewhere, go to www.chiroalliance.org or www.chiropractic.org to search for subluxation reducing Chiropractors.

Chapter 12

Recovery 101

"Taking care of your mental and physical health is just as important as any career move or responsibility."

— Mireille Guiliano

You are the Boss

Trying to write a complete guide to recovery would be like trying to write the complete guide to life, which is far beyond the scope of this book. I am working on a book which goes into this topic in more detail, so register on www.glennduffy.com, or scan the QR code at the end of the chapter if you want to get updates. Meanwhile, let's go over some easy-win, subluxation-reducing strategies.

As mentioned in Chapter 2, there are three main sources of subluxation stress: physical (traumas), emotional (thoughts), and chemical (toxins). To truly optimise your recovery process, you would ideally address all three. But for the scope of this book, we will go over some of the "low hanging fruit." These are simple exercise and postural principals which apply to most spinal health; however, please take the principals within the context of the professional advice your doctor gives you.

> Chiropractors are lucky to "save" thousands of people from disc surgery every year. I can remember in detail every client of mine who has gone on to have surgery (there have only been a few over my 20 years in practice). One stands out. Mark was a 32-year-old specialist firefighter. He is one of very few of my clients to have undergone spinal surgery, despite following my recommendations. He worked at London Heathrow Airport, so was specially trained to board a burning plane. His training and preparation was vigorous. His wife studied and lived in Canada, where he was due to emigrate to rejoin her the following year. He planned to carry on as a firefighter

> in Canada but needed to pass a tough physical exam to get the job. The problem was that he had a degenerative disc in his lower back, which would flare up when he lifted weights. He was a strong, fit, but heavy guy. He responded well to adjustments, but he just kept getting re-injured. He even took a month off work, but that seemed to make no difference. With every option exhausted, he was on the list for lumbar disc surgery. The week before he went for surgery, he mentioned in passing that he Skype-called his wife early every morning for about an hour. It emerged that he chatted to her every day on his laptop, sitting on a low sofa, bent over the coffee table! He had been doing so for the past 18 months. There could be no worse habit for a degenerative disc than to get out of bed and sit bent forward in flexion for an hour. No wonder he was not recovering. Sadly, he was too close to the surgery to make any changes to his plans. He had surgery and soon after emigrated. I do not know what became of him, but I do wonder what would have happened had he changed that one simple but damaging habit sooner...

Remember that your doctor cannot follow you around all day long, watching every habit you have. If you want to get well, it serves you to observe what habits you have which may be holding you back. No one can do it all for you. You are the boss of your own healing.

Will I Get Better?

When you reduce subluxation in your spine, you will always get better. What an arrogant statement, don't you think? But it is as simple as it is true. When you are more connected, you are better off, even if a particular pain or problem persists. If you want to know how much you can gain from chiropractic care, a better question is, "How suitable is the chiropractic approach for me?" My experience shows that most clients start in one of three places.

1. "I carry on either way, so *click my spine* so I can be out of pain."

Perhaps you are more used to the crisis care paradigm. Some people in your position start care but stop long before seeing the true rewards.

This does not mean you cannot get a lot out of the chiropractic approach, but you will need to show patience as you learn a different way to associate with your body and your health. If you can do this, the rewards are great, but you have to invest first. You run the risk that your doctor might care more for your long-term health than you do. This can cause a conflict of expectations: them making recommendations for your health, and you seeking something short-term. If that is the case, you might be better off sticking with what you know until you feel the time is right to make lasting changes. Getting adjusted is still a great idea… it will help, but be mindful of the difference in expectations.

2. "*I know* what I need and how this works. I have had other injuries and care before—let's get started."

You are already health-aware and prepared for a wellness-oriented journey, which is great. But some clients in your position get great results and later stop their wellness journey, as they already feel great and forget their long-term goals. You will need to be aware of a possible resistance if things don't go quite how you expected. And as you move into wellness care, you would be well served by doing regular reminders of your goals, perhaps with the help of your wellness doctor.

3. "This is the missing piece of my health jigsaw. *You tell me* what to do next."

If you are already on a wellness journey, you already tend to make wellness-oriented choices. It is likely that your family and peers see you as very health-informed, perhaps even calling you to ask health questions. If you are not already working in health, you may have considered it! You will do brilliantly with the chiropractic approach, especially if you keep two things in mind. Firstly, be open to finding problems, gaps, or injuries which you were not aware of. Even the well-cared-for body has hidden secrets. Perhaps, you can learn a different perspective on your body in order to understand these findings. If you feel resistance, be mindful that it could slow your growth. Secondly, embrace the vitalistic element which you are already aware of. There is a spiritual level of growth which is beyond wellness. Keeping your nervous system clear, your mind open, and trusting in the unknown will allow you to reach higher levels of health, happiness, and enlightenment.

Exercise for Success

The effects of that chronic survival state which we discussed in Chapter 9 live in your posture. If I say "flexed forward," you think of bending from the hips, right? Well, all joints can flex, and to imagine what a totally flexed person looks like, imagine the foetal position: knees to your chest, chin tucked down, and hands curled under your chin. It was a great position to be in when we were in the womb. It is even a great position to be in should a bear attack you. It is also not such a bad position to be in when you sleep. Neurologically, a fully flexed posture represents a defensive, fight or flight position. Human beings spend way too much time in flexion, mostly while sitting, but also during sports. Too much flexion is not good news.

This ruins your spinal curves, causing the three most common and severe spinal alignment problems. A flat neck is an overly flexed cervical spine. A hyperkyphosis (hunchback) is an overly flexed thoracic spine. A flat back (lumbar hypolordosis) is an overly flexed lumbar spine.

But it doesn't stop at your spine. Rounded shoulders are overly flexed shoulder blades. A tipped pelvis is overly tight hip flexors. Not being able to bend to touch your toes without bending your knees is overly tight knee flexors. You start to get the picture. We all spend too much time in flexion, and for many of us our flexor muscles are too tight.

This is worsened further when we get pains in the muscles which have to fight that flexion. Yes, the most symptomatic or painful muscles in our bodies are generally the extensor group. This is because they spend so much time fighting to hold back this excessive flexion bias. So many gym instructors and physical therapists will recommend stretching these muscles, as they feel tight. And you get temporary relief. But, most ironically, this only biases flexion even further and adds increased spinal stress to the mix.

During 2003-2004 I was invited to guest lecture at the University of Surrey on their postgraduate programme. I lectured in my "specialty," which was Clinical Rehabilitation. Despite already being fully qualified and having extensively researched pelvic biomechanics, my understanding of these neurological concepts was lacking. I look back on what I taught in those lectures: flexion stretches, strengthening, and balance training. I would have better spent my time teaching the neurology of extension, of how to bring someone back into postural and neurological balance. My understanding now is that 50% of what I taught was *wrong and/or ineffective.* Now, some 20 years later, I know better. But many practitioners are still bound to that old, ineffective model of care.

Had tight neck muscles? You will have been told to stretch your neck downwards. Temporary relief, but long term worsening of the problem.

Had tight buttocks? You will have been told to stretch your knee to your chest. Feels better, right? But it does nothing to redress the deep imbalance and nervous stress that lies beneath.

All of this flexion not only stresses our spines, our posture, and puts us more into a stressed state, but it also projects badly both socially and in the workplace. Someone hunched forwards with rounded shoulders and head poking forward does not project the same ease and confidence as someone upright with open shoulders.[132] It is not coincidental that good public speakers work on being in an upright, extended posture. The posture of success.

Many sports worsen this still. I am a big sinner when it comes to flexion sports. My main sports over recent years have been cycling and kayaking. Both involve bending forward at the hips and then exercising in that posture, sometimes for hours on end. It is no wonder that most cyclists, kayakers, and rowers have appalling postures.

Stand Tall to Thrive

So from a postural perspective, how can we favour our parasympathetic, rest digest nervous system. Or put another way, what exercises increase our extensor tone? Many neutral sports give us an opportunity to stay upright. These do not necessarily correct a hunched posture. If you are already bent forwards, you need first to remedy it. Sports, such as aqua-aerobics, hiking, running, football, swimming, and basketball, are all more neutral. Tennis and racquet sports are a little more flexion-dominant, but are still good choices. Other healthy sports include dancing, and for the sufficiently patient among us, golf.

The only easy-access sports which are strongly extensor-dominant are walking or running *uphill* and rock-climbing. This is good news for anyone who lives near a mountain. But a set of stairs or even a stair-climber or inclined treadmill at the gym can do a good job. Walk uphill, keeping your chest upright, taking long strides, pushing off fully behind you, and letting your arms swing. You are now doing one of the most efficient forms of hip, lower back, and leg rehabilitation. Your buttocks and lower back are forced to strengthen into extension. Your knees get stronger with minimum impact. And you get fit fast with minimal shock to your body. Do take care coming back down, as it is easy to damage your knees, hips, or lower back if you rush. Hills are our friends, and it is no coincidence that many of the healthiest, longest-lived communities on earth live in hilly environments.[133] Keep hill walking for as long as you can walk, and it will repay you handsomely.

Unfortunately, the few hours per week which most of us throw at exercise pales against the tens of hours we spend sitting. The research is clear—you cannot undo an excess of sitting with three visits to the gym per week.[134]

Sitting Kills

The research implies that this is not an *association* but *causation*. Sitting kills. It is not *associated* with deaths; it *causes* deaths.[135] According to the American Cancer Society, sitting makes you more likely to die of 14 specific diseases, including cancer, heart disease, stroke, and Alzheimer's.[136] Indeed 7% of deaths over the age of 45 years old are attributable to diseases from sitting too much.[137]

If you sit just ten hours per day, you have a 34% increased all-cause mortality risk.[138] That is 34% increased statistical risk of dying from *any* cause, in *any* given year. Put that into context of an average day: 20 minutes over breakfast, 30 minutes in the car, train, or bus to work, 8 hours at work, plus 40 minutes over lunch, 30 minutes to get home again, 30 minutes over dinner, and an hour of television or reading before heading to bed. There, you have easily sat for 11.5 hours in just one day. That does not include the time on the toilet, reading magazines, or browsing your social media accounts! Most people are shocked when they add up all the time they spend sitting.

The full details of *why* sitting leads to illness are not yet fully understood. Some of it has to do with blood flow, which stagnates when you stop moving. But why sitting would cause cancer is not yet clear.

The effects that sitting have on your spine are better studied. The greatest damage is done by two different mechanisms.

Firstly, when you sit in certain postures, you stretch the discs and ligaments in your spine. After just 20 to 30 minutes these tissues start to "creep."[139] This means that they start to deform in a permanent way. Sit in a bad posture for long enough, and you literally change the shape and length of your ligaments and discs. How are your lovely spinal curves then? Peak disc loads during sitting can be three times your body weight. As mentioned in Chapter 6, a 70kg person can have 210kg sitting on their lumbar discs as they sit in a poor posture. It is no wonder that so many of us suffer from herniated discs nowadays. It is not because of lifting or exercise. It is because of the weakness after so much sitting.

Unfortunately, exercise cannot magically undo this damage. I am not saying stop exercising, but I am saying that you need to move a lot more. If you want to remove yourself from the high probability of paying the price for sitting too much, you have to make changes.

Rules for Sitting

Firstly, come to terms with how much you sit. Over breakfast, you can calculate all of your sitting hours and write down the three places you sit the most. We all sit a lot more than we want to admit, and right now, as you read this, you are probably sitting and looking down at the book. We all become unconscious to our posture when we are engaged in something. So let's not fool ourselves by saying we will "win the posture war" with willpower alone. We need to be more clever than that.

I do not believe the *"no pain, no gain"* adage. To crudely paraphrase the movement master and founder of the Feldenkrais technique, Moshe Feldenkrais; "Where there is will, there is no skill." Or put another way, if you need to use willpower and force the result, you have not used skill to get the result. *Forced postural changes are untenable.* Here are the key skills in order to lessen the burden of sitting on your health.

Check out my Youtube channel for some tips on sitting and sleeping postures. Scan the QR code to learn what exercises to do at your PC.

If you look up "Dr Duffy, Happy Spine," on YouTube, you will find videos explaining other postural themes. Subscribe for new content!

1. Short-chunk your day. You know that spending long periods in one posture is counter-productive. So chop your time between different tasks as much as possible.
2. Use every opportunity to move. Telephone calls do not need your bum to be on the seat. Get up and walk around, even carrying a notepad if needed.
3. Set alarms. Set one for every 30 to 40 minutes to get up and move around. Do your "spinal wake-ups" (on my Youtube channel) or take a walk. Your best posture is your next posture. Keep moving.
4. Avoid static stretching to relieve postural strain. One of the most used and abused ways of temporarily relieving postural strain is holding stretches for 30 seconds or more. It may give temporary relief, but more and more static stretching just "kicks the can down the road," meaning more problems later. Get checked by someone properly qualified.
5. Laptops are for occasional use only. The lowest hanging fruit to be picked is to avoid using a laptop more than occasionally. See the story at the end of "You are the Boss" in Chapter 12 for a real warning. A laptop stand, bluetooth keyboard and mouse will cost you 60 euros, weigh next to nothing, and change your postural health for life. Seriously, when people do not take this advice, I am dumbfounded. Relatively cheap, easy, and hugely impactful on your health.
6. Consciously choose how you sit without needing to force your posture. There are two distinctively "healthier" ways to sit, active vs,

passive. But the problem happens when you get caught in no man's land, neither active nor passive. You should be able to "set and forget" these two positions and let yourself focus on your work until your movement break alarm goes off.

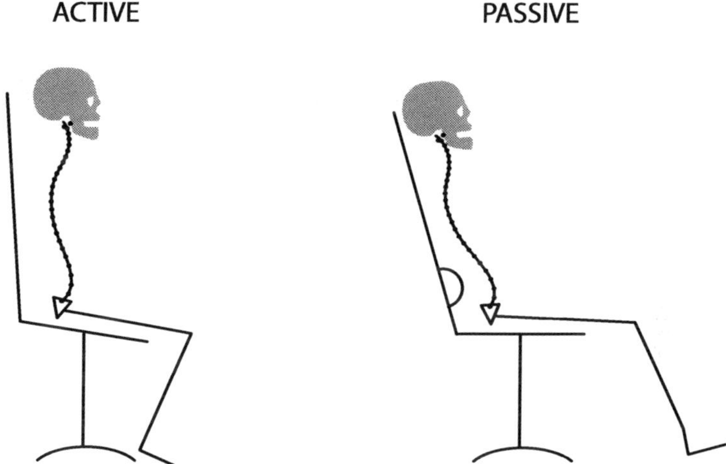

Figure 29. Two contrasting models of sitting. One does not even need a back support, as your posture is self-maintaining. The other uses full support. The problem occurs when we get caught in "no man's land"

The active model of sitting has your knees lower than your hips, your pelvis rocked forwards, your screen *very high*. This is active sitting. It is like fooling your spine that you are standing up. Your spine should be aligned and should *naturally stay so*. If your screen is not high enough, you will slouch, and you are in no man's land. This posture will need three key ingredients: a tilting base to your chair (you may need to add a wedge cushion), a height adjustable screen (it should force you to keep your head up and back), and a keyboard/mouse close to your tummy (which keeps your elbows by your sides, unloading your shoulders). Active sitting works well for focused, repetitive tasks.

The passive model of sitting acknowledges that your spinal muscles will rest, so do it in a fully supported posture. This means leaning back in the seat and using the backrest, relaxing and using all the support you can get. This is almost a working "sofa posture."

Your knees should be in line with your hips, and you should consider a low back support (yes swapping cushions during the working day is good practice!). Passive sitting works better for mixed, creative tasks and should not be used for prolonged periods.

If you sit a lot at just one or two workstations (and most of us do), a sit-stand workstation may be one of your best lifetime investments. A cheap station could cost under 100 euros. Even popping your laptop on top of a filing cabinet and standing for 30 minutes a few times a day is better than nothing and costs nothing. A professional setup can cost less than 600 euros. Research shows that these workstations will save lives by improving health.[140] Could your life be one of them?!

Make small changes and put them at the top of your to-do list or in your diary. Changing everything at once may well cause you back pain and other problems. Make changes bit by bit. I encourage all of my clients to write their daily to do list, starting with the investment that they will make in themselves. So the top of your to-do list could read "stand 2 x 30min," and then have a list of the other tasks for your day. Make sure you can tick off the most important thing!

Sleep for Your Brain

Perhaps the most under-rated way to improve your overall health is to improve your sleep quality. Poor sleep quality or quantity means slower recovery times, more neurological stress, and poorer health. Sleeping fewer than seven hours per night increases all-cause morbidity by 12% and is associated with a 2 to 3 times increased risk of pulmonary fibrosis (lung scarring and thickening). Chronic insomniacs have a threefold increased annual death risk. The gravity of this cannot be understated; people who sleep too little live poorer quality lives and die sooner.

We all need 7 to 9 hours of sleep. You are more likely to win the lotto than to genetically "not need" this amount of sleep. If you think you do not need seven hours, you have gotten used to a lack of sleep.[141] When you constantly get more, you will improve your health. Period.

Improved sleep quality is one of the most common side effects of good quality spinal care and improved neurological health, so it ends up being a conversation I often have with clients. But rarely on the first visit. Most sleep-deprived people have no idea that they are sleep deprived. We normalise sleep deprivation so much, we become so used to functioning with poor sleep, that we are oblivious to it. It mostly damages things in a subtle, but profound way. Poorer creativity, impaired concentration and memory, irritability, and feeling tired are things which become normal, without us ever realising how they damage our quality of life. Read over Chapters 4 (especially "Your Neck Feeds Your Brain") and 9 ("Flexible Brainwaves, Happy Life") to recap how your brain is "washed down" and nourished overnight. Removing quality of sleep stops these deep brain waves, meaning your brain never gets a proper "clean." Perhaps, this is why poor sleep quality is linked to early onset dementia.

I regularly see new clients who say they sleep well, but it turns out they use melatonin daily or even lorazepam or lithium to help them sleep. Sometimes, they have been using these for years, against all evidence and good practice. Or they "self-medicate" with alcohol or cannabis before bedtime. They have (or had) no psychological "problems" but are now dependent on these drugs to sleep. The evidence is clear, even "natural" melatonin should not be needed long-term. *All substances which help you to sleep* affect the normal cycles and quality of sleep and promote dependence. If you feel that you need to take something to sleep, you have a problem. I feel slightly bad writing this, because I know that if it applies to you, it may feel uncomfortable. But I would rather say it and you have a chance to change it than for you carry on oblivious to this problem.

I know, I know, if you are suffering insomnia, this "news" does not fix anything, and might even be more stressful. Perhaps, however, it is the wake-up call that you really need to seek a sustainable solution. And in my experience, for nearly all insomniacs, there are at least improvements which can be made. At review, 36% of our clients say that they have improved sleep. But as new clients, fewer than 5% recognise poor sleep quality. Nearly all of our clients stop taking their "sleep aids," as they no longer need them. It is hard to put a finger on just one reason why this happens. A peaceful nervous system allows you to release your stressors, rather than carry them with you and store them. Instead of your mind racing when you lie down, it soon calms down and allows you that time which your body so badly needs to rest and recover. Bliss time.

Sleep for Your Spine

But your brain is not the only thing which relies on sleep to get a good "feed." Unlike your brain, certain tissues of your body have a very small and delicate blood supply. These are mostly the heaviest weight-bearing tissues of your body. Bones, cartilage, and ligaments. Imagine these were to have a bigger blood supply… they would be too vulnerable to support all of the load you place on them. So instead, when you load these tissues, you squeeze some blood and fluid out of them. And when you unload them, they "suck up" fresh blood and fluid. They act like the sponges of your body, only a lot harder than any sponge. Squeeze out toxins and used blood under load, suck up fresh fluid and blood as they rest.

And their greatest period of rest is…you guessed it, overnight. As mentioned in Chapter 6, you can gain 2cm overnight, simply as your spinal discs rehydrate. Not only the amount you sleep but the posture in which you sleep can impair this process. Imagine you lie down with your spine still compressed and stay like that overnight. How can your discs rehydrate? Or you lie twisted in rotation (for example on your belly) overnight, with the walls of the discs wound up. You can see that the rehydration cannot be balanced. Unbalanced rehydration of the discs may be one of the reasons behind a phenomenon known as internal disc derangement, where your discs are unstable with no apparent cause. If every night you sleep with your L4 disc compressed on the right but loose on the left, how can you expect it to behave well, let alone to age well?

Rules for Sleeping

Sleep, like everything else we do, is driven by our habits. Excusing the pun, don't expect them to change overnight. For when we are already in the sleep zone, it is too late to go organizing new ways to sleep. Upgrading your sleep means taking stock, writing a short action plan, and seeing it through, as a priority, until it becomes habit.

Let us look at general "Sleep Hygiene" before addressing sleep posture.

1. Waking up at the same time every day has a profound normalising effect on sleep habits. Big lie-ins on weekends cannot recover lost sleep during the week. You are better off getting to bed a little earlier every night and getting up *near* the same time, including on weekends. This time-discipline has far-reaching long term impacts.
2. As much as is possible, use your bedroom for sleeping in your bed. Not as an office. Not as a TV room (the idea makes me shudder). Even scrolling on your phone should not be done around sleep time. Blue light exposure from screens disrupts the normal melatonin release cycle needed for sleep. You should have dim lights and avoid screens for the last 60 minutes of your day. Give your brain a break from the phone and do not look at it for the first 30 minutes of your day. Your messages and emails will still be there for you 30 minutes later, while your brain will be happy to wake up more gently.
3. Napping is a marvellously healthy habit and associated with longevity. But napping too late in the day will mess up your next night.[142] In order to respect natural sleep cycles, naps should be *either short* (15-30min) *or long* (60-90min).[143]
4. A pen and paper should live by your bed. Write just ten words, or as many as you like, before sleep. If it ends up being 2000, great. If it ends up being just ten, that is great too. It gives your brain the chance to "offload" concerns and "shelve" them until the next day. See if you can finish the list by writing some positive things, like things you are grateful for. This seeds your brain to focus on these as you go to sleep.
5. Likewise, if you awake and struggle to return to sleep, don't lie there fretting. Turn on the light and write whatever comes to mind until the pen stops moving... it may surprise you how much this helps to clear your mind and get back to sleep.

Sleeping posture should be 1/3rd of your daily postural stress, so it is worthy of consideration.

1. Practise the "long spine posture" no matter which way you lie. This unloads and stretches your spine, allowing it to fully recover while you sleep. It is just not something that can be described in words. Scan the QR code to watch a YouTube video for a full explanation.
2. Front-sleeping is a bad idea for just about everyone. It requires you to jam your neck into rotation-extension and your lower back into extension and then leaves your poor spinal discs there for hours on end. To wean yourself off front-sleeping, use a pillow under one side of your chest as if you were in "recovery position," before gradually transitioning onto your side.
3. Side posture sleeping is a good solution but needs a little care. A very hard mattress can cause your spine to end up too bent and twisted in side posture. Use a pillow between your knees to lessen that twisting effect and keep your pelvis more vertical, in line with your shoulders. If you have wide shoulders, you may end up squashing the shoulder you are lying on, causing a decrease in blood supply and shoulder ache and degeneration. Worse still, your neck can end up bent to the side all night long...not good news. Ensure you have a supportive, contoured pillow (give up that duck-down softness) and a mattress topper—a layer of softer foam—to offset this problem. You may even consider another pillow in front of your chest to help you stay more square between hips and shoulders.
4. Back sleeping posture is generally the best, yet many people cannot tolerate it. This is because their hip flexibility pulls on their lower back, compressing the discs. Practising the "long spine posture" (see point 1 above) can really make back-sleeping a viable option. You may also place a pillow (or two) under your knees to release this pressure. Make sure that any head pillow in this posture only supports your neck. Anything under your head itself will bend your neck forward, damaging the curve and causing long term problems.

All sound a little overwhelming? If so, pick up your diary and put a "sleep check" date in your diary for every three weeks, repeating four times over the next three months. On each date, open this chapter again, review your progress, and make a small change or two. Trying to make all these changes today and tomorrow could be too much. Better make small changes for life than big changes for just a few days!

Chapter 12 Checklist

- Don't rely on anyone to fix all of your postural habits. Only you can do this. You are the boss.
- You are always better when vertebral subluxations are reduced. Aligning your personal expectations towards long-term wellness, instead of short-term relief, will optimise your results.
- Chronic tightness and tiredness should be dealt with as a nervous stress and/or alignment problem. Just stretching, massaging, and strengthening misses the point.
- Upright sports, or those favouring back strength, tend to help your nervous system and posture, while "bent forward" sports can be damaging.
- The best posture is your next posture. Sitting kills. Get up and move. Lots.
- Not honouring your real need for sleep and rest is very expensive in terms of health and happiness. Sleep time literally "washes" your brain, warding off age-related memory decline. It is also the time when your spinal discs "feed" themselves, recovering for the next day. Sleep keeps you young in every way.

Action Points

- Register on www.glennduffy.com for news on upcoming books and even online courses on this topic.
- Pull out your diary or organiser and make a date to re-read this chapter in three months time. Bringing these important themes back into focus regularly is key to sustained health gains.

If you are near Marbella, Spain, go to www.duffyquiropractica.com to find out how to work with Dr Duffy.

If elsewhere, go to www.chiroalliance.org or www.chiropractic.org to search for subluxation reducing Chiropractors.

Chapter 13

Drugs and Surgery

"The best and most efficient pharmacy is within your own system."

— Robert C Peale

The Way it Should Be

The Intervention Stairs

Having been anaesthetised seven times by the age of 17, fractured a few bones, and had another surgery since, I know the surgical world very well as a patient. I have worked with many orthopaedic surgeon colleagues — both friendly and absurdly hostile — through all of my professional life. Many of my clients and some of my closest friends are surgeons. Good surgeons know the limitations of surgery. They are aware of the problems with the medical approach, and often seek health care for themselves and their families outside of the medical system. When we chat and debate, we are mostly in agreement. Putting all of this knowledge together, I can describe what makes the best surgeon for you and have drawn this person for you in Figure 30.

Figure 30. Picture of the best surgeon for you. The best surgeon is the one you never see.

I mentioned before that much of our medical system sees no other option for you other than drugs or surgery. In fact, the lack of proactive recommendation implicitly means that they are waiting either for your symptoms to go away or for you to need surgery. If there is nothing else offered, then at some point drugs and surgery will be the only options. It is a self-fulfilling prophecy. And the prophet is the medical specialist who told you nothing other than surgery could be done.

You have learnt that my focus professionally is adding health rather than removing illness. But for the purposes of this discussion, let us imagine that we are only aiming to remove illness. Let us see what the generally agreed approach should be.

I like to call this simple concept the *Intervention Stairs*. This assumes that an "intervention" is needed. It is a logical, simple way to deal with injuries and symptoms. You start at the bottom step on the stairs, and having given sufficient time to ensure that you have exhausted that step (intervention), you proceed to the next step until satisfied (your symptoms have gone). When satisfied, you exit the stairs. This is basic, logical reasoning. Common sense.

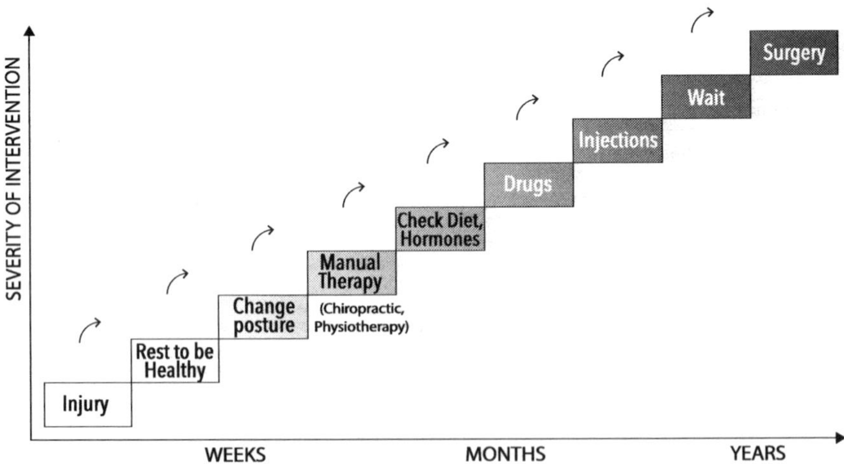

Figure 31. The Intervention Stairs. If you skip steps or start too high up, you cannot turn back. Taking time to let each intervention work respects your body's need for time to heal. This is common sense.

We could spend quite some time arguing over the order of these steps, but the point is to start at the bottom first. If you jump straight to the top step of the stairs, you cannot come back down again.

The most health-enlightened approach allows time for your body to heal, leaving surgery as the last option. The principal of surgery last does not mean diagnostic testing last. Diagnostic testing can often rule out more sinister problems and allow you to fully commit to natural healing above all else. It makes sense to test sooner, operate later.

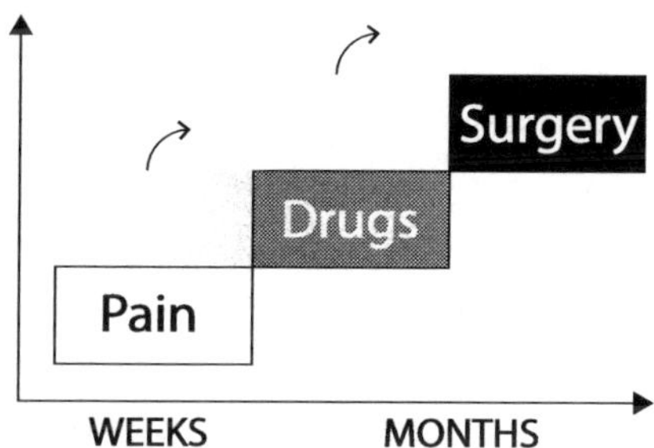

Figure 32. Bad practice in illness care. When all you have to offer are drugs or surgery, the Intervention Stairs looks like this. Jumping straight to drugs or surgery without a chance to heal naturally increases the chance of an unnecessary or failed surgery. Except in genuine emergencies, this approach does not make sense.

The unfortunate fact is that, especially when you have private health insurance,[144] many people jump most of these steps, going straight to drugs, injections, and surgery. This is tragic. Why? Because someone who follows the advice of rushing straight to surgery has no coming back.

What Painkillers Should I Use?

If you are trying to put off surgery and are doing everything in your power to recover naturally, what drugs or painkillers could help? Let me put my answer in a little context.

There are thousands and thousands of good, fair, caring people who work in the pharmaceutical industry, trying to help humanity. Certain drugs have saved countless lives, while others have made challenging illnesses more bearable.

If you read the industry news, it becomes obvious that drug companies have a history of professional deceit and lying on a scale which makes politicians and the mafia look like amateurs.[145] If the public were to have an idea of how many fines these companies receive every year for the illegal practices for which they are *actually caught*, the trust level toward all of these companies would be very different. Let's ask a few questions...

Surely we know the safety data in real time before any drug is on the market?

The history of the drug thalidomide is a sobering story. It was first used in 1956 in order to stop pregnant women from feeling morning sickness. But many babies were born with deformities, missing arms and legs. It was banned in the UK in 1961. Thalidomide was manufactured by Grunenthal, the same pharmaceutical company who still make esomeprazole, the highly popular acid reflux-suppressing drug (often sold as Nexium) and many other "household" drugs, including migraine drugs, to this very day. In 1961, Grunenthal wrote an internal letter to its Spanish HQ, telling them *not to tell the spanish medical community why the drug was being banned worldwide.*[146] Thalidomide continued to be used in Spain until its ban in...1985. 24 years later! At least 10,000 deformed babies were born, with countless lives damaged.[147] In fact, it is estimated that 90% of these babies died during childhood. In the very clear name of corporate profit, nothing else. The most shameful part is that the Spanish thalidomide victims are still fighting for compensation,[148] whilst Grunenthal continues to post record profits on drugs in Spain.[149]

Yeah, but some drugs are really just like supplements, like to help digestion...

Speaking of stomach acid suppressants, esomeprazole (a stronger form of omeprazole), may be prescribed to reduce acid reflux symptoms after eating. Sold by the same company behind the thalidomide scandal, this is a drug which should normally be used for two weeks,[150] or the shortest time possible.[151] There is occasional cause to prescribe it for longer, even over eight weeks, but such use carries an increased risk of kidney disease[152] and stomach cancer,[153] to name just two. Vitamin B deficiencies can occur in people who take these longer term. Yet I routinely see young clients who have been using this for many years with the understanding that they will take it for the rest of their life. Despite there being multiple calls for this to stop, many of which come from within the medical establishment, the routine over-prescribing of acid-suppressing drugs continues.

Ok. But surely painkillers are safe? I mean, everyone uses them, right?

You may have heard some of the press about the brilliant "opioid" painkillers called Oxycodone, Oxycontin, or similar. If you had severe, chronic back pain over the past 20 years, there is a fair chance that you were prescribed an opioid painkiller. The problem is that, on withdrawal, the clients need more and more of the drug, causing an inevitable addiction. This was known to Purdue, who manufactured Oxycontin. By 2019, they were selling 76 billion Oxycontin pills a year, fuelling a drug addiction epidemic greater than anything that heroin or cocaine could ever compare to.[154] In fact, the drug had caused 450,000 deaths in the USA alone by 2020 and destroyed countless families and lives. Opioids continue to be the biggest killer of under 50 year-olds in the USA every year and cause the most drug-related deaths in Europe. I have personally seen clients addicted to these drugs. Spain has seen an 84% increase in these prescriptions between 2009[155]. Some believe the same epidemic is about to hit Europe. Purdue were eventually brought to pay damages in the region of 10 billion USD.[156] That is not a misprint. 10 billion dollars. And then they were dissolved.[157] Did the private individuals who perpetrated this crime lose their salaries and their careers? I'll let you guess.

But that is a "strong" painkiller; what about milder drugs like anti-inflammatories?

Then there is the famous case of Vioxx (known as Rofecoxib in Spain). Vioxx is a non-steroidal anti-inflammatory (NSAID) drug, approximately like ibuprofen, enantyum, naproxen, or diclofenac. Some 80 million people worldwide took this drug between 1999 and 2005.[158] You or a family member could be among them. It is estimated that *up to* 500,000 people were killed by Vioxx worldwide.[159] That is up to 100,000 deaths per year over 5 years. Eventually, Merck settled to pay 4.85 billion dollars[160] in fines and a limited 50,000 compensation claims. Yes, nearly 5 BILLION DOLLARS. To put it in perspective, Merck recouped that 5 billion dollars with their following year's profits.[161] Do you remember seeing the headlines about this? Neither do I. There was press coverage, but not mainstream. If you had back pain during those years, you would likely have received this prescription, and with it, the increased risk of death.[162] The main risk is of heart conditions and heart attacks. This is not unique to this one drug, but generally true for all non-steroidal anti-inflammatories (NSAIDs).[163] Diclofenac doubles your risk of dying from a heart attack,[164] and most other "household names" increase the risk by 70% or `thereabouts.[165] And yet, these continue to be the most prescribed painkiller group for ageing clients...precisely those who already have increased heart disease risks. Even conservative estimates show that this drug killed more people than American soldiers died in the 10-year Vietnam War. Was this just "the cost of business?"

OK, so that is if you take them regularly, or for a long time, but I only take them once a year...

It is true that taking anti-inflammatories like NSAIDs briefly is less risky, but there is still risk. They cause gut damage and bleeding, especially when taken for longer periods. This is why acid suppressants (above) are so often prescribed at the same time. But they do damage, even in small quantities. You lose the equivalent of one cup of blood per day from gastrointestinal bleeding after *only three days of use* of NSAIDs.[166] Many people are already aware that we need to "restock" our gut's immune system, the probiotics, after taking antibiotics. But NSAIDs also kill your gut microbiome,[167] also damaging your immune system.[168] Short-term relief (maybe), long-term ill health.

So, not even paracetamol? I guess you are going to tell me those are dangerous too?

Well, if they were to work, perhaps paracetamol may be the "best" option, having a lower risk profile. But alas, the research is very clear—they do not relieve chronic pain[169] when compared to placebo.[170] In fact, paracetamol only has evidence of moderate painkilling effect level for headaches, and nothing else.[171] Not only that, but even a mild overdose of paracetamol—like getting the timings wrong—can provoke permanent liver damage.[172] You start to wonder if it is really worth it.

So all drugs are bad, always?

The simple fact is that ill health is *never* caused by a lack of factory-manufactured chemicals in your body. When you see illness as lost health, things become clearer. There is no drug that is fully safe. Every drug has at least some secondary effects. I am not saying that drugs cannot save lives—they do. But in a healthy society, we would treat these as the last option, not the first, let alone the *only* option. This is the marvellous success of the pharmaceutical industry's marketing division.

Not only through advertising, but also through "campaigning" with medical doctors, they have succeeded in making drugs the first option for the "treatment" of just about everything. And the public has bought the story, paying with both money and their health, as popping a pill promises convenience.

What do I do when my back is in pain or in "crisis?"

The best relief is usually moving your body gently, using ice, heat (if it is a chronic problem), and getting your spine adjusted. Personally, the first thing we do in our family is to get adjusted, so our bodies can heal faster. We use natural anti-inflammatories such as turmeric, breathing techniques such as Tummo or the Wim Hof method, and homoeopathic remedies before we touch any synthetic drugs, such as Ibuprofen or paracetamol. I recently broke my foot, and only needed the above support, recovering quickly and without any painkillers. I am happy to try anything which does not have the risks of drugs. Anything that helps to get past the "intolerable" period while my body can start to heal. I would be happy to take even a placebo, if they sold it in pill form. For me and my family, the risks of taking drugs mostly outweigh the marginal gains.

If you feel that a particular painkiller helps, that is your choice. My point here is not that all drugs are bad. But when any news of drug effectiveness or side effects is published, it has to be taken with a lot more than a pinch of salt. This is an appeal to our sense of individual responsibility. For you, for me, for all of our family members, there is a risk-benefit assessment for any drug we take. Let us choose wisely.

What drug or drugs are currently being prescribed to your family and mine, which we will later realise were ineffective and dangerous? Many years are needed to assess the true risks of any drug. Many drugs that we were told were effective and very safe are neither effective nor very safe. Scepticism is healthy and should be encouraged.

If you are given a "lifelong" medical prescription with no date to review, you have to ask questions. The most common lifelong prescriptions which I see in Spain are painkillers, stomach acid suppressants, sleeping "aids," and anti-cholesterol pills. A real concern is when you receive a prescription and your doctor does not even review all of your current medications to see whether there may be negative interactions. Perhaps in some cases, a drug may be needed long-term. But that should be a very serious, case-by-case decision, never taken lightly. Ask questions. What are the alternatives? How long will I need to take this? What is the plan to come off this? What are the side effects? Can I see the prospectus please? If your doctor doesn't like the questions or cannot or will not answer them, find a new doctor. This is your life and your health. Don't allow anyone to take it lightly.

Should I Get Surgery First?

"We still have to come to terms with the absurd reality that it is significantly safer to board a commercial airplane, a spacecraft, or a nuclear submarine, than to be admitted to hospital."
- Philip Stahel et al.[173]

Blame Portugal

In 1935, a famous Portuguese neurologist called Dr Egas Moniz performed the first frontal lobotomy in Lisbon. He drilled a few holes in a patient's skull, stuck a needle in, and scraped it around. And severed the connections between the frontal lobes of the patient's brain and the rest of their brain.[174] In 1949, he won the Nobel Prize for his work. Meanwhile, 1000 lobotomies were being performed annually in the UK alone.[175] The procedure was used to cut the connection in the brain which was deemed responsible for "excessive self-reflection." The results were profound. Highly stressed, manic people seemed to "relax" and sit still. Peace, at last. But the procedure caused countless ruined lives, mostly in rendering the clients "brain dead," socially retracted, and disconnected. The manic behaviour had gone, but so had the person. In 1967, the last such procedure was performed,[176] but it told the most dramatic story of fundamental misunderstanding of human beings and nature. The story is that "nature got it wrong," and the surgeon could play God and cut it out to put it right. The belief system which wrote that story is still pervasive in medicine, in fact, in society, today.

We used to think that the appendix was a useless vestigial organ. We now know it is a storehouse for healthy bacteria, used to reboot your gut health after diarrhoea. When it is removed, it removes a key part of your immune system.[177] A Finnish study showed that 74% of appendix inflammation could be treated without surgery.[178] Yet in the USA alone, over 300,000 appendix removals are performed each year.[179] Recognising that it is *designed* to be there could change our approach to this organ removal.[180] But where is the incentive in that?

The knee arthroscopy industry is worth 4 billion USD annually in the USA alone[181]. Of these 750,000 procedures, the most common procedure is to cut out the damaged cartilage in the knee. A Norwegian study shows that after two years, there is no clinical difference (in pain and function) between those who did and did not undergo surgery! At least 75% of the surgery could be avoided.[182] Many people give up on conservative care like physiotherapy, saying it is not working.[183] Unfortunately, research shows that when they choose surgery, they are no better off two years later than if they had no surgery at all. So the statement, "I need surgery," is more often a statement of personal belief than a medical fact.

Surgery saves lives, yet also costs lives.

I personally believe that you are beautifully designed. There are no design errors. All your bits are meant to be there. I believe that, with a clear nervous system, good nutrition, and movement, there should be no need for surgeries. And yet surgeries have no doubt saved countless lives.

Heck, I have personally had plenty of surgery. Here are a few examples: I have had my eye muscles cut and shortened twice—both unnecessary and ineffective. I have had my appendix removed. It seemed to be a good idea at the time. I miss it. They once gave me an anaesthetic to surgically remove a stone which I had managed to get wedged inside my wrist—very necessary, and I am very grateful. I had surgery to sew my ear back on after it got pulled off while playing rugby. I am happy, because I prefer having two ears. My last surgery was an inguinal hernia repair to sew up a "hole" in my lower abdomen, caused by lifting beyond my capacity. I am grateful to not have my gut bulging through that hole. There are more, but you get the idea. Some of these were down to my misadventure, the others, in my opinion, were unnecessary. Or put another way, the crisis surgeries were a good idea, the rest were not.

Medical error continues to be the *third leading cause of death* in the United States, approaching half a million deaths per year. That is not a misprint. I invite you to look it up. The World Health Organisation (WHO) says that 2.6 million people are killed by medical errors worldwide every year.[184] About five people die *every minute* due to medical error, while a further 140 million are injured by medical care annually. When you are aware of these statistics, you can take steps to avoid becoming a part of them.

So what parts of your spine do you not need? Which parts are design or manufacturing errors?

I am writing this book in 2022, at the end of a two-year, relentless period of lockdowns and restrictions. The "non-essential" surgeries list has been all but stalled for many months, in many countries.[185] And in one way that stall may have been a blessing in disguise. Because many health services have suddenly realised that a large proportion of those surgeries were not just "non-essential," but also not necessary![186]

This has led to the $100 billion back surgery industry being called "mostly a hoax," with up to 90% of surgeries deemed unnecessary.[187] One commentator noted that spinal fusion ... *"with a price tag averaging $80,000, has a success rate of about 35%. Those most likely to benefit are the young, trim, and athletic, not the typical surgery candidates."*[188] Profitable, but unnecessary. Unnecessary means that they produce no better outcomes than other, far less risky options, such as chiropractic care, physiotherapy, and exercise. This is an ongoing debate.[189] Surgery is a product like any other, and needs a growing market to survive.[190] At what cost? Profitable surgery has become the default outcome in the medical system, simply because it has become normalised.[191]

Each surgery carries different risks, but no surgery, even minor surgery, is without risks. One study showed that over one quarter of spinal surgery results in complications.[192] Another study shows that surgeons believe what they do is safer and more effective than it really is.[193] Perhaps because when things go wrong, the patients look elsewhere. As long as surgery is financially incentivised,[194] what is best for the patient starts to get blurred.[195]

Pushing spinal surgery on patients, while saying that things like chiropractic are dangerous, is like a heroine dealer telling their client that an organic diet is dangerous.

The real miracle is that our bodies can even recover from surgery.

When ligaments, muscles, and bones are cut open, there is only one force which can fix them: the self-healing intelligence which is organised over your nervous system. No surgeon can re-knit a bone. Some say that surgeons must have the greatest insight and belief in God, because they trust that after the surgery, your body can perform a miraculous recovery.

A surgeon colleague once explained that the thing he most feared was "revision surgery." Revisions are when you need to go back and operate on the same thing for a second time. Revisions are never pretty and happen more often with unnecessary surgeries. I wish that all surgeons were like this guy. He coached patients away from unnecessary surgery, meaning that any surgery he did was when there were no other options left. He had an excellent reputation, not just for his effective use of other therapies like physiotherapists and chiropractors, but because he had an extremely low revision rate. Put another way, he only used surgery as the *last* option.

Always get a second opinion from an expert in *non-surgical management*, not from someone who is also invested in operating. Research clearly shows that surgery rates are higher where there is a financial incentive.[196] Like it or not.

If you are considering surgery, first totally explore and patiently exhaust all other options. If you do end up needing surgery, then you will already be healthier, and success is more likely. If you jump into surgery because it sounds easier and faster than persevering through months of rehab or because your "health" insurance pays for it, the risks are high. **Surgery does not add health back into your spine.** It can only cut out, rearrange, or fuse an area of your spine.

There is nothing sadder than seeing a recently operated spine, which is still just as unhealthy as it was before surgery. First, get as healthy as possible.

Chapter 13 Checklist

- "Best practice" means intervening *only as much as necessary.* Unfortunately, this principle is not followed, and countless drugs are dispensed, or spines are cut open, without honouring your body's natural ability to heal.
- No drug is totally safe. Every pill that is ever prescribed or sold over the counter should come with a three-part assessment. 1. What are the risks, relating to you and your history. Not just the published risks, but the *possible* risks, including interactions with any other drugs you may be taking. 2. What are the real benefits, as backed by *independent research, specific to your condition and age group*? 3. Could you attain your goals with an alternative, safer "intervention?"
- Only you can guarantee that this individual assessment is made. Especially referring to long-term prescriptions, YOU are the person who will live with the consequences.
- Surgery is a high-risk, irreversible approach. It may be "the best course" after exhaustion of other possibilities and approached with extreme caution. But surgery cannot make an unhealthy spine healthy again.
- Surgery in an unhealthy spine is less likely to "succeed." First, take time to rebuild good spinal health, then review things. How many surgeries could be spared every year?

Action Points

- Have you or a loved one become "used to" using a drug without researching the risks? Or have a prescription for "whenever you need it," or even "for life?" Review and research this decision. Seek a second opinion. Your health depends on it.
- Know someone who thinks that spinal surgery is "the only option?" Invite them to read this chapter, and then perhaps the whole book. Seek a second opinion, as there may be a safer alternative.

If you are near Marbella, Spain, go to www.duffyquiropractica.com to find out how to work with Dr Duffy.

If elsewhere, go to www.chiroalliance.org or www.chiropractic.org to search for subluxation reducing Chiropractors.

PART IV

Next Steps

"You don't have to see the whole staircase, just take the first step."

— Martin Luther King, Jr.

Chapter 14

Choosing Your Doctor

"A healthy outside starts from the inside."

— Robert Urich

If Health Were a House

We had a leak in our roof the other day. It started dripping water all over the lounge floor. I looked online and called up a company called "Therapist Builders." The man quickly came out and said he would fix the problem right away. He went to his van and got a bucket and a mop. Within half an hour, he was all done. No water on the floor and only a bit of damp on the ceiling. Our problem had gone away, which was great because it was pizza night and we wanted to watch a movie. What a lovely guy.

Unfortunately, the next week we had the same problem, but the same builder was quick to come and fix it again. He was definitely efficient and quite cheap, and he was great to chat to, which always made me feel a lot better. And we only ever needed to see him once as he fixed the problem every time. He just said, "Call me when you need me," and was always available at short notice. Which was good, because we did need him again. Again and again and again until the house started to stink of damp. But the therapist builder had a solution for that too, because the next time he came over, he lit scented candles and put on whale music, and it was a lovely experience.

My wife got irritated and decided that we should get a second opinion. She found a company called "Surgical House Repairs" and made an appointment. Better still, this was covered on our household insurance. Out came the man, very smartly dressed and authoritative. He looked like we should trust him. We told him of our wet floor and the smell of damp in that part of the house. He ordered a full image of that part of the house and concluded that it was rotten. That whole part of my house was rotten. He recommended we remove that room from our house, but my wife was having none of that. I argued that he was clearly the authority on such matters, that we should never argue with him, but she put her foot down. She had put up this lovely new wallpaper which she did not want to ruin with all the dust and works. In fact, the reason she had put up this wallpaper was that the paint on that wall had been flaking and cracking off. He said if I didn't want to have it removed yet, he could offer me a prescription for the problem. "A prescription?" I asked. "My roof is dripping; the floor of my lounge is wet; and it stinks of humidity. How is a prescription going to fix the problem?" He paid no attention to my protests as he wrote the prescription for pegs and hats. One peg on my nose and one hat on my head daily to be taken before watching TV. I could take them for as long as I liked, and when the problem got bad enough, I could come back and have the room cut out of my house. I tried his remedy for a bit, but my nose started to really hurt, and the hat only covered my head, so my pyjamas kept getting wet. But at least it was covered by our insurance, so we didn't have to pay anything.

This was clearly crazy, so I called back the first Therapist Builder. He was much better after all and always available. Always smiling and happy to chat, I always felt better after he came over. But as previously, the problem just kept getting worse.

Finally, my wife had it with me. She suggested I go to see a different specialist about the problem. Her friend had seen this person and it had changed her house completely. "But what else can be done? It clearly needs to be removed," I protested. "You heard the surgical specialist. He was even wearing a white coat and a tie! Not only that, but the insurance will reimburse us fully for cutting our house open!" She didn't listen and booked me in with some weird specialist. She could not even properly describe what they did. On arriving, they asked quite a lot of questions, including questions about other parts of my house. Nothing to do with the problem of the water on the floor and the damp smell. It was none of their bloody business! At first, I suspected they were casing my house for a robbery; I was very sceptical. Then they started poking various different walls, probing them with special measuring devices. They pulled back a cabinet and found mould against one of the walls. I did not like what they were inferring about my house. My house was a beautiful house, and they were busy finding problems which I did not like. They even asked about how I maintained my house! Cheeky.

They then seemed to suggest that the cracking paint on that wall my wife had redecorated could be coming from the same problem. As if this was all not crazy enough, they then made their way onto the roof. They were clearly looking in the wrong place. After a while of pondering and poking, they came down, and before they went to leave, they gave me a bill for their work! At this stage, I was outraged. They had not mopped the floor or lit any scented candles. They had not chatted at length about the traffic or the sports results, and they wanted me to pay them for this? At least the insurance had covered the bill for the other "specialist." My wife was embarrassed so I reluctantly paid the bill.

A few days later, we got the results. This specialist produced a short report and told us that the problem stemmed from the spine on our roof. That the gutters had been blocked, and the dirt and debris had backed up, dislodging some tiles. Now to fix the problem, they would have to lift the tiles from the whole area. In fact, in this respect, the problem could get worse before it would get better. Then they would have to relay a healthy defence system, a damp-proof course. But in order to do that, they had to wait for the area to dry out. Finally, they would replace the damaged tiles and gutters, and then the work would be finished. It would take a lot of time and multiple visits. Oh and if that was not enough, he also said that we would need to clean our gutters regularly, forever. I mean, not just for a while, but he was suggesting that we maintain our house properly, forever. And all at a cost not covered by the insurance.

I was in a state of shock. Surely it would be better to mop the floor and maybe even repaint the mouldy wall, but this was outrageous, not to mention very expensive.

Before he left, in shock, I asked one further question. "What will you do about the wet floor and the mouldy wall?"

"Oh nothing," he replied. "Once the water ingress has stopped, those problems will dry up and stop recurring. I am not a painter-decorator!"

So this charlatan was going to work on the spine of our house without touching the damp or the mould or the damaged paintwork, without any scented candles, and without even chatting about the sports results from the weekend. And charge us for it all. I was angry. Angry not just at his prices and his proposal, but he was suggesting that our beautiful house, which looked lovely from the outside, had long term problems *and* that we needed a strategy to look after it long term.

This passage is absurd. And this is how absurd the normal "treatment" approach is. And how many of us choose our doctor based on how "easy" they make it for us. Based on how "matey" they are. Or worse still, based on whether or not our "illness insurance" covers it. Totally absurd. In this passage, there were three choices. One, to rub it so it feels better, as your house continues to rot. Two, to mask it or cut it out, covered by insurance. Three, to look to the cause and rebuild a healthy, waterproof home. These three choices are made blindly by millions of people every day, unaware that they even have the choice.

Living consciously means making conscious and critical choices not just about ourselves but also who supports our health goals, in other words, the doctors or therapists we use. It may take a little searching before you find more "health-enlightened" help. But that investment will pay great health dividends in the long run.

I understand that finance can be a big pressure when choosing health care. And I have seen poorly paid cleaners afford and benefit from care that wealthy bankers refused simply because the cleaner made their health their genuine priority. We all invest based on our priorities, our authentic values, and I do not judge people on it. Although called *health* insurance, these policies are only concerned with getting you out of the *illness* crisis and no more. But what price would you put on your *health*? What price do you put on your spine? 1000 euros? 2000 euros? How about 80-150 euros per month? For most people, regaining and maintaining spinal health is affordable when you truly value it. If ever you think that getting and staying healthy is expensive, you should compare it to the cost of being ill.

Measure Your Doctor

You may have noticed that I use the word "client" instead of "patient" through this book. Although I have spent most of my career calling my clients "patients," good chiropractors do not really "treat" any illnesses. And so, you are not a chiropractic patient, but a chiropractic client. The difference is that, instead of removing illness from you as a patient, we are restoring health in you as a client. If this is what you want, to add health, then it makes sense to consider how much health your doctor or therapist aims to add.

This makes choosing your doctor a lifestyle choice. Just like choices you make around where you live, what job you have, your sports and past-times, family holidays, or diet, this choice will make a difference to your experience of the world. Focus is not on the years in your life, but the life in your years.

Is the practitioner specialised and totally prepared?

Imagine this scenario. It is the World Cup soccer final. It is a nil-all draw in the last minute of extra time. But suddenly a penalty is granted to your side. For some reason, there is a delay, during which the manager has to choose who will take the penalty. The commentators quickly draw up the season statistics for the two main penalty takers.

One is really famous; he is always in the newspapers. He has scored seven penalties this season. He might have scored more but was busy training in tennis and golf because he was considering a career change. Breaking his conversation with the other players (they are arguing over which pub to go to after the game), he starts trying to convince the manager why he is the best man for the job. The last time he took a penalty, he missed, because he heard someone calling his name from the crowd. "But it'll be okay today," he argues, because today he is wearing his lucky boots. What's more, he recently went on a weekend course on how to massage balls. And today, he is going to massage the ball before taking the kick, because a YouTube video he watched said it could help score goals.

The other one is quieter but has scored 23 goals from penalties this season. He has attended all of the training sessions and usually stays behind to practise his penalty shots. He studies his opponent before every game. He has researched and knows how the goalkeeper is likely to react. He is eyeing up the goal and simply says, "I am ready, Coach."

Which should the manager choose? The fun and chatty, persuasive one or the one who has properly prepared and is focused on nothing other than this moment in time?

Put another way, do you want your balls massaged, or do you want to win the game?

Choosing your doctor based on how nice, chummy, or persuasive they are is like choosing your striker based on how good they look in shorts rather than how many goals they score.

Is adjusting your neck any less important than such a penalty kick? Is relieving pressure from your brain stem less important than which team wins the cup?

It is no secret that I meditate. A lot. No matter how well or badly my day goes, I meditate on the beachfront before I enter the clinic. And if something rustles me, I go out back and centre myself before returning to adjusting. My job, your adjustment, is too important for me to be at anything less than 100% focussed. For me, every adjustment is like a game-deciding penalty kick in a Cup final.

If a chiropractor is doing massage, ultrasound, or taping your joints, perhaps they really wanted to be a physiotherapist. A bit like a professional football player who spends more than half their time playing tennis and golf, they will never be very good at football. When I want physiotherapy, I go to a full-time physiotherapist. When I want nutritional advice, I go to an experienced, well qualified nutritionist. When I want chiropractic, I go to a doctor of chiropractic. The most effective tool available to the chiropractor is the adjustment. The training takes years and then an ongoing commitment to practice and mastery. The delivery of all of that training and expertise takes just a few minutes, to make a life-changing adjustment. Anything else is filler, or pretending to be or do something that is not chiropractic.

I would not want to be adjusted by someone who is not committed to the training and mastery needed to adjust well and neither should you.

Are they efficient and fully present?

I personally get adjusted at least 52 times per year. On average, once per week. For most adjustments, I drive an hour each way, then park, and walk to the practice of a chiropractor who takes two minutes to give me a life-changing adjustment. My overall trip is typically three or four hours. I go there not to have a chat, nor to tell the story of what is hurting, but to get an expert adjustment, where the chiropractor is listening to nothing other than my body. I go such a distance to get adjusted by someone for whom, in that moment, nothing else exists other than my spine and nervous system. Every time I get an adjustment, it is with presence, connection, and loving intention.

Chiropractors who chat lots while they adjust me freak me out. It's like that soccer player taking that penalty kick. While taking the kick, he is chatting to the referee, trying to convince him that the ball is going in. I'd rather someone who is 100% efficient and present. Because freeing up the pressure on my brainstem from a subluxation is more important than any penalty kick.

Which heart surgeon would you rather have: the inexperienced one who spends an hour faffing about or the experienced one who spends just minutes with the same results?

When you choose your doctor, choose someone who works as efficiently as possible and is totally focused, totally present.

Do they have a plan, a vision of you being healthy?

When I hire an architect, I want them to visit my property, not just look at the plans. How on earth could you design a great house without studying the property? I want them to look at it in a way which I cannot, to see problems and opportunities to which I am blind. Then, I want them to listen to my goals and to come up with a vision of how to realise those goals in a healthy, sustainable way. I do not expect them to explain their 5 to 7 years of training or their decades of experience to me. But I do expect them to explain the vision, so I can be onboard in supporting the steps to realise the vision. I know that the build process will not look like the finished product. I assume that as they lay the foundations it may look downright ugly. Most importantly, I know that I can trust in their professionalism and expertise.

When a practitioner does not have a plan, a recommendation, it is a bad sign. A good professional should have a recommendation not just for the next few weeks, but for the next months and years. This should be a minimum expectation from anyone who you expect to improve your spinal health. They should examine you and discuss what vision you have of your future health. How you are today is more important than what happened in the past, so there is no point on dwelling on the past.

Then, they should draw up a plan to rebuild your health in a sustainable way. They need not give you every detail of every technique they will do. They are the expert. They might explain that the process is not the end product. If you want everything to look perfect when the work has just begun, your expectations are unrealistic. They should see you on a schedule, holding the vision of where you are going, not how you are feeling just today, as the guide.

Are they congruent? Do they walk the talk?

If there is something I really value in people, it is authenticity. I can never find it authentic when someone tells their clients to do ABC, when they would never do it themselves.

So here is a great question to ask of your chiropractor or any other therapist: "What do you do yourself to look after your spine and health?" Or put another way, "What would you recommend I do if I were your brother/uncle/mother?" The way I see the world, there should be *no difference* between what your doctor recommends to you and what they recommend to their family. I mentioned this in Chapter 2. Realising this was a big turning point in my career. Your health as a client should be treated with the same respect and vision as if you were a member of my family.

In this same light, if you are seeing a chiropractor who does not get adjusted regularly, something is wrong. In fact, if your chiropractor does not recommend lifelong care to you, something is wrong. If you were taking a totally natural pill, free from any side effects, that improved the quality and quantity of life, would you not want to share it? Would you keep it a secret?

Do they know where to press?

When I take my car to the mechanic, I tell them what I think is going on and then leave it to the professionals. "I hear a noise coming from the right side" is all I need to say. Then I expect them to know where to look, what to rule out, and how to diagnose the condition of the car before using the right tools and parts to fix the problem. I don't stand over their shoulder, telling them that they could use a spanner instead of a screwdriver. I am not a mechanic.

Pain and discomfort are only a fraction of what is going on in your body and nervous system. Trying to understand your body based on pain is a bit like diagnosing an engine problem without leaving the drivers seat. Of course symptoms matter to you, but don't let that get in the way of your progress.

You should not need to give your therapist constant feedback about what hurts or where to press, or "what feels good." If it is all about your pain each visit, then there is probably no plan.

If you say, "It hurts here," and they instantly manipulate in the same place, that is not chiropractic. I freely admit that this is exactly what I did at the start of my career, and I now apologise to the clients I saw at that time for selling them short.

Chiropractors are doctors for a reason and should choose to adjust what is most affecting your nervous system and your health. The subluxation may not even be where you have a pain at that moment. Any well qualified chiropractor should quickly know what needs doing, where, when, and with what technique. If they "listen" to or "read" your body, they will know things about your body which you were unaware of. Your spine is like a "telltale," if only we listen. A good chiropractor will constantly surprise you by knowing a scary amount about your body, without your ushering a single word.

At your new client visit or at review appointments, it is normal to check-in with any symptoms you have, because that is a small part of the very big puzzle—but it should not distract from the goal of positively changing your body. If you need to tell them what to do every visit, something is off. Can they not hear your body?

If you fell down the stairs or had a bereavement in your family, then it is important to share that. But if you are evolving and changing positively, then the best thing to do is to keep quiet and let the doctor concentrate and listen to your body.

A late friend of mine in England was a specialist knee surgeon and Clinical Director of Orthopaedics at the Royal Surrey County Hospital. Neil was a remarkable guy, an ex-rugby player, larger than life. I was invited to the inaugural lecture series at a new private hospital, where he introduced me to other surgical colleagues. He said, "This is Glenn. His job is to put us out of business, but otherwise he's an okay guy!" I received a slightly confused but warm welcome. Neil was right. A good chiropractor's job is to put surgeons out of business. Not by robbing their clients or by treating their injuries but by rebuilding healthy spines and healthy bodies which don't need to see the surgeon.

Do they see your x-rays, your problem, or YOU?

My best friend in the UK is an excellent chiropractor and an extremely caring, kind person. He does a lot of structural work, permanently improving his clients' spines. He has x-ray facilities in his clinic and has seen thousands of spinal x-rays through his career. I was getting changed after he first took x-rays of my spine, and I saw him looking deeply upset. I mean tearful. I kind of suspected he was reading an email on his PC. Perhaps he had received some really bad news. But no, he was looking at my spine x-rays! My spine was so degenerated and twisted that he could hardly believe it. You see, he and I spend a lot of time in the mountains together, running, climbing, and generally acting half our age. And what he was seeing on the x-rays—the severity of the degeneration, particularly in my neck, low back, and hips—was, as he put it "from another person, not someone who can jump from rock to rock as he climbs a riverbed." I have a big history of contact sports, lifting weights, running long distances, doing stupid things, and of course, having accidents. That I have a lot of joint degeneration is no real surprise. But I proactively look after myself now in many ways. I am not my x-rays. I am not my hip degeneration. I am not my herniated discs. I am not my scoliosis. None of these things stop me from having an active, fun life, and I intend to keep it that way.

Bob was the son of a professional golfer, and he himself played off scratch. He was a successful property developer, spending hours in the car between site visits. This took its toll, and he got sciatica from a bulging disc in his low back. One day he came into the practice, doubled over, sweating, with his hands on his knees. It was a Tuesday. Between tears and moans, he told me that on Thursday he was flying to Lanzarote for a golf tournament, returning next week. I told him that it was doubtful. He had clearly severely herniated the disc. I adjusted him and ordered some MRIs to be taken the next day. I adjusted him again on Wednesday, and he was already upright and moving better. I gave him words of caution before he took his flight. I received his MRIs on Thursday morning. In the centre of his low back, the disc had bulged all the way to the back wall of his spinal canal. It looked like there was *no space* for any of the leg nerves to pass through. He had such a large, central disc hernia that it was amazing he could even stand up at all. He had an appointment on the following Tuesday. I prepared his report and prepared myself to give him some bad news. Honestly, I had assumed that he had not even travelled to Lanzarote. But Bob got out of his car and strolled in with a huge smile on his face, carrying a huge trophy! Not only had he gotten there and played the tournament, he had also won. This is one of many "ridiculous" or "miracle" stories which any experienced chiropractor can tell you. His hernia had not stopped him, nor would it stop him. He was much more than an MRI.

Some professionals are obsessed with your tests and images. It is not uncommon for a patient to see a "specialist" who does not physically examine them at all. Maybe they do not even ask what you do for a living or if you do sports. There is an assumption that all humans need the same thing. The fact that you sit all day driving a taxi or stand all day as a pharmacist or cycle 25 hours per week, or run every day to stay sane, or play five rounds of golf per week, is just irrelevant to them. What is relevant to them is what your MRI looks like. From that alone, your "specialist" can tell you what surgery you need.

When you bring your MRIs or x-rays to your first visit, expect a good doctor to put them to one side until they have seen *you*. An x-ray or MRI is just a photo; it is not a story, a movement, a feeling, let alone a whole person. You and your body have more to say than any image.

Others doctors can only see where you say you have pain. If all they offer is surgery, then I can forgive them (though not entirely). But if you have back pain and go to see a chiropractor or physiotherapist, then they should thoroughly examine your neck… your whole spine. You! If they do not, then there is something missing—they have not read the research or do not understand how a human body works.

You are more than an x-ray. You are more than a diagnosis or a problem. A good doctor will see you as a *whole* person, with an amazing potential to heal. A good doctor is determined to find *how* to unleash your healing potential.

Undoctor Your Life

"If you want to go fast, go alone; if you want to go far, go together."
— African proverb

Many of us, myself included, would prefer to never see any health professional for any support. We would prefer to do it all alone. We were made perfect, so eating well and exercising is all we need to do.

But unless you grew up in the forest, eating only what you hunted or collected, without stress or pollutants, this is probably wishful thinking.

We have all suffered moments of excess stress, toxic exposure, poor nutrition, chronic postural trauma, and even accidents. If we want to live well and long, we need to employ strategies to regain our fullest health and stay that way. If you live a life with zero physical, emotional, or chemical stress, in the forest without any digital devices or seats in sight, you probably don't need ongoing support. But for the rest of us, we do.

The undoctored life involves not needing the emergency care system. Not needing medical crisis care. It does not mean living without a health support network.

Think about it. Planet Earth was, and would be, healthy and happy without interference. The human body was, and would be, healthy and happy without interference. But interference, in all those forms we mentioned above, is a *fact of life.* And with interference comes problems. Interference has created endless problems for modern humankind. And we have two ways of dealing with them. Wait for them to become crisis or move proactively to live without that interference, to live the undoctored life.

Chapter 14 Checklist

- Never choose your therapist or doctor based on 1) How "nice" they are, 2) How "well-presented and authoritative" they are, or 3) whether your illness insurance reimburses the care. Consider choosing insurance which at least includes some payment towards natural therapies such as chiropractic.
- Put your health first, finding someone who works on the *cause of problems* and provides a *plan to restore health.*
- Signs of the "best doctor" include:
    1. Being specialist in exactly what you need, rather than a "one-stop shop" for everything.
    2. They see you before any x-rays or images. You are not a set of 2-D images.
    3. They "walk the walk" and *have a plan for building your health* long-term.
    4. Being highly attentive and present, using expertise rather than filling time with idle talk.
    5. They know where to adjust and are not limited to "poking the painful bit."
    6. They are happy for you to see other doctors and understand that only you are responsible for your health.

Action Points

- Use this guide to get the best from your care, no matter what professional you are seeing. If you cannot get the "perfect" doctor, do the best you can.
- Commit to *actively* live an undoctored life—being proactive so that you are unlikely to ever need crisis care.

If you are near Marbella, Spain, go to www.duffyquiropractica.com to find out how to work with Dr Duffy.

If elsewhere, go to www.chiroalliance.org or www.chiropractic.org to search for subluxation reducing Chiropractors.

Chapter 15

The Choice is Hope

"As soon as healing takes place, go out and heal somebody else."

— Maya Angelou

Building Your Health Approach

Putting together your own healthcare support team should be a process. Your team may evolve over the years. You may have more need in different areas as you evolve. But beware of becoming a "health shopper."

Health Shoppers

In healthcare we have clients that we call "health shoppers." Most "health shoppers" don't even know that is what they are. A health shopper tries one thing for a little while before becoming bored and moving on. Effectively, they are shopping for better health. The story is that "nothing has ever worked" or that "the problem kept coming back." It is hard to know really, because they never give anything a long enough chance to really have a big impact. For some, it is truly that their case needs a different approach. But for most, the only thing all of those therapies and doctors have in common is that client who "tried them" for a short while. If the only thing that all of the "failed" therapies have in common is you, then perhaps how *you* are using them is the thing that needs to change.

Health is a marathon, not a sprint. If you are looking for lifelong wellness, you are not choosing a therapist just to poke a problem but for a longer term relationship. As you choose any therapist, commit to giving them time (I would suggest a year) to allow their work to really take effect. If that therapist does not have a vision of how you can be and what you should be doing in a year, perhaps they do not hold real health goals for you.

Shopping for health does not work. Commit to something and give it, and more importantly *give yourself*, a real chance. Don't be a health shopper!

Your doctor should not need you but must at least like you.

No one ever talks about this, but it is important.

When I start to work with a new client, it has to be a two-way relationship. You like me, I like you. You trust me to give the best recommendation and care as if you were a family member, and I trust you to follow your care schedule and make the occasional lifestyle adjustment I ask of you. Brilliant. We can work together. Anything less in a therapist-client relationship is not healthy.

Over the years, I have recommended to many clients that they find someone else, that I am not going to provide care for them. I have no interest in working people who fail to keep their part of the deal, unreasonably make up their own care schedule, or worse still, blame me for the condition of their body or how they feel. This is a real problem in proper health care, and no one talks about it. If you are seeing a therapist or doctor who "needs" you as a client, the relationship will not work. At least not long-term.

Your doctor needs to be happy to be just one player in your team.

In an ideal world, both chiropractic and medical doctors would know what they can and cannot do, what their scope should be. The chiropractic doctor frees your innate ability to heal, rebuilding health, guiding you away from illness, and generating long term wellness. This is wellness healthcare. When there is something suspicious, they know to recommend further testing.

The medical doctor helps with diagnostic testing to rule out pathology, then leaves you alone unless you are in crisis. They recommend that you see someone to rebuild your health instead of using unnecessary interventions. If you are in crisis, they know what tools to use and when to get you out from under illness care and back into healthcare, as quickly and non-invasively as possible.

They are both happy that you are seeing other practitioners as a part of your health team. If your doctor puts down other therapists or suggests you stop seeing them without good reason, look elsewhere.

Beware of doctors who espouse opinions outside their field of knowledge. For example, someone who has never even been to see a chiropractor, but says "that doesn't work" or "that is dangerous" or even "that will damage your herniated disc." I have heard this more times than I care to remember. More accurate re-definitions of those three statements would be: "I have not read the evidence around this or visited a chiropractor myself, but I heard of one case where someone got hurt later the same day after seeing a chiropractor, and not knowing anything about their training or impeccable safety record, I am guessing that it must be dangerous. In any case, surgery is the only thing which can help people with disc hernias." In all of these cases, should the person in question actually visit a chiropractor or learn about chiropractic, their opinion is instantly changed. We have many medical doctors and orthopaedic surgeons as clients. Some of my best friends are orthopaedic surgeons. Some of the biggest promoters of chiropractic are from the medical profession. If your doctor gives opinions on things they know nothing about, do your own research.

When I managed clinics in the UK, I was blessed by having a multidisciplinary team who were real experts, the best you could find. They did things that I do not do. A good nutritionist can identify and deal with a big nutritional deficit. A physiotherapist can help you recover from an ankle sprain, an accident, or teach you exercises to re-strengthen an injured area. For the most part, your doctor or therapist should be happy for you to also see another therapist—this just makes sense. If there is some momentary clash or overlap, then that can be addressed. But you are the manager, and the "team" should work for YOU, not for any one of the players.

My Family's Health Approach

It is pretty obvious that my family's health team is led by a chiropractor. We are blessed, due to my work, to be surrounded with health support. We have a conscious wellness lifestyle, which includes chiropractic care. I go to great lengths to visit my own chiropractor. I could not be healthy and well-adjusted, nor could I serve my clients or family without my regular chiropractic adjustments. All of my family in Spain come to my practice to get adjusted, and my close family in Ireland get adjusted too.

Both my wife and I also have long-term "mentors," for want of a better description. They keep us true to our missions with the goal of being the best parents, companions, and people we can be.

We both meditate regularly, attend or lead personal development courses, and belong to meditation groups. These keep us accountable to do the "practice."

We are both active sports people. In the past, we would stay motivated by events such as races. That is more challenging with family life, so we use a different approach now. My wife gets motivation from attending regular classes; for example, tennis lessons. I am more challenge-driven, doing one or two 100-day challenges per year. For example, it may be to cycle x number of kilometres in 100 days. I also regularly do my own yoga, pilates, and calisthenics routine. Some people self-motivate to stay fit, while others need a little nudge. I certainly need a little nudge!

In case of specific issues, our family also has physiotherapists, a homoeopathic doctor, and trusted medical doctors whom we call upon.

Does that sound like a lot? To be honest, I had to think hard to remember all of the support network which we have. It just *is*. Our health regime has evolved over decades and is now a mature, strong support network. We did not build it overnight. You may already have built a team without being aware of it. It is up to you how much you avail of it, leverage it, to create long term health.

What if I cannot find "the right doctor"?

"Chiropractic is like sex. When it's good, it's wonderful. When it's bad, it's still pretty good." – Reggie Gold

Earlier in my career I dedicated a lot of time to managing practitioners and support staff across multiple locations. As a joint owner of a struggling bicycle brand and competitor in cycle races at the same time,

I was under a huge amount of stress. I was also nowhere near as skilful a chiropractor as I am today. I did not dedicate the time and attention to be the best chiropractor I could be. Yet, I still did a pretty good job with my clients. They still had huge health breakthroughs, despite my limitations. At the time, I was the perfect person for them. I have family members who cannot see a chiropractor of the standard I would wish, but their chiropractor is still good enough to totally alter their health future. My point is that getting adjusted by a properly qualified chiropractor, even if not perfectly aligned with your long-term health goals, is better than not getting adjusted at all!

What if you don't have any support yet? Start by finding a good chiropractor. I can honestly say that making life changes with a clear nervous system is hundreds of times easier than making those same decisions when you feel under pressure. About 90% of our overweight clients lose weight. Do I give them dietary advice? No. But as they feel more connected to their body, more confident in themselves, they make different choices. They start to feel good about themselves again. Health is an inside-out job, and skilful chiropractic can reconnect you with that power inside you. I suggest you start by upgrading your master control system—your spine and nervous system. Use the above guide to find the best person for you. Develop a relationship. And ask them for suggestions as to what else would help.

The Curse of the Educated

"The greatest power that a person possesses is the power to choose"
— J Martin Kohe

When is ignorance bliss?

You have already come a long way. Do you remember when you really, truly knew little or nothing about health? I do. The bliss of ignorance. The folly of youth. How much easier was life then? You could eat what you wanted, behave how you wanted, be as lazy as you wanted, without a care in the world, but while ignorance was bliss, it also carries a hidden price tag. Hidden and sinister.

The graveyard is full of people who never knew the habits they had were killing them. For decades, those were the smokers, though they are literally "dying out." There are the heavy drinkers. And not to forget the fast-food consumers. Or the sugar addicts. Now, if those bad habits had brought happiness and relaxation, positivity and cohesion, enjoyment and fulfilment, only to have that persons life cut unnecessarily short, then that was a life well spent, right? But the sad reality that most smokers die horrible, protracted deaths of suffering. Heavy drinkers spiral into full alcoholism or get caught by liver disease and die a slow and painful death. These pleasure-fixes cannot, and do not, ever, ever bring lasting happiness.

If these bad habits could ever provide happiness, then I would be the first to recommend them. But let us not confuse pleasure with happiness. A deeply sad person can experience temporary pleasure, given the right "drug." But it does not change their sadness, and more often, it will only worsen it.

These short-lived pleasures also rob people of true happiness and fulfilment. For in the moments between those fixes, when the drug has worn off, how does life look? When the tub of Häagen Dazs is empty, the bottle of wine alongside it, how do you sleep?

So the idiom was wrong; ignorance is NOT bliss. Ignorance is confusion and suffering. Ignorance produces victims. Victims of the tobacco industry. Victims of the fast food industry. Victims because they knew no better.

And although many of us identify most easily with nutritional health, this concept extends WAY beyond what we eat. It extends to how we exercise, what postures we choose, our mental hygiene, and our emotional literacy. And of course, it extends to our nervous system clarity. Our connectedness. Connectedness to ourselves. To others. To a whole lot more.

If you have gotten to this part of the book, it cannot be said of you that you are ignorant. You know, for better and worse. Once you know, ignorance is no longer an option. You cannot "un-know" what you know! And that knowledge comes with something hidden up its jumper. It's there. You can see the bulge. You are aware of it, whether or not you want to see it. It is a fact.

More knowledge does not just give you more power. More knowledge gives you the power to choose differently. And making choices creates responsibility. There you have it, the "R" word. Ouch. Does that not feel burdensome? Does that mean that I am to blame for my health? I felt that I was already to blame for enough, without having to add my health to the list.

Let's be super-clear here. No, you are not to blame for your health. Your state of health is made up of a lot of past decisions made by you, your family, your doctors, and the media you were exposed to. But you are *responsible* for your health. Every choice that you have made in your life was to protect you from real or perceived threats and move you towards happiness. If your conditioning and habits meant that you chose to lock the front door and binge watch *Bridget Jones's Diary* for two days while eating nothing other than Doritos, then that was right for you in that moment. In fact, you can even thank yourself for doing that, as that experience has led you to here, now, this point. And here, now, in *this moment*, you get to choose again. And there will be many, many more opportunities to choose again.

So every extra bit of knowledge brings choice. Every choice brings responsibility. This is the curse of the educated. Some wear this better than others. You can choose to celebrate every great decision or feel guilty for every bad one. That too is a big choice!

The Guilt Trip Goes Nowhere

You know how it goes. There are things we love until some new knowledge turns it into a guilt trip.

I love a tuna steak. When my wife got pregnant, it was on the list of BANNED items for her to eat. It was recommended that she get injections, take supplements made in a laboratory, have multiple ultrasound scans, and a whole lot of other things, but eating tuna from the sea was too dangerous? Tuna can have a relatively high level of mercury toxicity. So I still eat tuna steaks, just not so often.

Cycling is my favourite sport. I bend over in a hunched posture, produce as much power as I can through my legs while barely exercising my arms, and generally go for too long and too fast, at least for my fitness level. No one can meaningfully argue that cycling improves your posture. And yet, I plan to cycle regularly, for as long as I can.

So the knowledge does not mean we have to stop what we are doing. Nor does it mean that we have to ruin every dinner party! But it gives us the choice to make more conscious decisions.

If the knowledge you have gleaned through this book has changed your understanding, share it with your friends and family. Give them the opportunity to take back control of their health, to live a pain-free and liberated life.

Connect—Change—Celebrate—Repeat

Two Actions to Change

In my practices in the UK, we had a whole team of professionals who worked together to implement big lifestyle changes. We did exercise plans, shoe orthotics, running analysis, biomechanical bicycle fits, nutritional plans, coaching, physiotherapy, and of course, chiropractic care. You may well have ended up spending hours per day, not to mention money and effort, on our recommendations. And for *some* people, this worked wonders. Yes, we had great results with some people. I could never admit it at the time, but it is very clear to me now—for *most* people, it was too much.

I do not regret how I worked early in my career. I helped a lot of people turn their life around, start a new sport, find a new partner, study a new profession, even to have "miracle" babies. But I would never go back to working like that again. We were trying to change *everything at once.* And for a lot of people, it resulted in overwhelm, dropping out of care, and ultimately, returning to the cycle of ill health and suffering.

I have learned that things can be far simpler, and the results speak for themselves. Reducing subluxation with chiropractic adjustments produces something far greater. It triggers health transformations, miracle healings, personal rebirths, which continue to leave me in awe. Every week, I get to witness *awesome* things.

Once you have made the decision we discussed in chapter 1—the decision to change health direction towards life and for life—you then only need to take two actions.

1. Get Connected

The first action is to clear the connection, to have the power switched on by having a clear nervous system and a good connection to your body, to yourself (the best version of yourself), and therefore to others, including the world around you. That means reducing subluxations in your spine. Nothing more and nothing less. Once you are clearer, everything else becomes far easier. Befriending gravity will make you feel light again. When you no longer fight it, it feels like it releases you.

2. Change One Habit

The second action can be as simple as you wish, and I encourage you to make it very simple. It involves changing *one* habit. Just *one* habit. Once you have changed that, wait until this new habit becomes normal. When that new habit is now normal, consider changing just *one* habit again. Yes. That is it, just *one* at a time.

What habit? Well a good practitioner may guide you to the "low hanging fruit." This is different for each of us. Do you already know what it is? It may be setting an alarm to get up from sitting and move your spine every 25 minutes while at work. Or turning off your mobile phone an hour before bed. It may be stopping to take three deep breaths in gratitude after you get out of your car in the morning. Whatever it is, make it just *one* thing. Then CELEBRATE it!

Connect—Change—Celebrate—Repeat

Our clients in wellness care choose to stay healthy and conscious long-term. They choose to leave the life of reactive, pain-centred, crisis care behind them. They choose to get adjusted to stay connected. And we encourage them to change *only one habit,* every three to six months. And they do. Nothing dramatic. Small things. Then celebrate.

And as each year passes they improve their health maybe only 5%, but consistently so. When you improve 5% every year, year on year, the sky is the limit. Our wellness clients are some of the healthiest people I know.

Connect—Change—Celebrate—Repeat

Be the Change

What next?

The way in which society on the whole "ages" is sad and causes years of pain, suffering, and disability. The statistics are horrible, and to beat the statistics, we each must choose to do something different. That starts with believing in your body's *own* ability to heal. When you know that your body is a healing miracle, the only course is to reduce obstacles to that healing.

Vertebral subluxation gets in the way of your body's ability to heal, and living subluxation-free is like changing the lens on your whole world.

A spine with vertebral subluxations causes your stresses to store in your nervous system. Even when the mortgage has been paid, your mother-in-law has left, or the exam is over, after all the stress has gone, it remains in your nervous system. Your mind and body cannot find real peace or happiness.

Chiropractic can free your spine, your body, your nervous system, and your full and happy self. Connecting your body to your brain, and staying connected means your body wants to be healthy again. Your healthy body makes healthy choices and has lots of fun on the way.

Aligning the four bones of your spine so they all balance in line means you can befriend gravity and stand tall, free, young, and happy about yourself and the world. When you befriend gravity, it releases you, and you feel like a weight has been lifted from your shoulders.

Staying subluxation-free, young, and supple, allows this state of flow in you and your life, meaning that you get to choose what is next, no matter what your age or condition.

The greatest gift to yourself, your friends, and your family is to turn up as the best version of you. The pain-free, flexible, young, and happy YOU. As they see your bright, shining light, they will be inspired to the same. No convincing or brow-beating will be needed. They will ask you how, and then I hope that you can share this book and your experience with them.

If you want to see a better world, less suffering, more connection, more happiness, it starts with you. Be the change that you want to see in the world.

Chapter 15 Checklist

- Even if you previously neglected your health, you are only a few steps from starting the wellness journey.
- Just as you brush your teeth daily, integrate more healthy habits into your lifestyle, always giving an approach plenty time to work for you. Avoid "shopping around."
- If you cannot find "the best doctor," that is okay. Getting adjusted by someone you trust is the most important thing.
- Once you *know* how to take control of your health, all of the responsibility lies with you. With knowledge comes power. Power to choose differently!
- You can never "guilt-trip" yourself into real health or into feeling good about yourself!
- I recommend two steps for everyone: 1) Get adjusted, get reconnected. 2) Change one health habit. Then CELEBRATE, and repeat!
- The greatest impact you can have on your family and friends is not by changing them. ***Be the change***. Show them the way by setting an example.

Action Points

- Regularly celebrate your good health choices. Things grow when you water them with positive attention.
- Next time you notice a "bad health habit" in a friend or family member, rather than telling them what to do, consider how you can lead better by example.
- If this book has inspired you, then p*lease please please* gift it on to someone who could benefit from the same. If one particular part relates to a person you know, hand it to them, telling them to read the relevant chapter.

If you are near Marbella, Spain, go to www.duffyquiropractica.com to find out how to work with Dr Duffy.

If elsewhere, go to www.chiroalliance.org or www.chiropractic.org to search for subluxation reducing Chiropractors.

Thank you and Please...

This book was a real labour of love. Not so much the writing of it... to be honest my fingers struggled to keep up with my mind at some times, as the text came flowing out! But the referencing, diagrams, editing, cross-referencing, modifying, compiling, and all those other "hidden steps" were a steep learning curve. I have a renewed appreciation and respect for all authors... It is no small challenge. But that is all worth it, as long as the book is useful to *you, your friends, and family.* I dearly hope that this book may help you make a better health choice, or support a friend or family member in changing direction in their health decisions.

Please leave a helpful review on Amazon, letting me know what you thought. This book is the start of my writing career. Your review will make a huge difference to how many people I can reach.

I am working on the "sequel" to this book... so your review will be really helpful. Remember to let me know what you want to learn more about!

Review in UK & Ireland

Review in USA

Review in Spain

Are you interested in the other projects that I am working on?

I am currently working on a number of book titles, *and* some online course material. Yes, I like to stay busy!

Upcoming Books:

When I set about writing *Befriend Gravity*, there were just too many ideas, and too much content. This book could easily have ended up over 1000 pages long, so instead I have separated out some other projects, which I am working hard on. Here is a sneak preview of one of the working titles:

Break Free. Journey from stiff and stressed to flexible and happy.

How to upgrade your experience of the world by "biohacking" your own nervous system

Release your inner Zen and learn the practices of those who seem forever young.

Scan the QR code to be the first to find out about these titles, or visit www.glennduffy.com.

Courses:

I already have online courses available to our clients, but plan to extend some of these to be available to non-clients. If you sign up at the link above, I promise to let you know!

Acknowledgements

As I have no formal literary training, the development of this book is the work of many hands. Friends and family have read and re-read the manuscript, hauling it into something which hopefully has legs enough to change many lives.

My friend Vismai Schonfelder originally motivated me to write, and gave much early direction. Lynn McAvenia, with all of her literary prowess and eagle-like insight, whipped me into shape with amazing efficiency. A big thanks goes to the honest and challenging criticism from Jaqui Philips, Stew Bittman, Max Jacobs, my mother Doreene Duffy, and best friend Tim Wood. Tim and Max especially put in a lot of effort, quickly replying to my ongoing edits and changes. Your friendship and contribution are priceless.

Jose Lebron worked hard to illustrate some complex medical topics in simple forms. And Alan Cooper pulled the whole manuscript together into presentable form. Thank you all for your hard work!

Farah and the kids put up with me being unavailable and coming out from a writing binge in any given mood. Whether excited after writing about a client story, or angry after writing about the corruption in the medical system, they coped with it all. Thank you, thank you, thank you!

References

1 Dittman, M, (2004) Protecting children from advertising- APA's council of representatives supports a call for stricter regulations on ads geared to kids, *American Psychological Association, https://www.apa.org/monitor/jun04/protecting*

2 Guttmann, A. (2021, June 5). U.S. pharma TV ad spend 2020. Statista. https://www.statista.com/statistics/953104/pharma-industry-tv-ad-spend-us/

3 Passarino, G., De Rango, F., & Montesanto, A. (2016). Human longevity: Genetics or Lifestyle? It takes two to tango. *Immunity & Ageing, 13*(1), 1-6.

4 Dugdale, D.C. (2021 July 9). *Cell Division.* National Library of Medicine. https://medlineplus.gov/ency/anatomyvideos/000025.htm.

5 Ackerman, S. (1992). Discovering the brain. National Academies Press (US)

6 *What cells in the human body live the longest?* (2013). Science Focus. https://www.sciencefocus.com/the-human-body/what-cells-in-the-human-body-live-the-longest/

7 *Scientists learn what makes nerve cells so strong* (April 15, 2013). Science Daily. https://www.sciencedaily.com/releases/2013/04/130415172021.htm

8 Taylor, H. H., Holt, K., & Murphy, B. (2010). Exploring the neuromodulatory effects of the vertebral subluxation and chiropractic care. *Chiropractic Journal of Australia, 40*(1), 37-44..

9 Haavik, H., Kumari, N., Holt, K., Niazi, I. K., Amjad, I., Pujari, A. N., Türker, K. S., & Murphy, B. (2021). The contemporary model of vertebral column joint dysfunction and impact of high-velocity, low-amplitude controlled vertebral thrusts on neuromuscular function. European Journal of Applied Physiology, 121(10), 2675-2720.

10 Seaman, D. R. (2016). Toxins, toxicity, and endotoxemia: a historical and clinical perspective for chiropractors. *Journal of Chiropractic Humanities, 23*(1), 68-76.

11 Gatterman, M. I., & Hansen, D. T. (1994). Development of chiropractic nomenclature through consensus. *Journal of Manipulative and Physiological Therapeutics, 17*(5), 302-309.

12 Seaman, D. R. (2016). Toxins, toxicity, and endotoxemia: a historical and clinical perspective for chiropractors. *Journal of Chiropractic Humanities, 23*(1), 68-76.

13 Holtzman, S., & Beggs, R. T. (2013). Yoga for chronic low back pain: a meta-analysis of randomized controlled trials. *Pain research & management, 18*(5), 267–272. https://doi.org/10.1155/2013/105919

14 Swain, T. A., & McGwin, G. (2016). Yoga-Related Injuries in the United States From 2001 to 2014. Orthopaedic Journal of Sports Medicine. https://doi.org/10.1177/2325967116671703

15 Holton, M. K., & Barry, A. E. (2014). Do side-effects/injuries from yoga practice result in discontinued use? Results of a national survey. *International journal of yoga, 7*(2), 152–154. https://doi.org/10.4103/0973-6131.133900

16 Campo, M, Shiyko, M.P, Kean, M. B., Roberts, L, & Pappas, E (2018) Musculoskeletal pain associated with recreational yoga participation: A prospective cohort study. with 1-year follow-up, *Journal of Bodywork and Movement Therapies, 22(2)*

17 Cramer, H., Quinker, D., Schumann, D. et al. (2019) Adverse effects of yoga: a national cross-sectional survey. *BMC Complement Altern Med 19*, 190 . https://doi.org/10.1186/s12906-019-2612-7

18 Harrison, D. E. , & Oakley, P. A. (2022). An Introduction to Chiropractic BioPhysics® (CBP®) Technique: A Full Spine Rehabilitation Approach to Reducing Spine Deformities. In M. Bernardo-Filho, R. Taiar, D. C. de Sá-Caputo, & A. Seixas (Eds.), Complementary Therapies. IntechOpen. https://doi.org/10.5772/intechopen.102686

19 White, A. A. & Panjabi, M. M. (1990). *Clinical biomechanics of the spine.* (2nd Edition). Lippincott-Raven publishers, Philadelphia, New York.

20 Harrison, D. E., Betz, J. W., Harrison, D. D., Hass, J. W., Oakley, P. A. & Meyer, D.W. (2007). *CBP®* structural rehabilitation of the lumbar spine. Harrison, CBP Seminars, Inc.

21 Plaugher, G. (1993). *Text book of clinical chiropractic: A specific biomechanical approach*. Williams and Wilkins, a Waverly Company.

22 Alexandru, D., & So, W. (2012). Evaluation and management of vertebral compression fractures. *The Permanente Journal, 16*(4), 46.

23 White, A. A. & Panjabi, M. M. (1990). *Clinical biomechanics of the spine.* (2nd Edition). Lippincott-Raven publishers, Philadelphia, New York.

24 Keller, T. S., Colloca, C. J., Harrison, D. E., Harrison, D. D., & Janik, T. J. (2005). Influence of spine morphology on intervertebral disc loads and stresses in asymptomatic adults: implications for the ideal spine. *The Spine Journal, 5*(3), 297-309.

25 Harrison, D. E., Colloca, C. J., Harrison, D. D., Janik, T. J., Haas, J. W., & Keller, T. S. (2005). Anterior thoracic posture increases thoracolumbar disc loading. *European Spine Journal, 14*(3), 234-242.

26 *Health and cervical lordosis* (2008) Practicing Chiropractors' Committee on Radiology Protocols. http://www.pccrp.org/ P181

27 Bakris G, Dickholtz M Sr, Meyer PM, Kravitz G, Avery E, Miller M, Brown J, Woodfield C, Bell B. (2007) Atlas vertebra realignment and achievement of arterial pressure goal in hypertensive patients: a pilot study. *J Hum Hypertens. 21*(5):347-52. doi: 10.1038/sj.jhh.1002133.

28 Lin, S. Y., Hsu, W. H., Lin, C. C., Lin, C. L., Tsai, C. H., Lin, C. H., Chen, D. C., Lin, T. C., Hsu, C. Y., & Kao, C. H. (2018). Association of Arrhythmia in Patients with Cervical Spondylosis: A Nationwide Population-Based Cohort Study. *Journal of clinical medicine, 7*(9), 236. https://doi.org/10.3390/jcm7090236

29 Harrison, D. E., Harrison, D. D., & Hass, J. W. (2002). *CBP®* structural rehabilitation of the cervical spine. Harrison, CBP Seminars, Inc.

30 *Mouth of God.* (n.d.). Michael Hane. https://www.michaelhane.org/mouth-of-god-page..

31 Parisio-Ferraro, A.L. & Alcantara, Joel. (2013). The chiropractic care of an infant female with a medical diagnosis of strabismus: A case report. *Chiropractic Journal of Australia.* 43. 15-18.

32 *Headache disorders*, World Health Organisation Fact Sheets (April 2016). https://www.who.int/news-room/fact-sheets/detail/headache-disorders

33 Harrison, D. E., Harrison, D. D., Troyanovich, S. J., & Harmon, S. (2000). A normal spinal position: it's time to accept the evidence. *Journal of Manipulative and Physiological Therapeutics, 23*(9), 623-644.

34 Moustafa, I. M., Diab, A., Shousha, T., & Harrison, D. E. (2021). Does restoration of sagittal cervical alignment improve cervicogenic headache pain and disability: A 2-year pilot randomized controlled trial. *Heliyon, 7*(3), e06467.

35 Gerstin G, Oakley PA, Harrison DE. (2020) The treatment of dizziness by improving cervical lordosis: a Chiropractic BioPhysics case report. *Journal of Physical Therapy Science. 32*(12):864-868. DOI: 10.1589/jpts.32.864

36 Moustafa IM, Diab AA, Harrison DE. (2017) The effect of normalizing the sagittal cervical configuration on dizziness, neck pain, and cervicocephalic kinesthetic sensibility: a 1-year randomized controlled study. *Eur J Phys Rehabil Med. 53*(1):57-71. doi: 10.23736/S1973-9087.16.04179-4

37 Miller, D. (2014 March 6). *Carpal tunnel syndrome: It's time to explode the myth.* Insurance thought leadership. https://www.insurancethoughtleadership.com/life-health/carpal-tunnel-syndrome-its-time-explode-myth

38 *Did you get a carpal tunnel misdiagnosis?* (2020, April 28). CarpalRx. https://www.carpalrx.com/post/carpal-tunnel-misdiagnosis.

39 Kaehr, R. E. (2010). What's a Librarian to Do? Literature Review: The Carpal Tunnel Syndrome. *The Christian Librarian, 53*(2), 66-76.

40 Newington, L., Ntani, G., Warwick, D., Adams, J., & Walker-Bone, K. (2021). Sickness absence after carpal tunnel release: a multicentre prospective cohort study. *BMJ open, 11*(2), e041656.

41 *Evaluating concomitant lateral epicondylitis and cervical radiculopathy,* (March 7, 2010) The Journal of Musculoskeletal Medicine Vol 27 No 3, Volume 27, Issue 3

42 Cleland, J.A, Whitman, J.M, Fritz, J.M (2004) Effectiveness of Manual Physical Therapy to the Cervical Spine in the Management of Lateral Epicondylalgia: A Retrospective Analysis. *Journal of Sports and Orthopaedic Physical Therapy, 34*(11)

43 Bokshan, M. L, De Passe, J. M, et al (2016) An Evidence-Based Approach to Differentiating the Cause of Shoulder and Cervical Spine Pain. *The American Journal of Medicine 129*, 913-918

44 Gao, K D, Zhang, J, et al. (2019) Correlation between cervical lordosis and cervical disc herniation in young patients with neck pain. *Medicine 98*(31)

45 Whedon, J. M., & Glassey, D. (2009). Cerebrospinal fluid stasis and its clinical significance. Alternative therapies in health and medicine, 15(3), 54–60.

46 Katz, E. A., Katz, S. B., Fedorchuk, C. A., Lightstone, D. F., Banach, C. J., & Podoll, J. D. (2019). Increase in cerebral blood flow indicated by increased cerebral arterial area and pixel intensity on brain magnetic resonance angiogram following correction of cervical lordosis. *Brain circulation, 5*(1), 19-26.

47 Eide, P.K., Valnes, L.M., Lindstrøm, E.K. *et al. (2021)* Direction and magnitude of cerebrospinal fluid flow vary substantially across central nervous system diseases. Fluids Barriers CNS ***18,*** 16. https://doi.org/10.1186/s12987-021-00251-6

48 de Leon, M. J., Li, Y., Okamura, N., Tsui, W. H., Saint-Louis, L. A., Glodzik, L., Osorio, R. S., Fortea, J., Butler, T., Pirraglia, E., Fossati, S., Kim, H.

J., Carare, R. O., Nedergaard, M., Benveniste, H., & Rusinek, H. (2017). Cerebrospinal Fluid Clearance in Alzheimer Disease Measured with Dynamic PET. *Journal of nuclear medicine : official publication, Society of Nuclear Medicine, 58*(9), 1471–1476. https://doi.org/10.2967/jnumed.116.187211

49 Li, Y., Rusinek, H., Butler, T. *et al.* (2022) Decreased CSF clearance and increased brain amyloid in Alzheimer's disease. Fluids Barriers CNS **19,** 21 https://doi.org/10.1186/s12987-022-00318-y

50 Han F, Chen J, Belkin-Rosen A, Gu Y, Luo L, Buxton OM, et al. (2021) Reduced coupling between cerebrospinal fluid flow and global brain activity is linked to Alzheimer disease–related pathology. *PLoS Biol 19*(6). https://doi.org/10.1371/journal.pbio.3001233

51 Moustafa, Ibrahim M. et al. (2016) Addition of a Sagittal Cervical Posture Corrective Orthotic Device to a Multimodal Rehabilitation Program Improves Short- and Long-Term Outcomes in Patients With Discogenic Cervical Radiculopathy. *Archives of Physical Medicine and Rehabilitation 97*(12) 2034 - 2044

52 Moustafa, I. M., & Diab, A. A. (2014). Multimodal treatment program comparing 2 different traction approaches for patients with discogenic cervical radiculopathy: a randomized controlled trial. *Journal of chiropractic medicine, 13*(3), 157–167. https://doi.org/10.1016/j.jcm.2014.07.003

53 Moustafa, I.M., Diab, A.A., Hegazy, F. *et al.* Demonstration of central conduction time and neuroplastic changes after cervical lordosis rehabilitation in asymptomatic subjects: a randomized, placebo-controlled trial. *Sci Rep* **11,** 15379 (2021). https://doi.org/10.1038/s41598-021-94548-z

54 Fortner, M. O., Oakley, P. A., & Harrison, D. E. (2018). Non-surgical improvement of cervical lordosis is possible in advanced spinal osteoarthritis: a CBP® case report. Journal of physical therapy science, 30(1), 108–112. https://doi.org/10.1589/jpts.30.108

55 Wilkes, C., Kydd, R., Sagar, M., & Broadbent, E. (2017). Upright posture improves affect and fatigue in people with depressive symptoms. *Journal of behavior therapy and experimental psychiatry, 54*, 143-149.

56 de Zambotti, M., Goldstone, A., Colrain, I. M., & Baker, F. C. (2018). Insomnia disorder in adolescence: diagnosis, impact, and treatment. *Sleep medicine reviews, 39*, 12-24.

57 Philipp, J., Zeiler, M., Wöber, C., Wagner, G., Karwautz, A. F., Steiner, T. J., & Wöber-Bingöl, Ç. (2019). Prevalence and burden of headache in children and adolescents in Austria–a nationwide study in a representative sample of pupils aged 10–18 years. *The Journal of Headache and Pain*, *20*(1), 1-12.

58 *CBP®* Protocol of care. (n.d.). Chiropractic BioPhysics. https://idealspine.com/cbp-protocol-of-care/

59 *Thoracic disc syndrome - Physiopedia*. (n.d.). Physiopedia. https://www.physio-pedia.com/Thoracic_Disc_Syndrome

60 Harrison, D. D., & Harrison, S. O. (2002). *CBP®* Technique. CBP seminars, Inc.

61 Harrison, D. E., Colloca, C. J., Harrison, D. D., Janik, T. J., Haas, J. W., & Keller, T. S. (2005). Anterior thoracic posture increases thoracolumbar disc loading. *European Spine Journal*, *14*(3), 234-242.

62 Kaminskyj, A., Frazier, M., Johnstone, K., & Gleberzon, B. J. (2010). Chiropractic care for patients with asthma: a systematic review of the literature. *The Journal of the Canadian Chiropractic Association*, *54*(1), 24.

63 Sardar, Z. M., Ames, R. J., & Lenke, L. (2019). Scheuermann's Kyphosis: Diagnosis, Management, and Selecting Fusion Levels. *The Journal of the American Academy of Orthopaedic Surgeons*, *27*(10), e462–e472. https://doi.org/10.5435/JAAOS-D-17-00748

64 Lam JC, Mukhdomi T. Kyphosis. [Updated 2022 Jan 15]. In: StatPearls [Internet]. Treasure Island (FL): StatPearls Publishing; 2022 Jan-. Available from: https://www.ncbi.nlm.nih.gov/books/NBK558945/

65 *Forward Head Posture – It's Effects On The Young And The Aging* (31/10/2017) Australian Spinal Research Foundation https://spinalresearch.com.au/forward-head-posture-effects-young-aging/

66 Kado, D. M., Huang, M. H., Karlamangla, A. S., Barrett-Connor, E., & Greendale, G. A. (2004). Hyperkyphotic posture predicts mortality in older community-dwelling men and women: a prospective study. *Journal of the American Geriatrics Society*, *52*(10), 1662-1667.

67 Imagama, S., Hasegawa, Y., Wakao, N., Hirano, K., Hamajima, N., & Ishiguro, N. (2012). Influence of lumbar kyphosis and back muscle strength on the symptoms of gastroesophageal reflux disease in middle-aged and elderly people. *European Spine Journal*, *21*(11), 2149-2157.,

68 Koelé, M. C., Lems, W. F., & Willems, H. C. (2020). The clinical relevance of hyperkyphosis: A narrative review. *Frontiers in endocrinology*, *11*, 5.

69 Pyykko, I., Jantti, P., & Aalto, H. (1990). Postural control in elderly subjects. Age and ageing, 19(3), 215-221.

70 Lorbergs, A. L., O'Connor, G. T., Zhou, Y., Travison, T. G., Kiel, D. P., Cupples, L. A., Rosen, H., & Samelson, E. J. (2017). Severity of Kyphosis and Decline in Lung Function: The Framingham Study. *The journals of gerontology. Series A, Biological sciences and medical sciences*, *72*(5), 689–694. https://doi.org/10.1093/gerona/glw124

71 Wilkes, C., Kydd, R., Sagar, M., & Broadbent, E. (2017). Upright posture improves affect and fatigue in people with depressive symptoms. *Journal of behavior therapy and experimental psychiatry*, *54*, 143-149.

72 Nishiwaki, Y., Kikuchi, Y., Araya, K., Okamoto, M., Miyaguchi, S., Yoshioka, N., Shimada, N., Nakashima, H., Uemura, T., Omae, K., & Takebayashi, T. (2007). Association of thoracic kyphosis with subjective poor health, functional activity and blood pressure in the community-dwelling elderly. *Environmental health and preventive medicine*, *12*(6), 246-250.

73 Preidt, R. (2013, April 19). *Older Adults' Posture May Predict Future Disability.* Consumer Health News. https://consumer.healthday.com/senior-citizen-information-31/misc-aging-news-10/older-adults-posture-may-predict-future-disability-675263.html.

74 Lorbergs, A. L., O'Connor, G. T., Zhou, Y., Travison, T. G., Kiel, D. P., Cupples, L. A., Rosen, H., & Samelson, E. J. (2017). Severity of Kyphosis and Decline in Lung Function: The Framingham Study. *The journals of gerontology. Series A, Biological sciences and medical sciences*, *72*(5), 689–694. https://doi.org/10.1093/gerona/glw124.

75 Lowery, E. M., Brubaker, A. L., Kuhlmann, E., & Kovacs, E. J. (2013). The aging lung. *Clinical interventions in aging*, *8*, 1489–1496. https://doi.org/10.2147/CIA.S51152

76 Nishimura, H., Ikegami, S., Uehara, M., Takahashi, J., Tokida, R., & Kato, H. (2022). Detection of cognitive decline by spinal posture assessment in health exams of the general older population. *Scientific Reports*, *12*(1), 1-8.

77 McGill S. M. (1998). Low back exercises: evidence for improving exercise regimens. *Physical therapy*, *78*(7), 754–765. https://doi.org/10.1093/ptj/78.7.754

78 Harrison, D. E., Colloca, C. J., Harrison, D. D., Janik, T. J., Haas, J. W., & Keller, T. S. (2005). Anterior thoracic posture increases thoracolumbar disc loading. *European Spine Journal*, *14*(3), 234-242.

79 Keller, T. S., Colloca, C. J., Harrison, D. E., Harrison, D. D., & Janik, T. J. (2005). Morphological and biomechanical modeling of the thoracoc-lumbar spine: implications for the ideal spine. *Spine Journal, 5*, 297-309.

80 Hides, J. A., Richardson, C. A., & Jull, G. A. (1996). Multifidus muscle recovery is not automatic after resolution of acute, first-episode low back pain. *Spine, 21*(23), 2763-2769..

81 Machado, G., Lin, C. & Harris, L. (2018, February 19). *Needless treatments: Spinal fusion surgery for lower back pain is costly and there's little evidence it'll work*. The Conversation. https://theconversation.com/needless-treatments-spinal-fusion-surgery-for-lower-back-pain-is-costly-and-theres-little-evidence-itll-work-91829.

82 *Low back pain and sciatica in over 16s: assessment and management NICE guideline* (30 November 2016) National Institute for Health and Care Excellence www.nice.org.uk/guidance/ng59

83 Consumer Reports Health Ratings Center. Back-Pain Treatments. (July 2011) ConsumerReports.org

84 Kiapour, A., Joukar, A., Elgafy, H., Erbulut, D. U., Agarwal, A. K., & Goel, V. K. (2020). Biomechanics of the sacroiliac joint: anatomy, function, biomechanics, sexual dimorphism, and causes of pain. *International journal of spine surgery, 14*(s1), S3-S13.

85 Whedon, J. M., & Glassey, D. (2009). Cerebrospinal fluid stasis and its clinical significance. Alternative therapies in health and medicine, 15(3), 54–60.

86 Capozzolo, K. (2022, January 20). *Tiger woods reveals his secrets about recovery and returning to Golf - EIN presswire*. EIN News; EIN Presswire. https://www.einnews.com/pr_news/561107963/tiger-woods-reveals-his-secrets-about-recovery-and-returning-to-golf

87 Turner, T. (2018, April 17). *JAMA: Unnecessary joint replacements cost americans $8.3 billion*. (n.d.). Drugwatch.Com. https://www.drugwatch.com/news/2018/03/19/jama-unnecessary-joint-replacements-cost-americans-8-3-billion/

88 New study projects the future volume of primary and revision TJAs in the US. (2018, March 6) International congress for joint reconstruction. https://icjr.net/articles/new-study-projects-the-future-volume-of-primary-and-revision-tjas-in-the-us

89 *Infertility* (n.d.). National Health Service, Uk. https://www.nhs.uk/conditions/infertility/

90 *Overdue babies.* (n.d.). Better health channel. https://www.betterhealth.vic.gov.au/health/servicesandsupport/overdue-babies

91 Leach, J (2021) *Anomaly scan 20 weeks*, BabyCentre, https://www.babycentre.co.uk/a557390/anomaly-scan-20-weeks

92 Drukker, L., Bradburn, E., Rodriguez, G. B., Roberts, N. W., Impey, L., & Papageorghiou, A. T. (2021). How often do we identify fetal abnormalities during routine third-trimester ultrasound? A systematic review and meta-analysis. *BJOG: An International Journal of Obstetrics & Gynaecology*, *128*(2), 259-269.

93 Froehlich, R. J., Sandoval, G., Bailit, J. L., Grobman, W. A., Reddy, U. M., Wapner, R. J., ... & Human development (NICHD) maternal-fetal medicine units (MFMU) network. (2016). Association of recorded estimated fetal weight and cesarean delivery in attempted vaginal delivery at term. *Obstetrics and gynecology*, *128*(3), 487.

94 Dip, S.M. (2022, May 31). *Giving birth to a big baby - 5 Reasons why it doesn't mean it will hurt more.* BellyBelly; https://www.facebook.com/BellyBellyBaby. https://www.bellybelly.com.au/birth/giving-birth-to-a-big-baby-doesnt-hurt-more/

95 *Big babies don't always need a C-section delivery*. (2017 April 7). CHPSO. https://www.chpso.org/post/big-babies-dont-always-need-c-section-delivery

96 Dekker, R. (2019, August 21). *What is the evidence for induction or C-section for a big baby?* Evidence based birth®. https://evidencebasedbirth.com/evidence-for-induction-or-c-section-for-big-baby/

97 Kiapour, A., Joukar, A., Elgafy, H., Erbulut, D. U., Agarwal, A. K., & Goel, V. K. (2020). Biomechanics of the sacroiliac joint: anatomy, function, biomechanics, sexual dimorphism, and causes of pain. *International journal of spine surgery*, *14*(s1), S3-S13.:

98 Sawyers, N. (2019, October 25). *Chiropractic care during pregnancy: The Webster Technique*. Northern star doula. https://northernstardoula.com/blog/chiropractic-care-during-pregnancy

99 Craig, M. E., Sudanagunta, S., & Billow, M. (2018). Anatomy, abdomen and pelvis, broad ligaments. StatPearls Publishing, Treasure Island (FL).

100 Borggren, C. L. (2007). Pregnancy and chiropractic: a narrative review of the literature. *Journal of Chiropractic Medicine*, *6*(2), 70-74.

101 Fallon, J. M. (1994). *Textbook on chiropractic & pregnancy*. International

Chiropractors Association. Arlington, VA: International chiropractic association, 52, 109.

102 Marcin, A. (2022, January 31). *Webster technique for breech babies: Benefits and risks*. Healthline. https://www.healthline.com/health/pregnancy/webster-technique#success-rates

103 Lenz, M., Oikonomidis, S., Harland, A., Fürnstahl, P., Farshad, M., Bredow, J., Eysel, P. & Scheyerer, M. J. (2021). Scoliosis and Prognosis—a systematic review regarding patient-specific and radiological predictive factors for curve progression. *European Spine Journal, 30*(7), 1813-1822.

104 Marty-Poumarat, C., Scattin, L., Marpeau, M., de Loubresse, C. G., & Aegerter, P. (2007). Natural history of progressive adult scoliosis. *Spine, 32*(11), 1227-1234.

105 Negrini, A., Negrini, M. G., Donzelli, S., Romano, M., Zaina, F., & Negrini, S. (2015). Scoliosis-Specific exercises can reduce the progression of severe curves in adult idiopathic scoliosis: a long-term cohort study. *Scoliosis, 10*(1), 1-7.

106 Janicki, J. A., & Alman, B. (2007). Scoliosis: Review of diagnosis and treatment. *Paediatrics & child health, 12*(9), 771-776.

107 Bjerkreim, I., & Hassan, I. (1982). Progression in untreated idiopathic scoliosis after end of growth. *Acta Orthopaedica Scandinavica, 53*(6), 897-900.

108 Yochum, T. R. & Row, L. J. (1995). *Essential of skeletal radiology* (2nd Edition). Williams and Wilkins, a Waverly Company.."

109 Kadowaki, E., Tamaki, J., Iki, M., Sato, Y., Chiba, Y., Kajita, E., ... & Yoneshima, H. (2010). Prevalent vertebral deformity independently increases incident vertebral fracture risk in middle-aged and elderly Japanese women: the Japanese Population-based Osteoporosis (JPOS) Cohort Study. *Osteoporosis international, 21*(9), 1513-1522.

110 What are brainwaves? (n.d.). Brainworks. Retrieved from http://www.brainworksneurotherapy.com/what-are-brainwaves.

111 Porjesz, B, Begleiter, H (2004) Alcoholism and Human Electrophysiology, *National Institute on Alcohol Abuse and Alcoholism,* https://pubs.niaaa.nih.gov/publications/arh27-2/153-160.htm

112 Huang, J., Ulke, C., & Strauss, M. (2019). Brain arousal regulation and depressive symptomatology in adults with attention-deficit/hyperactivity disorder (ADHD). *BMC neuroscience, 20*(1), 43. https://doi.org/10.1186/s12868-019-0526-4

113 *Tourettes Syndrome/Tic Disorder* (nd.) Neurofeedback Alliance - The science of Neurofeedback, https://neurofeedbackalliance.org/tourettes-syndrometic-disorder/

114 Sujith Vijayan, S, Klerman, E.B, Adler, G.K, Kopell, N.J (2015) Thalamic mechanisms underlying alpha-delta sleep with implications for fibromyalgia, *Journal of Neurophysiology* 114:3, 1923-1930 doi=10.1152%2Fjn.00280.2015

115 Barwell, R., Long A., Byers, A. & Schisler, C. (2009). A four case study. *The Chiropractic Journal,* 1-6..

116 Kiani, A. K., Maltese, P. E., Dautaj, A., Paolacci, S., Kurti, D., Picotti, P. M., & Bertelli, M. (2020). Neurobiological basis of chiropractic manipulative treatment of the spine in the care of major depression. Acta bio-medica : Atenei Parmensis, 91(13-S), e2020006. https://doi.org/10.23750/abm.v91i13-S.10536

117 Labuschagne, L. R. (2017). *A Case Series Describing the Medium Term Effect of Cervical Manipulation on qEEG.* M.Sc. Thesis, University of Johannesburg (South Africa).

118 Navid, M. S., Lelic, D., Niazi, I. K., Holt, K., Mark, E. B., Drewes, A. M., & Haavik, H. (2019). The effects of chiropractic spinal manipulation on central processing of tonic pain-a pilot study using standardized low-resolution brain electromagnetic tomography (sLORETA). *Scientific Reports*, *9*(1), 1-12.

119 Schafer, R. C., & Faye, L. J. (1989). Introduction to the dynamic chiropractic paradigm. Motion palpation. 2nd edn. *The Motion Palpation Institute & ACA Press. www. chiro. org/ACAPress/Introduction_to_Dynamic_Chiropractic. html.*

120 Biedermann, H. (1992). Kinematic imbalances due to suboccipital strain in newborns. *Journal Manual Medicine*, *6*, 151-156.

121 Langkau, J., & Miller, J. (2012). An investigation of musculoskeletal dysfunction in infants includes a case series of KISS diagnosed children. Journal of Clinical Chiropractic Pediatrics, 13, 958-67.

122 Fysh, P. (1994). *Suboccipital strain in newborns.* Dynamic chiropractic, 12(12). https://www.dynamicchiropractic.com/mpacms/dc/article.php?id=41306

123 Scott, R. M., Kaufman, C. L., & Dengel, D. R. (2007). The impact of chiropractic adjustments on intracranial blood flow: A pilot study. *Journal of Vertebral Subluxation Research*, 1-8.

124 Sperry, R.W (1952) Neurology and the Mind-brain problem, *American Scientist 40*(2). https://www.jstor.org/stable/27826433

125 Seladi-Schulman, J. (2020, February 11). *What is the cerebellum and what does it do?* Healthline; Healthline Media. https://www.healthline.com/health/cerebellum

126 Ackerman S. (1992) Discovering the Brain. Washington (DC): National Academies Press (US) Foreword. Available from: https://www.ncbi.nlm.nih.gov/books/NBK234155/

127 *Yes, The Human Brain is the Most Complex thing in the Universe* (n.d, MARCH 17, 2022) Mindmatters News. https://mindmatters.ai/2022/03/yes-the-human-brain-is-the-most-complex-thing-in-the-universe/

128 Vernon, H. T., Dhami, M. S., Howley, T. P., & Annett, R. (1986). Spinal manipulation and beta-endorphin: a controlled study of the effect of a spinal manipulation on plasma beta-endorphin levels in normal males. *Journal of manipulative and physiological therapeutics*, *9*(2), 115–123.

129 Lohman, E. B., Pacheco, G. R., Gharibvand, L., Daher, N., Devore, K., Bains, G., AlAmeri, M., & Berk, L. S. (2019). The immediate effects of cervical spine manipulation on pain and biochemical markers in females with acute non-specific mechanical neck pain: a randomized clinical trial. The Journal of manual & manipulative therapy, 27(4), 186–196. https://doi.org/10.1080/10669817.2018.1553696

130 *ICA policy statement on spinal adjustment and spinal manipulation* (2017). https://www.chiropractic.org/wp-content/uploads/2021/05/The-ICA-Policy-Statement-on-Spinal-Adjustment-and-Spinal-Manipulation.pdf

131 Sarnat, R. L., Winterstein, J., & Cambron, J. A. (2007). Clinical utilization and cost outcomes from an integrative medicine independent physician association: an additional 3-year update. Journal of manipulative and physiological therapeutics, 30(4), 263–269. https://doi.org/10.1016/j.jmpt.2007.03.004

132 Cuddy, A.J.C., Wilmuth, C.A., Carney, D.R. (2012) "The Benefit of Power Posing, Before a High-Stakes Social Evaluation." Harvard Business School Working Paper, No. 13-027,

133 Poulain, M., Herm, A., & Pes, G. (2013). The Blue Zones: areas of exceptional longevity around the world. Vienna Yearbook of Population Research, 11, 87–108. http://www.jstor.org/stable/43050798

134 Scutti, S (2017, September 11). *Sitting too long can kill you, even if you exercise, study says - CNN*. CNN; CNN. https://edition.cnn.com/2017/09/11/health/sitting-increases-risk-of-death-study/index.html

135 Biddle, S. J., Bennie, J. A., Bauman, A. E., Chau, J. Y., Dunstan, D., Owen, N., ... & Van Uffelen, J. G. (2016). Too much sitting and all-cause mortality: is there a causal link? *BMC public health*, *16*(1), 1-10.deaths.

136 Patel, A. V., Maliniak, M. L., Rees-Punia, E., Matthews, C. E., & Gapstur, S. M. (2018). Prolonged Leisure Time Spent Sitting in Relation to Cause-Specific Mortality in a Large US Cohort. American journal of epidemiology, 187(10), 2151–2158. https://doi.org/10.1093/aje/kwy125

137 van der Ploeg, H. P., Chey, T., Korda, R. J., Banks, E., & Bauman, A. (2012). Sitting time and all-cause mortality risk in 222 497 Australian adults. Archives of internal medicine, 172(6), 494–500. https://doi.org/10.1001/archinternmed.2011.2174

138 Chau, J. Y., Grunseit, A. C., Chey, T., Stamatakis, E., Brown, W. J., Matthews, C. E., ... & Van Der Ploeg, H. P. (2013). Daily sitting time and all-cause mortality: a meta-analysis. *PloS one*, *8*(11), e80000.

139 Little, J. S., & Khalsa, P. S. (2005). Human lumbar spine creep during cyclic and static flexion: creep rate, biomechanics, and facet joint capsule strain. Annals of biomedical engineering, 33(3), 391–401. https://doi.org/10.1007/s10439-005-1742-x.

140 Gao, L., Flego, A., Dunstan, D. W., Winkler, E. A., Healy, G. N., Eakin, E. G., ... & Moodie, M. L. (2018). Economic evaluation of a randomized controlled trial of an intervention to reduce office workers' sitting time: the Stand Up Victoria trial. *Scandinavian journal of work, environment & health*, *44*(5), 503-511..

141 Walker, M. (2018) Why We Sleep. Harlow, England: Penguin Books

142 Lastella, M., Halson, S. L., Vitale, J. A., Memon, A. R., & Vincent, G. E. (2021). To Nap or Not to Nap? A Systematic Review Evaluating Napping Behavior in Athletes and the Impact on Various Measures of Athletic Performance. Nature and science of sleep, 13, 841–862. https://doi.org/10.2147/NSS.S315556's sleep.

143 *How Long Should a Nap Be?* (July 30th, 2020) SleepScore Labs https://www.sleepscore.com/blog/how-long-should-i-nap/

144 Englum, B. R., Hui, X., Zogg, C. K., Chaudhary, M. A., Villegas, C., Bolorunduro, O. B., Stevens, K. A., Haut, E. R., Cornwell, E. E., Efron, D. T., & Haider, A. H. (2016). Association Between Insurance Status and

Hospital Length of Stay Following Trauma. The American surgeon, 82(3), 281–288. https://doi.org/10.1177/000313481608200324

145 Dickinson J. (2014). Deadly medicines and organised crime: How big pharma has corrupted healthcare. *Canadian Family Physician, 60*(4), 367–368.

146 *Carta de* grünenthal en alemania a grünenthal en españa en 1961 comunicando que No informen a médicos y visitadores españoles del motivo real de la retirada de la Talidomida en el Mundo. (2016, March 3). Avite. https://www.avite.org/carta-de-grunenthal-en-alemania-a-grunenthal-en-espana-en-1961-comunicando-que-no-

147 *Thalidomide* (Dec 2019), Science Museum, https://www.sciencemuseum.org.uk/objects-and-stories/medicine/thalidomide

148 Badcock, J. (2016, December 23). *Spain's forgotten thalidomide victims see glimmer of hope - BBC News*. BBC News; BBC News. https://www.bbc.com/news/world-38386021

149 *Grunenthal Report* 2020/21 (n.d) Grunenthal Annual Reports https://features.grunenthal.com/gruenenthal-annual-report-2020-21/

150 *Esomeprazole (Oral Route) proper use.* (2022, June 20). Mayo Clinic. https://www.mayoclinic.org/drugs-supplements/esomeprazole-oral-route/proper-use/drg-20074322

151 University of Illinois. (2018, July 17). *Esomeprazole: side effects, dosage, uses, and more*. Healthline; Healthline Media. https://www.healthline.com/health/drugs/esomeprazole-oral-capsule

152 *Side effects of omeprazole.* (n.d.). https://www.nhs.uk/medicines/omeprazole/side-effects-of-omeprazole

153 *Esomeprazole: MedlinePlus drug information.* (n.d.). MedlinePlus; Health Information from the National Library of Medicine. https://medlineplus.gov/druginfo/meds/a699054.html

154 Higham, S., Horwitz, S., & Rich, S. (2019, July 17). *Largest U.S. drug companies flooded country with 76 billion opioid pills, DEA data shows - The Washington Post*. Washington Post; The Washington Post. https://www.washingtonpost.com/investigations/76-billion-opioid-pills-newly-released-federal-data-unmasks-the-epidemic/2019/07/16/5f29fd62-a73e-11e9-86dd-d7f0e60391e9_story.html

155 Deutsch, J. (2019, September 25). *Spain's cautionary tale on painkillers – POLITICO*. POLITICO; POLITICO. https://www.politico.eu/article/spains-cautionary-tale-on-painkillers/ to 2015

156 Mulvihill, J. & The Associated Press. (2021, September 1). *Sackler family to pay fines of $4.5 billion as OxyContin-maker Purdue Pharma is dissolved.* Fortune; Fortune. https://fortune.com/2021/09/01/sackler-family-fine-4-5-billion-oxycontin-purdue-pharma-dissolved/

157 Hoffman, J., & Benner, K. (2020, October 21). *Purdue Pharma Pleads Guilty to Criminal Charges for Opioid Sales*. The New York Times - Breaking News, US News, World News and Videos. https://www.nytimes.com/2020/10/21/health/purdue-opioids-criminal-charges.html

158 Krumholz, H. M., Ross, J. S., Presler, A. H., & Egilman, D. S. (2007). What have we learnt from Vioxx? *Bmj, 334*(7585), 120-123.

159 Cockburn, A. (2012, April 27). *When half a million Americans died and nobody noticed. The Week UK*. The Week UK; The Week. https://www.theweek.co.uk/us/46535/when-half-million-americans-died-and-nobody-noticed

160 *Vioxx: The downfall of a drug: NPR.* (2007, November 12). NPR.Org. https://www.npr.org/series/5033105/vioxx-the-downfall-of-a-drug?t=1643104529507

161 *All the justice money can buy: the Merck Vioxx story that can't be forgotten* (n.d.). HealthNewsReview.Org. https://www.healthnewsreview.org/2012/02/all-the-justice-money-can-buy-the-merck-vioxx-story-that-cant-be-forgotten/

162 Wilk, V., Palmer, H. D., Stosic, R. G., & McLachlan, A. J. (2010). Evidence and practice in the self-management of low back pain: findings from an Australian internet-based survey. *The Clinical journal of pain, 26*(6), 533-540.

163 European Medicines Agency. (2012). Assessment report for non-steroidal anti-inflammatory drugs (NSAIDs) and cardiovascular risk.

164 Gislason, G. H., Rasmussen, J. N., Abildstrom, S. Z., Schramm, T. K., Hansen, M. L., Fosbøl, E. L., Sørensen, R., Folke, F., Buch, P., Gadsbøll, N., Søren R., Poulsen, H. E., Køber, L., Madsen, M., & Torp-Pedersen, C. (2009). Increased mortality and cardiovascular morbidity associated with use of nonsteroidal anti-inflammatory drugs in chronic heart failure. *Archives of internal medicine, 169*(2), 141-149.

165 European Medicines Agency. (2012). Assessment report for non-steroidal anti-inflammatory drugs (NSAIDs) and cardiovascular risk.

166 *High doses of ibuprofen cause significant gi bleeding, despite safety profile* (2005, November 1). Science Daily. https://www.sciencedaily.com/

releases/2005/11/051101075630.htm

167 Rogers, M. A., & Aronoff, D. M. (2016). The influence of non-steroidal anti-inflammatory drugs on the gut microbiome. *Clinical Microbiology and Infection, 22*(2), 178-e1.

168 Maseda, D., & Ricciotti, E. (2020). NSAID–gut microbiota interactions. *Frontiers in pharmacology, 11*, 1153.

169 Leopoldino, A. O., Machado, G. C., Ferreira, P. H., Pinheiro, M. B., Day, R., McLachlan, A. J., Hunter, D. J., & Ferreira, M. L. (2019). Paracetamol versus placebo for knee and hip osteoarthritis. *Cochrane Database of Systematic Reviews*, 25(2), CDO13273.

170 Moore, R. A., & Moore, N. (2016). Paracetamol and pain: the kiloton problem. *European Journal of Hospital Pharmacy, 23*(4), 187-188.

171 Moore, A. (n.d). *What's the point of paracetamol?* University of Oxford. *https://www.ox.ac.uk/research/what%E2%80%99s-point-paracetamol.*

172 *Is long-term paracetamol use not as safe as we thought?* (2015, March 11). *Nursing Times*. https://www.nursingtimes.net/clinical-archive/pain-management/is-long-term-paracetamol-use-not-as-safe-as-we-thought-11-03-2015/#:~:text=A%20new%20review%20of%20previous,system)%20and%20impaired%20kidney%20function.

173 Stahel, P. F., VanderHeiden, T. F., & Kim, F. J. (2017). Why do surgeons continue to perform unnecessary surgery? *Patient Safety in Surgery, 11*(1), 1-2.

174 Levinson, H. (2011, November 8). The strange and curious history of lobotomy - BBC News. BBC News; BBC News. https://www.bbc.com/news/magazine-15629160

175 Anastasia, K. (1984). History of frontal lobotomy in the United States, 1935 1955. *Neurosurgery, 14*(6), 765-772.

176 Lewis, T. (2021, October 13). *Lobotomy: Definition, procedure and history.* Livescience. https://www.livescience.com/42199-lobotomy-definition.html

177 *What is the appendix, and what does it do?* (n.d.). Everyday Health. https://www.everydayhealth.com/appendicitis/guide/appendix/ forever.

178 Davis, N. (2019, December 4). *Unnecessary appendix surgery, performed on thousands in UK. Health. The Guardian*. The Guardian; The Guardian. https://www.theguardian.com/society/2019/dec/04/unnecessary-appendix-surgery-performed-on-thousands-in-uk

179 Tanner, L (2018), Pills for appendicitis? Surgery often not needed,

study says. *Associated Press.* https://www.statnews.com/2018/09/25/appendicitis-antibiotics-surgery-often-not-needed/

180 de Almeida Leite RM, Seo DJ, Gomez-Eslava B. (2022) Nonoperative vs Operative Management of Uncomplicated Acute Appendicitis: A Systematic Review and Meta-Analysis. JAMA Surg. doi:10.1001/jamasurg.2022.2937

181 Robert. (2020, April 20). *Knee arthroscopy: Should this common knee surgery be performed less often? - Harvard Health*. Harvard Health. https://www.health.harvard.edu/blog/knee-arthroscopy-should-this-common-knee-surgery-be-performed-less-often-2020042019507

182 Kise, N. J., Risberg, M. A., Stensrud, S., Ranstam, J., Engebretsen, L., & Roos, E. M. (2016). Exercise therapy versus arthroscopic partial meniscectomy for degenerative meniscal tear in middle aged patients: randomised controlled trial with two year follow-up. *bmj, 354.*

183 *Most surgical meniscus repairs are unnecessary.* (2016, July 22). *Science daily.* https://www.sciencedaily.com/releases/2016/07/160722093239.htm

184 WHO calls for urgent action to reduce patient harm in healthcare. (2019, September 13). World Health Organization. https://www.who.int/news/item/13-09-2019-who-calls-for-urgent-action-to-reduce-patient-harm-in-healthcare.

185 Harris, I. (2020, April 8). The coronavirus ban on elective surgeries might show us many people can avoid going under the knife. The Conversation; https://facebook.com/ConversationEDU. https://theconversation.com/the-coronavirus-ban-on-elective-surgeries-might-show-us-many-people-can-avoid-going-under-the-knife-135325

186 Elshaug, A. (2020, April 16). *Hospitals have stopped unnecessary elective surgeries – and shouldn't restart them after the pandemic*. The Conversation. https://theconversation.com/hospitals-have-stopped-unnecessary-elective-surgeries-and-shouldnt-restart-them-after-the-pandemic-136259

187 Machado, G., Lin, C. & Harris, L. (2018, February 19). *Needless treatments: Spinal fusion surgery for lower back pain is costly and there's little evidence it'll work*. The Conversation. https://theconversation.com/needless-treatments-spinal-fusion-surgery-for-lower-back-pain-is-costly-and-theres-little-evidence-itll-work-91829.

188 MacLellan, L. (2017, June 26). *The $100 Billion per year back pain industry is mostly a hoax, says investigative journalist Cathryn Jakobson Ramin —*

Quartz. Quartz; Quartz. https://qz.com/1010259/the-100-billion-per-year-back-pain-industry-is-mostly-a-hoax/

189 Epstein, N. E., & Hood, D. C. (2011). Unnecessary spinal surgery: A prospective 1-year study of one surgeon's experience. *Surgical neurology international, 2 (83).*

190 Watts, C. (2011). Response to unnecessary spinal surgery. *Surgical Neurology International, 2 (108).*

191 Smith, K. (2021, April 8). *Why unnecessary spine surgery is prevalent: The Discseel®* Procedure. DiscSeel - Regenerative spine procedure. https://discseel.com/unnecessary-spine-surgery/

192 Reis, R. C., de Oliveira, M. F., Rotta, J. M., & Botelho, R. V. (2015). Risk of complications in spine surgery: a prospective study. *The open orthopaedics journal, 9,* 20.

193 O'Connor, D. (2018, September 13). Needless procedures: knee arthroscopy is one of the most common but least effective surgeries. The Conversation. https://theconversation.com/needless-procedures-knee-arthroscopy-is-one-of-the-most-common-but-least-effective-surgeries-102705

194 Are many spinal surgeries unnecessary. (2011, August 23). Miller & Wagner. http://www.miller-wagner.com/articles/are-many-spinal-surgeries-unnecessary/

195 *Unnecessary operations.* (n.d.). Thomson Snell & Passmore; Ambitious Law Firm Based in Kent. https://www.ts-p.co.uk/news/unnecessary-operations

196 *Clemens, J., & Gottlieb, J. D. (2014). Do Physicians' Financial Incentives Affect Medical Treatment and Patient Health?. The American economic review, 104(4), 1320–1349. https://doi.org/10.1257/aer.104.4.1320*

197 Harrison, D. D., & Harrison, S. O. (2002). *CBP®* Technique. CBP seminars, Inc.

Index

D

E

F

G

M

N

O

P

R

S

T

U

V

W

X

Y

Printed in Poland
by Amazon Fulfillment
Poland Sp. z o.o., Wrocław
07 August 2023

3427c7b2-e2cf-440b-a998-bc1f01663b60R01